The Emergence of Feminism
Among Indian Muslim Women
1920–1947

The Emergence of Feminism
Among Indian Muslim Women
1920–1947

Azra Asghar Ali

OXFORD
UNIVERSITY PRESS

OXFORD
UNIVERSITY PRESS

Great Clarendon Street, Oxford OX2 6DP

Oxford University Press is a department of the University of Oxford.
It furthers the University's objective of excellence in research, scholarship,
and education by publishing worldwide in

Oxford New York

Athens Auckland Bangkok Bogotá Buenos Aires Calcutta
Cape Town Chennai Dar es Salaam Delhi Florence Hong Kong Istanbul
Karachi Kuala Lumpur Madrid Melbourne Mexico City Mumbai
Nairobi Paris São Paulo Singapore Taipei Tokyo Toronto Warsaw
with associated companies in Berlin Ibadan

Oxford is a registered trade mark of Oxford University Press
in the UK and in certain other countries

ISBN 0 19 579152 5

Printed in Pakistan at
Mehran Printers, Karachi.
Published by
Ameena Saiyid, Oxford University Press
5-Bangalore Town, Sharae Faisal
PO Box 13033, Karachi-75350, Pakistan.

To

Francis Robinson

CONTENTS

List of Abbreviations

C.P.	Central Provinces
IOL	India Office Library and Records, London
MEC	Muslim Educational Conference
M.L.A.	Member of the Legislative Assembly
n.d.	not dated
n.p.	not paginated
N.W.F.P.	North-West Frontier Province
U.P.	United Provinces

Acknowledgements

This research would have been very difficult without funding from the Ministry of Education, the Government of Pakistan, which permitted me to come to Britain and take advantage of the research facilities of Royal Holloway College, University of London. However, without the help of many other people also, this research would have been virtually impossible.

I wish to express my deep sense of gratitude to my Supervisor Prof. F.C.R. Robinson, from whom I have learned the first lessons of knowledge and perception. With his help, blessings and encouragement I have been able to pass through every stage of *marfat* and *agahi*.

My sincere and big thanks also go to Dr Sarah Ansari and Dr Khizar Ansari, a very ideal combination of eastern and western cultures. Throughout the course of my research, they not only encouraged me but also helped make my research easier.

I am also very thankful to the staff of the Department of History, Royal Holloway College, London, especially to Vanessa Ormesher who managed, against all the odds, to deal with my computer difficulties.

I would also like to thank my friends Nesa Abdul Majeed, Dr Lubna Tanveer, and the members of the Islamic Society, Royal Holloway, for standing by me through thick and thin.

Last but not the least, I wish to acknowledge the encouragement and constant support of my husband, Professor Asghar Ali without whom this work would certainly never have been done. I have to thank my children Fatima Asghar and Basit Habib Asghar whose support and presence have animated me during the hard times of my research.

INTRODUCTION

The nineteenth and twentieth centuries have witnessed far-reaching changes for Muslims. Faced with the assault of western power and values, many Muslims found themselves grappling with the problem of whether or not, or how, to reform their own societies in order to strengthen themselves under these changing circumstances. With political power slowly but constantly slipping out of their control, they turned their attention to the so-called private world as the focus for their reforming urges. Muslim women and their lives became crucial to this process of reform: they provided the barometer by which its 'successes' or 'failures' very often came to be judged. Facilitated by developments in communications which occurred alongside the expansion of western imperial power, Muslims in different parts of the world were drawn into similar kinds of responses as they tackled this dilemma.

Hence, in the Middle East and then in the Indian subcontinent, efforts at reform followed similar patterns. These patterns, however, were not necessarily identical and were often influenced by the local political and social context in which they took place. Muslims in India, for instance, while they shared the concerns of their co-religionists further west, were also affected by their particular circumstances, both past and present, which meant that, while they had much in common with Muslims in the Middle East in terms of outlook, they were affected by the changes taking place more widely in Indian society. The consolidation of British power in India sparked off intense debates over the question of the condition and rights of Indian women. They represented part of the broader transformation of Indian society which has often been regarded as a shift from tradition to modernity, but which in reality has been far more blurred than this clear-cut distinction suggests. All the same, the changes which began to take place within

Indian society during the nineteenth century involved the refashioning of ideas about women in the context of political, economic and social circumstances.

As, during the nineteenth century, the British moved to consolidate their power, the ability of Indians to control political and social changes became increasingly difficult. This led them to turn their attention towards adopting strategies necessary to overcome foreign occupation or to cope with it. The strategy adopted by many Indians to accommodate these changes was mostly based on ethnic or religious affiliations which led to competition between these groups; 'between their tongues, sects and communities there were intense competitions which under the circumstances of foreign rule mainly took the form of struggle for status.'[1] The symbol of status was not only used by many Indians to represent their powerful interests but also to reaffirm the continuing validity of their own values in the changing circumstances.

One such 'community' was that of India's Muslims who used these kinds of changes to improve their social condition as well as to gear themselves up for the internal consolidation to cope with and withstand the physical, social, and intellectual attacks which they perceived were taking place on their interests.[2] Two distinct movements emerged in the latter half of the nineteenth century. Both were cultural but potentially political: they emphasized the need for Muslim cultural regeneration, and helped create among Indian Muslims a greater awareness of themselves as a community.[3] The first involved *ulama* who sought to strengthen Islamic culture in India through the founding of new religious educational systems. One of the best examples of this was the establishment of the Dar-ul-Ulum at Deoband in 1867. Such institutions made reforms in the traditional curriculum which included the promotion of basic religious education and the observance of Islamic law in Muslim society. The other movement which centred on Aligarh under the supervision of Sir Sayyed Ahmed Khan, advocated western education for Indian Muslims. Education in English and the western sciences, it was argued, would lead to a quicker advancement of the community, surely bringing the advantage of employment in government and other professions, and ultimately continued access to power. The foundation of the Scientific Society of Aligarh (1864), for instance, can be seen as a step towards promoting cooperation between the community and the government. Likewise another important effort to impart western education to Indian Muslims was the foundation of Anglo-Muhammadan Oriental College in 1875, which, to mitigate any accusations of secularism, maintained religious education as an adjunct of the curriculum to strengthen community ties and reverse the 'irreligious' effects of western-style education.[4] By the closing years of the nineteenth century, like other Indians, Indian Muslims had developed a number of common strategies to deal with the socio-economic changes that were the outcome of political change in India. It led them particularly, to construct their own *sharif* culture almost as a private polity.

The subject of Muslim women was central to this *sharif* culture as it was generally assumed that the position of women provided an excellent indicator of the 'health' and 'progress' of Muslim society in India under the changing circumstances. Defenders of the 'community's interests', however, approached the question of reforming Indian Muslim womanhood in a variety of ways: reformist and modernist. The reformist approach was epitomized by Ashraf Ali Thanawi's book of advice for women, his *Bihishti Zewar*, which outlined the importance of *adab* (manners) on religious basis. The first stage of the modernist approach was represented by Nazir Ahmed and Hali's didactic works (*Mirat-al-Arus* and *Majalis-un-nisa*), which emphasized the importance of modern education for women similar to the one received by any well-to-doman. The second stage of the modernist approach was reflected in the curriculum advocated by Shaikh Abdullah, (Aligarh Zenana Madrasa and his journal *Khatun*), which, with its inclusion of English, prescribed for women the 'conservative' education similar to that of a modern middle-class man.[5]

The shift within *sharif* culture in the early twentieth century, away from localized 'traditional' norms to largely shared values, meant that it sought to expand its ideological discourse into the realm of the 'common middle class or new bourgeois class' which had emerged as a product of new economic relations and the erosion of distinct *qasbah* cultures in the face of urbanization. The demand for an 'enlightened' woman was an important characteristic of bourgeois culture. As many of the men of this class themselves were the product of western education and cultural influence, they therefore needed 'new women' as their partners, women who would be presentable in colonial society yet with a role that remained primarily in the home. These women had to show that they were the negation of everything that was considered 'backward' in the old society: they were no longer illiterate and secluded, with bound feet and minds.[6]

Thus, the concept of an 'enlightened' woman had roles which were divided into the private and the public spheres. The former idea was based on the 'dignity and status' of women within the family through the redefinition of normative gender ideologies of traditional Muslim society in India, as well as through legal prospects of marriage, divorce and property share. The latter was the essential result of the former, which helped to reconstruct the images of the new 'virtuous woman'. The concept of pure womanhood was not limited to woman's traditional role but also became part of her social awareness, a national role and, above all, her personal belief and self image. The visible attempt to regulate the mobility of women in public life was also seen in the communalization and identity politics of Indian Muslim society during the 1930s and 1940s. The manner and extent to which this communalization was developed not only reflected female efforts in the struggle for the creation of Pakistan but also their struggle to participate in public life.

The general question of the changing position and role of Muslim women in different parts of the world has attracted scholarly attention in recent years. This research has mostly investigated the importance of gender to the process of reform in Muslim societies both under formal and informal colonial rule. The key issues examined have included the socio-economic status of Muslim women, their education, their political identity, and various elements within their evolving consciousness. However, most of these works deal with major aspects of Middle Eastern women's lives. For instance, *Women in the Muslim World* (Cambridge, 1978), edited by L. Beck and Nikki Keddie, gives an overview of the general social position of Muslim women in the pre- and post-colonial periods. Another important work edited by Nikki Keddie and Beth Baron, *Women in the Middle Eastern Society: Shifting Boundaries in Sex and Gender* (Yale, 1991) helps to establish a higher profile for Middle Eastern women by sketching shifts in their position from ancient to modern times. Similarly, Leila Ahmed's *Women and Gender in Islam* (New Haven, 1992) looks at the tension between orthodox legal discourse and unorthodox movements which sought to provide greater scope and freedom to women, and is particularly concerned to illustrate the complex nature of Muslim women's response to modernity. In addition to these investigations, much work has also been published which deals with the perspective of women from the point of view of individual societies in the Middle East.[7]

In the same way, the response of Indian society towards women's issues in general has been highlighted in recent historical work looking at the subcontinent, most notably in Kumari Jayawardena, *Feminism and Nationalism in the Third World*, (London, 1986); Joanna Liddle and Rama Joshi, *Daughters of Independence: Gender, Cast and Class in India* (London, 1986); Kumkum Sangari and Sudesh Vaid, *Recasting Women: Essays in Colonial History* (Delhi, 1989); and Radha Kumar, *The History of Doing: An Illustrated Account of Movements for Women's Rights and Feminism in India, 1800–1990* (Delhi, 1993). But none of these volumes considers to any meaningful extent the responses of Indian Muslim society, focusing instead primarily on the majority Hindu community. This absence has been compensated for, to some extent, by work which takes Indian Muslims as its central subject, in particular a number of scholarly works which investigate the development of Muslim reformist ideas alongside issues connected with gender in the changing context of Indian society. For instance, contributions to *Modernization and Social Change Among Muslims in India* (Delhi, 1983) edited by Imtiaz Ahmed, examine the historical meaning and relationship of Muslim revivalism in relation to the changing meaning of gender and class in India. Likewise, *The Extended Family: Women and Political Participation in India and Pakistan* (Delhi, 1981) edited by Gail Minault, provides a framework for the analysis of changes in women's roles including their public place in society and a metaphor for the expansion of their social concerns. Minault's other works, such as 'Political Change: Muslim Women in Conflict with Purdah: Their Role in the Indian Nationalism Movement' in Sylvia A. Chipp & Justin J. Green (eds.), *Asian Women in Transition* (London, 1976); 'Purdah and Politics: The Role of Muslim Women in Indian Nationalism' in Hanna Papanek and Gail Minault (eds.), *Separate Worlds: Studies of Purdah in South Asia*, (New Delhi, 1982); 'Purdah's Progress: The Beginning of School Education for Indian Muslim Women' in J.P. Sharma (ed.), *Individuals and Ideas in Modern India*, (Calcutta, 1982); 'Urdu Women's Magazines in the Early Twentieth Century', *Manoshi*, (New Delhi, 1988) and 'Sayyed Mumtaz Ali and Huquq un-Niswan, 'An Advocate of Women's Rights in Islam in the Late Nineteenth Century', *Modern Asian Studies* (1990) provide insights into the past as well as open new topics of understanding Muslim women and gender in Indian society. In the same way, a groundbreaking translation of and a commentary on Thanawi's *Bihishti Zewar* is provided by Barbara Daly Metcalf's *Perfecting Women: Maulana Ashraf Ali Thanawi's Bihishti Zewar* (Berkeley, 1990). Another important and more recent volume is that of Zoya Hasan (ed.), *Forging Identities: Gender Communities and the State* (Delhi, 1994) which focuses on the various dimensions of the identity of Muslims in India and the way in which the process of identity formation is located in different historical moments and political and social conjunctures. These conclusions are shared to varying extents by other studies, such as Patricia Jeffery, *Frogs in a Well* (London, 1979); Roya Shibani, *Status of Muslim Women in North India* (Delhi, 1979); H.Y. Siddiqui, *Muslim Women in Transition: A Social Profile* (Delhi, 1987); Shahida Lateef, *Muslim Women in India: Political and Private Realities* (London, 1990); and Anjum Mohini (ed.), *Muslim Women in India* (Delhi, 1992). But, while these studies contribute considerably to understanding the changing position and relevance of Muslim women to society more generally, they tend either, as in the case of Minault and Metcalf's work, to focus on traditional reformers of Muslim womanhood, or, as with Lateef's work, they concentrate on the post-independence position of Indian Muslim women and so only looked very fleetingly at the years before 1947.

There still remains a gap, therefore, as far as understanding the chain of developments which gradually opened up a space for Muslim women in terms of their private and public lives. Indeed, the gradual process of increasing awareness of Indian Muslim women and the movement for their emancipation did not occur accidentally or by chance, but rather it was a historical process achieved through different stages. Without knowing these chains of development, it remains difficult to examine how Muslim society in general and Muslim women in particular responded to these changes and challenges during the decades leading to independence and the creation of Pakistan.

This work, therefore, seeks to fill the gap identified above as well as to offer some thoughts on the emergence of 'feminism' among Indian Muslim women. It does this by focusing on various kinds of 'spaces' in which Muslim women were increasingly able to participate in the public sphere, created in large part by changes emanating from the impact of the colonial state. Through the use of the term 'feminism' this study acknowledges its growing popularity in the Indian subcontinent during the period under discussion, albeit among growing Indian middle classes. Feminism in this context, can be defined as the awarenes of constraints placed upon women because of their gender system involving new roles for women and new relations between women and men.[8] The opening up of new public spaces within which these reassessed gender relations could develop was, therefore, central to the evolving position of Indian Muslim women from the end of the nineteenth century. Public space here means the visibility and audibility of middle class Muslim female population within their own cultural framework in the period under discussion in this work. In order to identify these challenges, this work employs a wide range of sources deposited in the Oriental and India Collection of the British Library in London, School of Oriental and African Studies, London and in different libraries of Pakistan. It includes, in particular writings about and of the women themselves as well as colonial records, both central and provincial. While the latter can present a number of problems, such as the stereotyping of various groups of women according to preset perception of their lives depending on their religious or regional identities, and the frequent failure of official statistical material to break down information according to community. Taken as a whole these sources reveal a range of new spaces which together constitute the arrival of Indian Muslims into a public arena.

While this study attempts a broad survey of these developments, it concentrates on non-official sources in Urdu. In doing so it reveals the changes taking place in the 'shared' culture' of many of the subcontinent's Muslims. This has meant that sources written in other regional languages, such as Bengali, are not used. However, to compensate for their absence and to gain access to what was occurring within the non-Urdu speaking world, care has been taken to include, for instance, articles contributed by Bengali Muslim women to nationwide Urdu publications. Likewise the study has incorporated material about only those princely states where Muslims were influential either in terms of numbers or state power; in the case of Hyderabad, Deccan, this means analysing the development of educational facilities for women within the state, whereas in Bhopal, where educational developments were far less, the study has utilized the literary writings and pioneering social activities of its female rulers.

Chapter 1 looks at the structural and cultural features of the transformation of Indian society with reference to women's status in the late nineteenth and the early twentieth centuries. The emergence of a new middle class among Indian Muslims and its active participation can be seen through the efforts which they made for the regeneration of their society. Analysis of the literary work, produced by Muslim social reformers in the form of a network of printed material in vernacular (mostly in Urdu), highlights the importance of women's education in fulfilling their traditional roles as mothers and wives. The formation of social reform associations and their concerns with women's issues further highlights the practical efforts of Indian Muslim society for the social uplifts of women in support of ideas of greater equality and greater freedom for them. Chapter 2 discusses the response of Indian Muslims towards new educational measures introduced for women's education during the period from 1920–47. One of the prominent features of this period was the growing interest taken by Indian society towards women's education as it was considered that educating a woman meant educating society as a whole. For women it was also a revolutionary step which was taken not only to improve their social condition but also to provide a space for them in public life. Chapter 3 highlights those measures which were taken to introduce the development of the idea of safe motherhood in India. The framework of vital information relevant to the maternity and child welfare movements is provided in this part. Most of the arrangements which were made by government and its affiliated agencies provide comprehensive information about the nature of maternity welfare work in different provinces. In the same way the cause of maternal mortality, the beginnings of the neonatal work, the growing interest of women in medical education explains not only the spread of the idea of safe motherhood but also how more spaces opened up for women's social activities. This new trend in health culture took place as much in the sphere of *Unani Tibb* as in that of western biomedicine.

Chapter 4 takes up the question of different kinds of social legislation which were introduced to redefine women's legal status in India. Three main pieces of legislation, the Child Marriage Restraint Act of 1929, the Muslim Shariat Application Act of 1937 and the Dissolution of Muslim Marriages Act of 1939, provide the main sections of this chapter. They examine those efforts, both by the government and the related communities. to raise the social status of Indian Muslim women The division of public opinion on a secular as well as on a religious basis indicates the range of attitudes towards women's questions. The interest of women in these pieces of legislation will be discussed in the context of the changes women were undergoing themselves. The construction of community identity emerges as an important part of this whole social process.

Chapter 5 discusses the constitutional developments (1919–35) *vis-à-vis* women's civil status in India which was the outcome of the development of the idea of sex-equality and women's full participation in public life. It highlights the way in which women's question became part of the formulation of a national identity as well as communal consciousness. The dual aspirations of Indian feminists (both Hindus and Muslims) on national and communal basis serve to indicate how women's organizations and associations incorporated their feminist agenda with that of wider contemporary political agendas. The active participation of Muslim women from all classes in the political arena highlights their greater mobilization in public life. Chapter 6 focuses on the ways in which Muslim women's search for a new definition of their role is reflected in their literary activities. The recovery of female voices through women's journals in Urdu provides a unique historical source. In this new literary form, this new public space, we can listen to women debating such issues as the necessity for a new kind of domestic literature, social transformation and the role of women and the reassessment of womanhood.

NOTES

1. Anil Seal, *The Emergence of Indian Nationalism: Competition and Collaboration in the Later Nineteenth Century*, (Cambridge University Press, Cambridge, 1968), p. 11.
2. Shahida Lateef, *Muslim Women in India: Political and Private Realities, 1890–1980*, (Zed Books, Ltd., London, 1990), p. 23.
3. Gail Minault, *The Khilafat Movement: Religious Symbolism and Political Mobilization in India*, (Oxford University Press, Delhi, 1982), p. 12.
4. Shahida Lateef, *Muslim Women in India: 1890–1980*, p. 25.
5. Faisal Fatehali Devji, 'Gender and the Politics of Space: The Movements for Women's Reforms, 1857–1900' in Zoya Hasan, (ed.), *Forging Identities: Gender Community and the State*, (Kali for Women, Delhi, 1994), pp. 22–37.
6. Kumari Jayawardena, *Feminism and Nationalism in the Third World*, (Zed Books Ltd., London, 1986), pp. 12, 13.
7. For example see, Beth Baron, *The Women's Awakening in Egypt: Culture Society and the Press*, (Yale, New Haven, 1994); N Abadan Unat, *Women in Turkish Society*, (Leiden, 1981); and F. Azari (ed.), *Women of Iran: The Conflict with Fundamentalism*, (London, 1983).

A NOTE ON SPELLINGS

It is often difficult to maintain consistency in spelling partly because Indians themselves have used a variety of spellings, and partly because of phonetic problems. To achieve a satisfactory compromise, and at the risk of losing a certain amount of linguistic precision, I have used spellings which reflect the way in which names are pronounced in the subcontinent, with all diacritical marks omitted. Place names, on the whole, have been spelt according to the *Imperial Gazetteer of India*, (Cambridge, 1939); however, where spellings used today differ from those of the *Gazetteer*, the former have taken precedence.

1

SOCIO-CULTURAL TRANSITION AND MUSLIM WOMANHOOD IN INDIA (1857–1920)

This chapter examines the redefinition of the role and status of women in the context of British India in the second half of the nineteenth century. During this period there developed, as a consequence of the economic and political impact of British policies, new Indian élites. More often than not, these élites looked to Europe as presenting a model of social and political progress. Among these ideas of progress were European concepts of greater freedom, greater equality and greater opportunities of personal fulfilment for women. These feminist concerns came to interact fruitfully with general élite concerns to regenerate their society in the colonial environment. This process led to the emergence of a public space for women.

The main concerns of this study of the process of Muslim women's emancipation in South Asia are:

(a) To investigate the efforts of these new Indian élites, and in particular, Muslim élites to reform the public and private spheres of women.

(b) To examine the nature of social reforms for the emancipation of Indian Muslim women in the broader context of South Asian culture and society.

(c) To analyse the development of new forms of literature, in particular Urdu literature, concerning the emancipation of

Muslim women, mainly published under the patronage of the government and by interested élites.

(d) Social reform associations and the question of women's emancipation.

THE EFFORTS OF NEW INDIAN ÉLITES TO REFORM THE PUBLIC AND PRIVATE SPHERES OF WOMEN'S LIVES

Victorian Britain had far-reaching effects both on the structure of colonial rule and on the local communities. Robbed of a political arena for action, Indians resorted to the arenas of religion and community. In the process they created their own private polities, founding associations, social reform organizations, colleges and schools.[1]

The impact of British imperialism and British culture was accommodated in large part in nineteenth century India through the emergence of a new bourgeois class. This was made up of clerks who serviced the bureaucracy, traders who managed the working of international trade, and the lawyers and newspaper editors who peopled the fledgling areas of Indian public life.[2]

These were the men who criticized the evils of *purdah*, widow burning, child marriage and female infanticide; these were the men who led the regeneration of their society under British tutelage.[3] In the process, for instance, of addressing the evil of *purdah* they redefined the public and private spheres of Muslim life, which, in turn, led to the questioning of the old patriarchal gender-based relations. Thus, they carried the social policies of their British rulers into their society. They did so at the same time as they themselves were developing as a class of intermediaries between the colonial state and their society.[4]

These new élites, however, were selective in what they borrowed from the British and careful to reinterpret their borrowing in terms of the needs and circumstances of their communities. Certainly, in general, the Western mode of life was considered more scientific, more hygienic and more civilized than existing Indian lifestyles. But Indian responses to the West tended to be moderate and evolutionary.[5]

Nineteenth century Muslim reformers responded to Western ideas and values without actually bringing about fundamental changes in the structure of their society. With regard to the position of women, for instance, it was considered more important to emancipate men from conservatism and backwardness rather than focus their efforts directly on Muslim women. Early Muslim educational institutions for women were established mainly to mitigate the effects of Christian missionary schools and Hindu revivalist activities.[6] Thus early efforts on behalf of women were less because women's emancipation was thought to be a good cause in itself, than in order to improve the image of the Muslim community in the eyes of the outside world.[7] Rudimentary education at home was considered sufficient for women, given to the practice of early marriage and the seclusion of women belonging to the well-to-do classes. The main emphasis was on religious education, household management and awareness of the maternal role. Early Muslim social reformers advocated the strategy of educating men first as it was anticipated that women would learn automatically from their male-kin such as fathers, brothers, and husbands. Towards the end of the nineteenth century, however, increasing numbers of Muslims began realizing the role of women in the regeneration of Muslim society. They made efforts to persuade Muslims to understand the need for women's education in the changing social context.

THE NATURE OF SOCIAL REFORM FOR THE EMANCIPATION OF INDIAN MUSLIM WOMEN

During the nineteenth century, efforts were made to elevate the status and rights of women in many parts of the world. New attitudes emerged towards the value and role of women. These developments were largely a result of the feminist movements of the United States of America and Western Europe that emerged from the impact of the European enlightenment and the Industrial revolution.

The impact of feminism in South Asia must be understood in the cultural context of colonialism and the particular concerns of social reformers. The reformers tended to envisage that the final emancipation of their society would take place only with the advancement of women's education and self-awareness alongside that of their men-folk.[8] Because the condition of women was used by their colonial critics to highlight the backwardness of their society, the Muslim intelligentsia sought a change in the position of women as symbolic of their desire for change in the whole social order. Through this they demonstrated their desire and quest for their own emancipation. At the same time, they rendered their society better-fitted to fight for political reforms.[9]

The strategy adopted by Muslim élites in South Asia was to reform women not according to the standards of the West but according to the standards which they generated for themselves in response to the West within their own Indian cultural framework. During the long development of Islam in South Asia, involving the conversion of large numbers of Hindus to the faith, the Muslim community had come to be influenced by Hinduism and had adopted many indigenous Indian practices. Muslim women were seen as the particular vehicle of Hindu traditions and indigenous customs within the Muslim community. They came to be the victim of a socio-cultural irony; on the one hand they enjoyed, in theory, the high status given to them by Islam; on the other hand, they were regarded as the bearers of influences which could destroy the Muslim community from within.[10]

Muslim work for the emancipation of women came in two forms. The first was concerned to achieve women's emancipation through the legislative machinery of the colonial state. The second was aimed at achieving this end through the enforcement of Islamic injunctions. The first involved creating organizations and associations to petition the colonial state in matters of educational and social reform relating to women. The second approach towards women's emancipation may be found in the changing discourse of religious institutions. European intervention and political domination led *ulama* and religious thinkers towards the revival of Islamic social and moral values. The early responses of *ulama* to British rule in the field of education came in the form of attacking the protagonists of English education and secular values.[11] By the late nineteenth century, the moral concepts of reorientation were explained through their efforts for the collective betterment of their society. They tried to provide such styles of religion that appealed to people who were part of an urban society, who moved from place to place and were an integral part of the political and social life of the times.[12] The practical guidance of Deobandi *ulama* through their *fatawa* reflected the preoccupation of Indian Muslims outside the charmed circle of those whom the British met socially.[13]

Ulama and other religious leaders emphasized mainly the traditional, moral, and religious education of Muslim women for the well-being of their families and children. They were of the opinion that such education and training could be helpful for a woman to lead her daily life more competently. The woman also could transform her personality to attain the balance and self-control that had long been the goal of *sufi* training.[14]

Ulama idealised woman's character as one of purity, loyalty, moral sensitivity and domesticity and as a very submissive wife and a good mother. Her religious obligations were considered more important for the purification of society than those of a man.

EARLY EFFORTS FOR THE SOCIAL UPLIFT OF WOMEN

The influence of Western movements for the emancipation of women, which may be considered as the main impetus for the development of feminism in South Asia, began to be felt in the early nineteenth century. The first stages of feminism in South Asia were quite different from those of the West. Whereas in the West there were strands of feminism which challenged the social and political structure, in South Asia the movement as a whole was concerned purely to reform social practices, to try to remove social abuses and to define the rights of women. Matters such as the predominantly patriarchal nature of South Asian society and the social segregation of women were hardly discussed.

Early pressure to improve the position of women came from missionaries and Hindu social reformers. They were concerned, in large part, with issues affecting Hindu women such as *sati* (widow burning), widow remarriage, female infanticide, child marriage and the seclusion of women. The last two issues, of course, applied equally to Muslims. *Sati* was the first abuse to be addressed. In 1829 missionary pressures led to the *Sati* Abolition Act which was followed by another act in 1856. By the second half of the nineteenth century *sati* was a relatively rare occurrence in Hindu society.

The Act of 1856 also addressed the issue of a widow remarriage, making it legally possible for a Hindu widow to marry a second time. This legislation received little support amongst Hindus at the time, and had been little followed in actual practice by themselves. Among South Asian Muslims, despite the fact that Islam encourages the remarriage of widows, due to Hindu social influence this rarely happened. This was a serious issue for Muslim social reformers in the latter half of the nineteenth century. However, unlike Hindu social reformers who made practical arrangements for the care of their widows, constructing refuges (widow houses) and arranging marriages, Muslim social reformers restricted their activities to speeches and writings. Not the least amongst the reasons for this was the prevalence of kin marriage and ignorance of Islamic law.

Female infanticide was another social abuse, common among Hindu Rajput families. Usually the birth of a girl was not announced or it was merely stated that nothing had been born. They used to kill their newborn daughters, either by refusing proper nourishment or sometimes by simply poisoning the nipples of the mother's breasts. The Female Infanticide Act was passed in 1870 in response to the forceful campaign from Hindu social reformers and Christian missionaries to combat this social evil.

Child marriage, in particular female child marriage, was widespread throughout South Asia and practised equally by Hindus as well as Muslims. Here again, Muslim society was influenced by the Hindu custom of child marriage, known as *chirk puja*. According to the Hindu practice, if the girl was not married at an early age, she would have to remain unmarried for the rest of her life. Such women were then ritually married to the gods and usually offered their services as prostitutes in temples.[15] The widespread practice of child marriage can be seen from the fact that during the last decade of the nineteenth century one Indian woman in five was a widow, a large proportion among whom were no more than ten years old, having become widows without their marriages having been consummated.[16] As far as Muslims were concerned, their women were generally married off after puberty, and child marriage was considered a matter of modesty and chastity. Although the Muslim female was a little older than her Hindu counterpart at the time of marriage, sometimes marriages took place between teenage girls and men of sixty years and over, since marriage was considered the only way for parents to get rid of the encumbrance of their unmarried daughters.[17]

Efforts to raise the age of consent of marriage were started on a large scale during the last decade of the nineteenth century, when Mr Dayaram Gidimul of the Bombay Statutory Civil Service wrote a series of articles in the *Indian Spectator* and brought the question more prominently before the Indian public. Later on, these articles were published in the form of pamphlets entitled *Notes on the Infant Marriage and Enforced Widowhood* by Mr Behramji Malabari, a Parsi social reformer, who circulated the publication among native leaders and urged them to consider the issue seriously. The matter came to a head in June 1890, when the horrible death of Phulmani Dasi—a twelve-year-old married girl—through forced sexual intercourse by her husband, emerged as a burning issue. Public pressure was put on government to take action and not the least by women: for instance, twenty-five Western lady doctors protested to the government as did 1,800 Indian women.[18] The first bill for the prohibition of child marriage was passed in March 1891 and was supported by many Hindus as well as by Muslims. It was an encouraging step taken by the government. In 1894 the state of Mysore passed an act prohibiting the marriage of girls less than eight years of age, and in 1897 the Maharajah of Jaipur fixed the age of marriage at fourteen after consulting the religious authorities at his court.[19]

The seclusion or *purdah* of Muslim women has for long been much discussed. Prominent among those who have focused their attention on this practice are social anthropologists, feminist writers and historians. Social anthropologists have interpreted *purdah* in terms of a custom that seeks to establish a standard of respectability, establishing a link between the seclusion of women and the maintenance of male honour and between the concealment of women and the separation of the world of men and that of women.[20] Scholars coming from a feminist background have referred to it as a system designed to achieve the physical and psychological dependency of women on men, or a facet of a male-dominated system in which women are controlled.[21] The historian I.M. Lapidus, however, offers a rather more subtle understanding which embraces the range of ways in which *purdah* is expressed, not just in Muslim societies alone. Lapidus emphasizes that although the veil is usually taken as a symbol of the domination of women by men, in fact it symbolizes the complexities of their relationship. It is not universal in Muslim societies, being found more commonly in urban than in rural societies. Moreover, it conceals significant ambiguities. On the one hand, it protects women against men and society against women, and, on the other, by concealing women it brings to them not only mystery and allurement but also freedom of movement.[22]

In South Asia the social concealment of women or *purdah* has been equally practised by Hindu and Muslim societies in different social contexts. In particular, the practice of *purdah* among the latter is considered necessary to safeguard their women from men outside the family and to keep them in their own separate feminine world, the *zenana*. The domestic and maternal role of Muslim woman has been linked to the concept of sexual purity and the honour or *izzat* of the male-centred group to which she belongs. Unmarried girls are protected by their fathers and brothers and after marriage they become the *izzat* of their husbands and in-laws.

Muslim *purdah* was the subject of strong attack by Christian missionaries. They criticized it in particular for its baleful impact on the education and the general health of women. This attack made the issue of *purdah* a critical one for Muslim reformers and religious thinkers. For these men the development of a new role for women was an inevitable part of their general attempt to achieve a social transformation of Muslim society as a whole. Their first concern, however, was to achieve advancement for women within the traditional structure and values of society; this they knew was the only acceptable and effective way at that time, of carrying the cause of women forward. This concern, however, was bolstered by the fact that the first aim of Muslim social reformers in the decades after the 1857 uprising was to build a bridge between the public world of Muslim men and the colonial state. Thus, although their work on behalf of women was many-sided, the issue of *purdah* was of secondary importance for them. For instance, the well-known social reformer and novelist of the latter half of the nineteenth century, Nazir Ahmed, acknowledged in one of his writings, *Mauizat-e-Hasna* (Good Advice), that the moral structure of Muslim society was based on the *purdah* of women but that this did not mean that Muslim women were to be confined to their homes or deprived of life's happiness. Such allegations were contrivances of the British Government and its panegyrists. In his opinion, it would look very odd if, after a long time in seclusion, women suddenly were allowed to come out of *purdah*. He was adamant that Muslims ought not to compare their women with English women who were superior as regards their knowledge and education. Instead, Muslim men first had to teach and educate Muslim women. For Muslim women to abandon *purdah* at this early stage amounted to a great mistake in his eyes.[23]

Contradicting these opinions of Nazir Ahmed were those expressed by his nephew Rashid-ul-Khairi, a leading Urdu writer of the early twentieth century. Unlike his uncle, Khairi was opposed to *rawaji purdah* (customary seclusion) but adopted a different stance on the matter of *shari purdah* as defined by Islam. He pointed out the contradiction between the fact that a woman could perform *Hajj* (pilgrimage) along with men, but yet remained so secluded in Muslim society that even for a stranger to hear her voice was considered *haram* (sin).[24] *Purdah* became even more horrible for women, Khairi noted in his *Aurat ki Intihai Tahqir* (The Extreme Disdain for Woman), when they had to face a double kind of *purdah*, which meant leaving the home wearing *burqa* and then having to sit in a *doli* (a kind of small sedan) which was already heavily covered.[25] Citing the example of the miserable condition of Muslim women of Bihar he further stated that they were not even allowed to come before strange, unknown women. The main reason for this was to prevent these unknown women from talking about them in public, for that was considered to bring great dishonour to their parents and relatives.[26]

The early reformist efforts targeting *rawaji purdah* were not warmly received by many Indian Muslims. However, Muslim social reformers gradually began to understand and express the view that *rawaji purdah* was the main hindrance to the development of their women and that there was no religious basis for it.

THE DEVELOPMENT OF A NEW KIND OF
LITERATURE ABOUT WOMEN

The growth of modern literature was a product of the colonial transformation of South Asia. It was part of a process in which South Asians interacted with developments in different parts of the world, in which they responded to new ideas and often did so by reinterpreting their cultural heritage in the light of these new ideas. The growth of the press from the early nineteenth century made possible a widening range of discourses on a steadily expanding number of topics. Among the new topics that began being discussed was a series of issues relating to women. The purposes of this literature about women and the forms it took may be classified as follows:

1. Works published with the patronage of government for the study of the condition of Indians and to make recommendations for their betterment. These took the form primarily of textbooks (in English and in the vernaculars), official records, reports and administrative documents.

2. Works produced by new political élites who were convinced that traditional education and learning had little to offer in the new economic and political circumstances. They wanted to bring about social transformation by introducing education patterns after a western fashion and by idealizing the status of the women of the West. A typical example of this approach was that of Badruddin Tyabji who sent his daughter, Attiya [Faizi], to be educated in England. He sought to fashion a new integrated Islamic society in which women enjoyed equal rights, better education, and a better domestic life. He believed that the greater presence of women in the public sphere would strengthen Muslim society.[27]

3. Works emanating from reformist *ulama* which responded to the fact of the colonial transformation but were concerned that Muslim society should not be wholly transformed by it. They had reformulated their religious ideas as part of the process of their resistance to the colonial state and, typically, these reformulations had come to be expressed through *madrasa* education, most notably for those who looked to the *Dar-ul-Ulum* at Deoband for a lead. A typical product of this school of thought was the *Bihishti Zewar* of the Deobandi *alim*, Maulana Ashraf Ali Thanawi, written in the early twentieth century. This book aimed to take reformist teachings into the home and did so with some success. The view of this section of the *ulama* was that if Muslim women

were to absorb reformist teachings, Muslim society would be better protected against the ravages wrought by the process of colonial transformation.[28]

4. Works produced by Muslim social reformers aiming to achieve a balance between the values of indigenous society and those of the world beyond. These bridge-builders were social activists mainly from a *qasbah* background, such as people who worked with the Aligarh movement but not necessarily committed to every thing it represented—men such as Nazir Ahmed and Altaf Husain Hali. They knew that the new demands required a reassessment of women's role in society but they wished that the answers should be pragmatic and feasible. For instance, they focused on the curricula prescribed in schools and addressed issues of female education in both Islamic and Western-style institutions.

The development of this new literature for Muslim women pointed to the emergence of Urdu as the common language linking *ashraf* Muslims in the various regions of India. Urdu was the medium of the new women's education, which became a part and parcel of *Sharif* culture and values, even though generally the prestige and the availability of education in Urdu declined with the introduction of government patronage towards English education. This new education which women were able to receive in Urdu, despite the fact that it was often rudimentary, enabled them to run their households and stimulate the minds of their children.[29]

Purdah restriction and class difference between *ashraf* (high class gentry), and *ajlaf* (lower class) made it difficult for the former to send their daughters to *zenana* schools; on the other hand special arrangements could be made for vernacular as well as English education at home. The role of the *atuji*, a female teacher, was appreciated in Urdu literature as well as in folk tales.[30] English education for women was considered as a matter of honour as well as enabling a good relationship to be established with the ruling class. For instance, the services of European ladies at Calcutta and other places who were involved in female education at homes, helped to strengthen ties with the British.[31] Many Muslim women of *ashraf* families showed great eagerness to seek knowledge and in particular modern education. Educated Parsi, Hindu, and Christian women were always cordially invited to teach them at home. A particular prestige attached to those families which educated their wives and daughters by European governesses and other female teachers. Modern educated Muslim women could speak and read English well and could go out to a theatre, but everywhere special arrangements had to be made—such as curtains—to protect their privacy.[32]

Urdu writings about Muslim women not only reflected the new socio-cultural experiences of British India but also represented different social classes of Delhi and Lucknow. The traditional rivalry between *Dabistan-e-Delhi* (the Delhi school), and *Dabistan-e-Lucknow* (the Lucknow school) began during the period of Burhan-ul-Mulk, the founder of the State of Oudh. The decline of the Mughal empire centred in Delhi drew the attention of local intellectuals towards Oudh, where the development of Urdu literature was at its climax during the second decade of the nineteenth century. But the Lucknawi intellectuals did not accept the Delhi school as they considered themselves more civilized in the context of their social background.

These differences were expressed in the writings of the two schools in the second half of the nineteenth century. For instance Rajib Ali Beg Saroor of Lucknow published *Fasana-i-Ajaib* (A Wondrous Tale) in response to *Bagh-o-Bahar* (Spring in the Garden) of Mir Aman of Delhi, whereas Daya Shanker Nasim of Lucknow wrote *Gulzar-e-Nasim* (The Rose Garden of Nasim) in response to *Sehr-ul-Bayan*, (Spellbinding Eloquence) produced by Mir Hassan of Delhi. Similarly, Muhammad Jamiluddin, the Lucknawi author, who published *Arsi Mushaf* (The Marriage Mirror) in response to Nazir Ahmed of Delhi's *Mirat-al-Arus* (The Bridal Image), criticized the Delhi school for confining its attention to the social lives of the bourgeois as compared to his own attention to the cultivated existence of Nawabi Lucknow.[33]

Urdu literature about women in the latter half of the nineteenth century also helps us to visualize various aspects of women's lives, for instance, the distinctive closeness of women to different local cultures, the local superstitions and customs they followed, the regional idioms, proverbs and parables that went to make the local language used only by women.

In this way modern Urdu literature operated as a force in which issues relating to the emancipation of Muslim women were discussed and at the same time enabled the world outside to see for the first time the rich, colourful, and often innocent culture which flourished behind the veil.

URDU WRITINGS FOR THE EMANCIPATION OF MUSLIM WOMEN

During the latter half of the nineteenth century, Muslim social reformers mostly concentrated on women's education, their domestic role, religious training and social consciousness. The reformist literature was mostly produced in the form of text books, social novels, folk tales, and contributions to journals and newspapers.

It is notable that there was a strong official support for furthering women's education. Both the Lieutenant-Governors of the Punjab and the United Provinces, Donald Macleod, (1865–70) and William Muir, (1868–74) and their Directors of Public Instructions, Colonel Holroyd and Matthew Kempson, were educated Orientalists who took pleasure in Urdu literature and sought to use it in developing the school curricula and especially female education. There were several books published during their period which aimed to improve the domestic life of Muslim families. Prominent among those were Muhammad Ismail's *Nairang-e-Nazir* (The Fascination of Eyes), Matthew Kempson's *Dastan-e-Jamila Khatun* (The Story of Jamila Khatun), Maulvi Wazir Ali's *Mirat-al-Nisa* (The Image of a Woman) and Muhammad Hussain Azad's *Nasihat ka Kiran Phul* (The Embellishment of Advice).[34] However, the two most important books were those of Wazir Ali and Azad. The former, who had religious reformist sympathies, was concerned with the social and moral reformation of women. Religious education was his answer and, being a countryman, his work reflected the village environment and expressed his message through local proverbs and examples.[35] The latter, whose interests were more than just religious, sought to communicate his message about female education in allegory. Thus the names of the characters reflect their special qualities—Sharif, a gentleman, Saeeda, a virtuous woman, and Adeeba, a female teacher of refined manners. The book revolved around Sharif, who was a merchant and lived with his wife and daughter Saeeda, in Lahore. He was a great believer in female education. He eventually persuaded his wife of the necessity of education for Saeeda and she arranged for Adeeba to teach her. Meanwhile Sharif travelled to China and Tibet on business and wrote letters to his daughter describing his experiences. The outcome of her lessons and her letters was that Saeeda was able to establish her own school for girls.[36]

The writers of reformist literature were further encouraged by an act of government. In 1868 the Lieutenant-Governor of North-Western Provinces, William Muir announced the annual award of prizes for literary works which would deal realistically with social problems. Many reformists were stimulated by this annual competition to produce works expressing their views on women's literacy, home economics and orthodox practices. In 1869, for instance, Sayyed Munir wrote his *Larkiyon-ki-Talim* (The Education of Girls) which was awarded a prize and which took the form of a series of dialogues between a mother and her daughter. The basic theme was to demonstrate the importance of education for mothers as they were responsible for the training of their children, in particular the upbringing of girls and their preparation for marriage. The mother advises her daughter that if she wants to be a good mother and a submissive wife, she must know her duties through knowledge, education and training. Sayyed Munir was keen to recommend the kind of education that was provided in government schools and which could be useful as a means of livelihood and enhancement of a girl's social status.[37]

A second prize-winning work was Inayat Husain's *Mufid-e-Khalaiq* (Of Benefit to the People), which was published in the same year and came to be adopted as a textbook in girls' schools in the North-Western Provinces, Oudh, and Rampur states. The work which was divided into four chapters, deals with the importance of women's education, recommendations for female curricula and its moral values. In the first chapter he outlined the advantages of female education and criticized those who opposed female education without having solid reasons for their opposition except considering it against prevailing customs. Such people as he noted did not understand that the illiteracy of women was harmful for their society and domestic life because illiterate women could not become the confident companions of their husbands. Moreover, they were likely to be unrefined and superstitious. Sometimes they could even bring dishonour to their families because they were unable to distinguish between right and wrong. In the second chapter Husain dealt with different aspects of modern education which would enable women to study the books of *hakims* as well as be able to read modern medical books which could advise them, for instance, as to how to vaccinate newborn babies against smallpox. In the third chapter, Husain referred to Quranic passages in which Muslim men and women both are enjoined to seek knowledge. He proceeded to outline the characteristics of famous Muslim women and advised his readers to follow their example. In the last chapter, he dealt with the pre-school education of girls and then with schools themselves. He suggested that there should be committees run by local gentry to make arrangements for women's education in government and private *purdah* schools under female teachers. If they were not available, then male teachers from Christian missions would also be suitable. Husain paid particular attention to the religious and moral content of the curricula of girls' schools and warned against the danger of romantic tales such as *Musnavi-Mir-Hasan*, *Qissa-e-Laila-Majnun*, and *Shireen Farhaad*.[38]

A major reformist work was produced by Nazir Ahmed who was educated at the Delhi College and was associated with the

Aligarh Movement. He challenged the behaviour of uneducated women who followed customary practices and were unfamiliar with Islamic teachings. Like others, Nazir Ahmed was concerned about women's education and their moral training but he was set apart from his contemporaries by his broader vision of education and by the quality of his literary technique which had a fascinating style, powerful dialogues and understanding of human nature. The popular appeal of his writings led people to consider him as a sincere friend who understood their problems and had acceptable solutions. His first social novel, *Mirat-al-Arus* (The Bridal Image) was published in 1869 and won the top prize of one thousand rupees. The names of the characters of *Mirat-al-Arus* mostly personified the nature of their work, for instance, Akbari (elder sister), Asghari (younger sister), Aqil (a wise man) and Kamil (the complete man). The basic theme of the story revolved around the tension between evil (ignorance) and virtue (education) and their impact on the part of women's lives.[39] Nazir Ahmed's other reforming work *Banat-un-Nash* (*The Daughters of the Stars*) which directed attention particularly to women's education, was published in 1873 and was considered to be a sequel to *Mirat-al-Arus* as far as its style, subject matter and educational recommendations were concerned formal education was not sufficient for women In his opinion so he divided his education plan into two parts. *Mirat-al-Arus* dealt with the first part, consisting of moral education and domestic affairs, while the second part, *Banat-un-Nash*, discussed the importance of physical education, geography and astronomy. His aim was that women should gradually understand the world at large and reduce the role of superstition in their lives.[40]

A rather less enlightened approach towards women's education was adopted by Maulvi Muhammad Ahsan from Bareilly in *Zad-ul-Mukhaddarat* (The Journey of Virtuous Women) in 1871. The book dealt with women from childhood to married life. He wished society to realize that the socio-moral education of Muslim women was the vital responsibility both of parents and female teachers. Knowledge about how to behave and religious education had to be sought through moral training and good books, taught by female teachers belonging to respectable families. A girl, after completing her education, should know her religious duties and social responsibilities towards her parents, in-laws and in particular, towards her husband so that she could be both a respectful and a respectable wife. He concluded by recommending books for female education which could be helpful in women's moral and social development.[41]

Another reforming work, *Kuhl-ul-Jawahir* (Chemistry of the Pearls) was written by Muhammad Muslihuddin in 1873. This was adopted as a textbook for vernacular girls' schools. The characters were developed through dialogues in very simple Urdu which idealized the picture of women's roles and their direct influence in the domestic sphere. Muslihuddin made it clear that homes were the basic unit of society and women were in charge of them. The main character, Liaqat-un-Nisa (a learned woman), talked about the proficiency of women in domestic affairs, learned from reading books and listening to elder female kin. The conversation of Liaqat-un-Nisa flowed from one subject to another in a simple style. In the beginning, she advised illiterate women to look after the general health of their families by using *unani* prescriptions and medicinal herbs. She also gave some useful prescriptions for seasonal fever, sunstroke and blood poisoning. Liaqat-un-Nisa then stated the importance of household management, expecting the educated woman to be a competent manager who always kept in mind the income of her husband and tried to extend a helping hand through her savings and handicrafts. She further advised women to be obedient to their husbands and to fulfil their obligations properly, as husbands were superior to their wives in all respects.[42]

At the same time some *ulama* were looking at the problems of women through their educational literature written from a reformist perspective. One of these was Muhammad Zahiruddin's work, *Fawaid-un-nisa* (Benefits for Women) published in 1873. For him education was the answer to what he felt was the need for women to deepen acquaintance with the traditional *madrasa* courses. So he recommended classic texts of the traditional *madrasa* system such as: *Kimiya-e-Saadat, Futuh-ul-ghaib, Lataif-e-Ashrafi, Akhlaq-e-Anwari, Musnawi Maulana Rum, Akhbar-ul-Akhbar, Madarij-ul-Nabuwwat,* and *Minhaj-ul-Salikeen.*

After religious education, Zahiruddin considered women's training in practical skills in domestic economy. He was concerned in particular with widows who were not able to remarry because of social restrictions. He emphasized skills that would enable widows not only to maintain themselves but also help to control sexual desire which could endanger society.[43]

A similar approach was adopted by Maulvi Shah Abdul Rahim Dehlvi who concentrated in particular on the issue of the remarriage of widows. It is gratifying to note that Rashid-ul-Khairi had a close relationship with Abdul Rahim, who started his career as a teacher in the Bengal Lancers, where he taught Arabic and Persian to English soldiers.

Abdul Rahim went to Mecca for *Hajj* in 1871. There he was able to discuss issues with *ulama* belonging to all the main *Sunni* schools of thought. Many issues related to women, in particular the serious problem of widows as many Indian Muslims thought their remarriage to be dishonourable. These *ulama* were shocked to discover the marriage practices of Indian Muslims and asked Abdul Rahim to write a *fatawa* for his people in the Urdu language with their endorsement. Abdul Rahim returned in 1873 and published his book *Randho-ki-Shahdi* (The Remarriage of Widows), in which he put forward his views both in poetry and prose that included the *fatawa* of *ulama* of Mecca and Medina. He appealed to Muslims to join him in his campaign for the remarriage of widows which was according to the traditions of Holy Prophet (PBUH). He appealed to every *imam* (a prayer leader) to pronounce this in the Friday sermons and to advise people to allow remarriage of their widows.[44] It is notable that Abdul Rahim was emphasizing this some twenty years before Altaf Husain Hali's *Ek-Bevah-ki-Munajat* in which the issue of the remarriage of widows was a major theme. (To be discussed later).

A notably important forward-looking book in the reforming mode was Altaf Husain Hali's *Majalis-un-nisa* (1874). This didactic work on female education was both awarded a prize by Colonel Holroyd, the Director of Public Instruction in the Punjab and recommended as a textbook in girls' schools in the Punjab and the United Provinces for decades afterwards.

The work was divided into two parts. The first part dealt with the relationship between a mother Bari Begum and her daughter Mahmuda Begum and the second part that of another mother Zubaida and her son Sayyid Abbas. The *Majalis*, as Minault has observed, accurately represented the conversation of upper-middle class women of Delhi and was written in a straight forward colloquial style, using idioms of the *zenana*. The characters in the work were developed through their dialogue; at the same time the atmosphere of the *zenana* became apparent. The discussion of *Majalis* flowed from one subject to another without any externally imposed scheme, but rather by free association.[45]

The opening conversation in the *Majalis* takes place between the Bari Begum, Mahmuda Begum, and Maryam Zamani, a close friend of the family. These three women are joined by *atuji*, an old family female retainer. One of the major themes of their conversation is the importance of female education. *Atuji* pointes out that the attitude of *ashraf* Muslims towards girls' education is quite different from their attitude towards the education of their boys. A girl is considered an unwanted child for her parents. But her parents would have to answer to God on the Day of Judgement for any injustice when He would say, 'We did not create girls so they could be pets in their parents' homes and then go to their husband's homes and there to pass their lives as slave girls. We created them so that they too, like the men, could use their minds and could benefit humanity, put order into a disordered household, and take care of their children.'[46] *Atuji* urges that women be educated just as in Europe where she believed that all the people were educated without sex discrimination.[47]

Atuji then mentions the case of Zubaida Khatun, an educated woman well-trained in household management. It is notable that the character of Zubaida Khatun is presented in the *Majalis* as that of an ideal woman. *Atuji* tells her story as if Zubaida herself is speaking. She (Zubaida) says that by the age of thirteen she had studied the *Gulistan, Bostan, Akhlaq-e-Muhsini, Aiyyar Danish*, in Persian, *Kimiya'sadat, Kalila-wa-Dimna* in Arabic, and the basic grammar, the common factor and the decimal factors in Arithmetic, Euclid's geometry, Geography and History of India and had practised both *naskh* and *nastaliq* calligraphy.[48] Zubaida was thus made to criticize the superstitions, heresies and social evils that were common among Muslim women under the influence of Hindu culture, claiming that it was difficult to remove this influence because people preferred customs to religion. For example, while Muslim widows were permitted to remarry according to the *Hadith*, Indian Muslims considered this practice immoral.[49]

Finally, Zubaida pays her gratitude to the British Government for its welfare work in the form of modern inventions, the press, hospitals and educational institutions.[50]

In 1876 another reformist work *Chasmah-e-Khirad* (The Spring of Wisdom) was published by Abdul Rahim Khan. It was awarded a prize and adopted as a textbook for girls' schools. In a colloquial style, Abdul Rahim elaborated the proper decorum of a patriarchal society in which an educated and talented woman could foster her family's well-being through correct household management and a proper relationship with her husband and his family. Abdul Rahim advised women to seek knowledge so that they could not only keep household accounts but, through their writing skills, also write letters to their husbands, fathers and brothers. He pointed out that an uneducated wife with an educated husband would have difficulties in holding his affection. Abdul Rahim admired the educated women of England who were getting compulsory primary education. He also appreciated educated women in India, from *ashraf* or ruling families, who organized the executive affairs of their states. Among those well known for their management skills whom he admired were Shahjahan Begum of Bhopal, Nawab Jaffri Begum of Shahmsabad, and Methab Kunwar, a Hindu lady of Kotla.[51]

Following his educational advice, the writer went on to emphasize the importance of women maintaining good relations with their in-laws. Some of his suggestions, however, reflected specific customary beliefs rather than Islamic practices. For example, he suggested that, whenever she returned back home from her parents' house, a wife ought to show deepest respect to her mother-in-law.[52] He further advised her never to laugh in the presence of her father-in-law and mother-in-law, never to talk to her husband in the presence of elder kin, and on the occasion of *Eid* and other festivals never to demand new clothes. Of course, if her mother-in-law gave her a gift, she should be very grateful to her.[53]

Abdul Rahim similarly forbade wives to make frequent visits to their parents' home as their mothers-in-law would suspect that they did not like their in-laws. He further advised that they should avoid speaking loudly in their husbands' homes and should cover themselves with a *dopatta*. If a wife had some complaint against her in-laws, she should not mention it before her parents. She had to be submissive to her husband.[54]

It is interesting to note the change of emphasis that occurred when some women of reformist principles, such as Shahjahan Begum, the ruler of Bhopal, came to write her *Tehzil-e-Niswan* (The Refinement of Women) in 1889. She did not stress the need for women to become submissive wives, good mothers, running a household or observing hierarchial relationships. Instead, she suggested something else more beneficial for her Muslim sisters and their lives. She surveyed all customary practices of Muslim women in the light of the Quran and *hadith*, and recommended a kind of 'purified' Islamic behaviour, by providing a general guidance for health conditions, the upbringing of children, and women's rights concerning marriage and divorce.[55]

What was particularly striking about this huge book was its commonsense approach to issues concerning Muslim women. It

was written in a most direct and accessible form of Urdu, and
dealt with key female concerns such as the various stages of
pregnancy, diets in pregnancy, the condition of labour rooms
and the duties of midwives. The different subject matter and
style of this work, the one reformist book by a woman in
nineteenth century India, highlighted the essentially patriarchal
nature of the bulk of other reformist authors who wrote during
the same period.

Nevertheless, the work of male authors did enable other
Muslim men to sympathize with the sentiments of their female
counterparts. In 1894, Hali, in his *Ek-Bevah-ki-Munajat*
(Supplication of a Widow), took the new step of making poetry
the vehicle for the discussion of social issues. Confronting the
problems of young widows, he expressed the misery of their
plight with such imaginative power that his readers felt the
desolation of South Asian widowhood from the bottom of their
hearts. He showed the agony of the young widow, who was
forbidden to satisfy her sexual desires, humiliated in society and
not even permitted to adorn her body. *Mehndi* (myrtle), *Kanghi*
(hair dressing), *Kajal* (eye liner), *Bali* (ear ring), *Kangan* (bracelet)
were prohibited for her. Miserable and mistrusted, nothing was
left for her, now that she was a widow. Robbed of all happiness,
she found that her only solace lay in the love of God.[56]

This said, the essentially patriarchal nature of reformist
writing was powerfully expressed by the most influential work
in this genre, the *Bihishti Zewar* (A Heavenly Jewel) which was
published by the Deobandi scholar, Maulana Ashraf Ali Thanawi
in the first decade of the twentieth century. This book, which
discussed women's issues in a religious context, was divided
into ten sections and ran to more than a thousand pages. It
contained exemplary stories of good Muslim women of the past,
rules concerning proper conduct and the formation of the
personality, lessons on how to manage a household, information
about *unani* medicine, requirements involved in ritual prayers,
and facts about Muslim personal laws. The book was designed
to save Muslim women from moral decline mainly as a result
of their insufficient religious education and training. Gradually

it became a part of the dowry of Muslim brides. They entered their husbands' homes with the Quran in one hand and *Bihishti Zewar* in the other.[57]

The strongest theme of this book is the submissive and constrained role of a woman. For Thanawi a woman's power lay in her submission. He described, for instance, the case of a woman in Lucknow whose husband was a scoundrel but who never complained and even sent out food for him to eat with his women from the *bazaar*. The argument was that when God ordered him to cease his bad conduct, he would become the slave of his wife.[58] It is astonishing that, despite clear statements in the Quran, there is no word of condemnation of the husband for committing the sins of fornication and adultery; the Maulana merely insisted that the wife should submit to her husband.

When it came to education the Maulana was particularly concerned with and anxious to control the knowledge which women should acquire. He produced a long list of books not suitable for female education, including, for instance, any commentary on *Sura Yusuf* of the Quran which tells the story of Yusuf (Joseph) and the wife of Aziz (Potiphar).[59] Women's association with the Quran was to be confined just to reading it as a religious duty and *sawab* (reward), and not for gaining guidance for daily life and its needs. It was as though the Maulana feared the revolutionary impact of the Quran on the social order of his time if women were able to discover for themselves the words of God.

THE EMERGENCE OF WOMEN'S JOURNALS AND NEWSPAPERS IN URDU

Christian missionaries were the pioneers in and the chief promoters of female education both in English and vernacular languages. The foremost amongst them were Methodists, who established themselves in India in 1856. In 1884 they founded the first journal for women *Rafiq-e-Niswan* (A Woman's Friend) with funds donated by American women. The journal was published twice a month in Urdu, Hindi, Tamil and Bengali. It was a broad sheet with eight pages and arranged in two columns per page. Articles on education, social moral training, household management and short stories from American and English history formed its main contents. Its target audience was native Christian women.[60]

The first Urdu journal specifically for Muslim women was *Akhbar-e-Nisa* (Women's Newspaper) published in 1887 by Maulvi Sayyed Ahmed, compiler of the world famous Urdu dictionary *Ferhang-i-Asifia*. This was followed by the publication of a large number of magazines for women. Prominent among these was the *Tehzib-e-Niswan*, founded by Maulvi Sayyed Mumtaz Ali and his wife Muhammadi Begum in 1898. Mumtaz Ali took up an agenda that was largely set up by the English. It revolved around the problem of polygamy, the age of marriage, *purdah* and the education of women. Like the *ulama*, he was keen for girls to be educated but he favoured a broader curriculum which included history, geography and science. It is not surprising that Mumtaz Ali's ideas were shared by many of those associated with the westernizing movement at Aligarh.[61]

As the first newspaper for women, published at a time when most Muslims were not in favour of female education, the publishing of *Tehzib-e-Niswan* caused resentment amongst conservative Muslim families. They accused Mumtaz Ali of inciting women to revolt, but he was not deterred from his reforming work. Gradually *Tehzib-e-Niswan* succeeded in establishing a circle of women writers who were able to play a vital role in emergence of a sense of Muslim sisterhood in South Asia.[62] Six years later, in 1904, Muhammadi Begum became the first sole female editor. She founded another magazine, the *Mushir-e-Madhar*, for the general guidance of mothers. This was followed by the production of a large number of didactic books for women in Indian idioms, the more remarkable being *Sughar Beti, Chandan Har, Safia Begum, Arsi*, and *Tin-Bahanoo-ki-Kahani*.

From 1904 efforts to improve the position of Muslim women became specifically associated with the Aligarh movement when

Shaikh Abdullah, a young lawyer, became the leading advocate of women's education. He started an Urdu journal, *Khatun*. His aim was to bring useful knowledge into the homes; he was particularly aware that, compared with men, Muslim women depended on books and literature for knowledge. He condemned those who considered the study of history, geography, mathematics and logic a waste of time for women, believing them worthy of only the most elementary texts.[63]

The achievements of *Khatun* during the early twentieth century were remarkable in that it transmitted the views of Abdullah and his supporters in their campaign for women's education and enlightenment.[64] Thus the fund raising scheme for his proposed girls' school at Aligarh and annual meetings of All-India Muslim Educational Conference were regularly reported in *Khatun's* pages.

The theme of *Khatun* was the contrast between the modernist and traditional approach towards women's education and its impact on Muslim society. The expression of these themes reflected the progressive attitude of its contributors, who saw the future of Muslim society in not only improving the domestic skills of women but also through the training of their minds, equal opportunities, and the development of greater self-awareness. *Khatun* idealized women as individuals who had duties and rights in society. Abdullah wished women to have the courage to voice their demands in exactly the same way as men would do; their traditional obedience and silence were not to be interpreted as the inferiority of their sex.[65]

It is notable that *Khatun* introduced a large number of women to each other through the publication of their writings and articles.[66] Characteristic of their views on issues such as child marriage, polygamy, *khulah*, and *purdah* was their sensitive approach towards these social problems. For instance, Zuhra Begum advised parents to obtain the consent of their daughters about the matter of their marriage, keeping in mind the consequences of an unsuitable marriage which could destroy the lives of their daughters. Although a girl's protest at such a time was considered disobedience, it could save her a lot of trouble.[67]

In 1908 journalism for women reached a new stage with the publication of Rashid-ul-Khairi's *Ismat*. The particular step forward represented by *Ismat* was that most of its contributors were women, who, as it happened, also brought to the field a higher standard of writing and a broader coverage of issues. These advances clearly bore fruit, for *Ismat* is the only Urdu journal for women that has been published down to the present day. After *Ismat*, Khairi published several journals which were all targeted at particular audiences known to be concerned with women's issues. None achieved the lasting popularity of *Ismat*. None had its distinctive style and interpretation, its variety of subject matter, and above all, its mission to cultivate the taste for reading among women and to change their views.

Ismat was not merely a women's journal, but its volumes relate the long history of the struggle of Muslim women to improve their status in the eyes of society while at the same time expressing feminist beliefs within the existing system. Alongside his female contributors, Rashid-ul Khairi also contributed to the journal. The message of his contribution was essentially that of a modern campaign to improve the position of women in the context of their traditional household and family role. Like Nazir Ahmed and Hali, he believed that the Western model of womanhood was inappropriate to the social context of eastern societies. In his view, women should have all the same social and religious rights as men, finding their identity and personal fulfilment within the traditional system.

There were two important vehicles for the dissemination of his vision. The first was the primary school for girls which he set up in Delhi under the title of *Tarbiyat ghah-e-Banat*. For this he developed a special curriculum.[68] A second vehicle was his creative writings, novels and short stories, many of which were first published in *Ismat*. It should be noted that many of his books about women were adopted as textbooks in different universities for the higher degree in Urdu.[69] His simple style, his powerful imagination and striking command of *zenana* idioms in Delhi usage made his writings popular. He articulated the misery of women's lives, their social exploitation and offered

possible solutions to their problems. His whole life was devoted
to the freeing of the Muslim woman.

He spoke in favour of her rights in *Bachchah-ka Kurta*
(published in *Ismat* in 1923), insisted on her consent in marriage
in *Sat Ruhhoon-ka Amalnamah* (The Record of Seven Souls),
urged for her shares in property in *Mahrum-e-Warasit* (Deprived
of Inheritance) and criticized those *mullas* in *Talaqan ka-Sufaid
Bal* (The Grey Hair of the Divorced Woman), who could destroy
women's lives with their cheap *fatawa*. For instance, he told the
story of Auzma, a mother of four children, who was given
permission by her mother-in-law to visit her parents' home.
Unfortunately, when Auzma began to leave, her mother in-law
tried to make an excuse for the second marriage of her son.
During the stay at her parent's home, Auzma went to see a
circus with another woman. When her father-in-law, who was
a *maulvi*, came to know, he got a *fatawa* from other *mullas*, to
dissolve her marriage charging Auzma with disobedience and
misconduct. At the last moment Auzma's husband refused to
divorce her and her marriage was saved.[70]

In addition to its social messages, *Ismat* aimed at providing
help to its female readers in their everyday lives: book reviews,
national and international news, cooking recipes, needle work,
fashion advice and information about female diseases and their
unani and allopathic treatments were published regularly in this
journal.

Along with the above mentioned popular women's journals,
many other magazines were launched from different places in
India in the first decade of the twentieth century. For example,
Mullaim-e-Niswan from Hyderabad, Deccan, *Purdah-e-Ismat*
from Lucknow, *Al Hijab* from Bhopal, all expressing reforming
views on social matters, the value of the individual, and demands
for civic and political rights for women.

THE CONTRIBUTIONS OF ENGLISH MAGAZINES

English printed media played a powerful role in the socio-
cultural transformation of British India. Although English was

read only by a tiny fraction of the population during the second half of the nineteenth century, reformists, wishing to attract the attention of the colonial state, used English language magazines as a vehicle for their views.

There were two types of reformist work commonly published in English magazines. First, there was the work of those reformers who wished to establish a new system in which all suppressed groups (mainly women), would be able to overcome age-old traditions, customary practices and social taboos through acquiring of equal rights in the eyes of state and society and consequently equal participation with men in the momentous events of life. These people were usually British, and often Christian missionaries, supported by some leading Indians. Second, English magazines provided an outlet for reformers who appreciated the views of the first group but felt that the transformation of Indian society should take place within the framework of their culture. These people belonged mainly to both Hindu and Muslim social élites.

With the founding of the reformist journal, *The Indian Magazine* in 1871 (issued by National Indian Association from London), local Indian communities had a chance to exchange their views on social problems with the assistance of government and voluntary associations. Another journal, *The Asiatic Review*, was also published from London in 1886. Its aim was to bring change in India by promoting social reforms with the mutual cooperation of both sexes on equal terms.

One of the most important magazines in English was *The Modern Review*, which was published from Calcutta in 1902 under the editorship of Ramananda Chatterjee. Its modern outlook was reflected in the writings of its contributors especially those which drew the connection between the regeneration of South Asian society and of the position of women who were characterized as sleeping one-third of their lives and spending the other two-thirds making beds and clothes, and cooking meals.[71]

The aim of *The International Review of Missions*, published in 1911, was to advertize the social services provided by

Christian missionaries in different parts of the world. The main objectives of the missions in South Asia were spreading education, confuting customary practises, especially strict *purdah* and winning support for the necessity of modern health arrangements.[72] All these voluntary services were reported and discussed in this journal by those who were directly or indirectly involved in missionary activities.

Turning to the second category that is those who wished to bring about social change within an Islamic cultural framework, note should be taken of the two journals launched by Khawaja Kamal-ud-Din of the Woking Mosque in England. *The Islamic Review* and *The Islamic Review and Muslim India* in 1912. He was particularly concerned with achieving a reinterpretation of Islamic social values through *ijtihad*. Note should also be taken of the *Indian Ladies Magazine* which was founded in Madras in 1909 and edited by Mrs K. Satthiananadhan. Like the other women's journals in English which were to come, it played a vital role in encouraging relationships among women from different communities and provided a forum in which they were able to address change first and foremost as women. The issues which it was particularly concerned to address were child marriage, infant morality and problems of child birth. In doing so, it appealed to educated women to offer their services voluntarily to improve the circumstances of their less fortunate sisters.[73]

Finally, note should also be taken of a women's journal which had a very different approach. *Stri Dharma* was introduced as the official organ of the Indian Women's Association founded by Mrs Annie Besant in 1917. It had quite a different reformist approach to other women's journals, especially on the question of the political rights of women, and it demanded Indian representation in local bodies and legislatures without sex discrimination.[74]

SOCIAL REFORM ASSOCIATIONS AND THE QUESTION OF WOMEN'S EMANCIPATION

This major evolution in ideas about society led Indian élites to support its further development. The main way in which they expressed their social concerns was through the foundation of different social organizations on a large scale. More commonly, the forums of social organizations were used as a means of obtaining two basic objectives. The first objective was to get information about the nature of contemporary social problems: efforts were made to discuss problems through debates and discussions. Regular meetings of the organizations were held at different places and resolutions were passed about general and local problems. Some organizations had their own journals which were used as the social organs of these particular societies and organizations. For instance, the National Indian Association published the Indian Magazine to project its social work.

The second concern of these reformers dealt with the emancipation of society through the practical efforts of their organizations. They tried to lessen the intensity of the class and caste based power structures of Indian society by promoting the ideas of equal opportunity and equal freedom. Above all, the traditional gender system was highly criticized by attacking social evils like *sati* and women's seclusion. In this way the matters of women's social uplift became the major concern of Indian élites in general, as they believed that the idea of women's emancipation would ultimately enable them to seek the final emancipation of their society.

The first organized reformist campaign which was started in Bengal and Calcutta became the centre of such activities. The *Brahmo Samaj* founded by Ram Mohan Roy in the early nineteenth century emphasized the education of women and the abolition of *sati*. The Association received much support from Christian missionaries who, in this respect, were working in the same directions. Another important organization, the *Majlis-e-Mubahasah* was started in 1861, under the patronage of the ruler of Benaras. The *majlis* did its work with the mutual cooperation of local Hindus and Muslims. The open debates of its participants particularly on matters of women's education and their seclusion were regularly published in its journal, the *Mujallah-e-Ilmia*.[75]

The first important social organization in north India was the *Anjuman-e-Shahajahanpore*, which came into being in 1862. Like other contemporary organizations, its social agenda was based on the problems of the remarriage of widows and female education. The *Anjuman* appointed Kazi Sarfaraz Ali, a local Muslim reformer, to write up the details of all customs which were badly affecting the lives of women who observed *purdah*. In later years the *Anjuman* succeeded in opening five branches in different parts of north India. Among its more prominent achievements was the establishment of three girls' schools. The *Anjuman* also launched its monthly journal, entitled *Rifah-e-Khalaiq*, which accurately projected its achievements.[76]

It is notable that, along with the local élites, English officers also took an interest in the social uplift of Indian society. For instance, in 1864, Dr Leitner, the Principle of Lahore College, founded the *Anjuman-e-Ishaat-e-Ulum* which was warmly welcomed both by Hindus and Muslims. Along with the development of modern literature, Muhammad Husain, the secretary declared that the *Anjuman* would aim to improve society, particularly to fulfil the financial needs of widows who were driven to prostitution due to their poverty.[77]

The above mentioned pattern was followed by *Anjum Tehzib-e-Lucknow* founded in 1867. Anyone could get membership irrespective of caste and creed and thereby had a chance to express their views on different social matters. Later the *Anjuman* regularly published these debates and discussions in its monthly journal, the *Risala*.[78]

The National Indian Association (1871) was another major organization founded in London to discuss the social problems of Indians on a broader scale with the mutual cooperation of British social reformers. Prominent among its achievements were annual social conferences held under the auspices of the Association in different parts of India. For instance, in 1888 the fourth social conference was held in Allahabad and was attended by about 1,000 people. The conference passed the resolution for the distribution of social reform literature in English as well in vernacular languages. It also emphasized the spreading of female education, the prevention of child marriage and the reduction of expenses on different ceremonies of childbirth, marriage and death.[79]

Similar but lighter work was done by the Debating Club Delhi in 1871. The prominent figures among Muslims and Hindus who attended were Sayyed Mahmood-ul-Hasan and Lala Hukum Chand, who actively participated in an attempt to resolve common social problems. They tried to persuade people to allow the remarriage of widows, in particular young widows, so as to reduce their social agony.[80]

Among Muslims, the first important social organization, the *Anjuman-i-Islam* (1876), was founded by Badruddin Tyabji in Bombay. His social experiences were quite different to those of Sayyed Ahmed Khan, who in the first place wanted to emancipate Muslim men rather than Muslim women. But the education of Tyabji abroad led him to forge relations with enthusiastic Hindu and Parsi social reformers such as Telang, Ranade, Sir Pherozeshah Metha, and Dadabhai Naoroji, all of whom sought to emancipate Indian society as a whole. Matters like Muslim female education and local custom of *purdah* were usually discussed through the forum of the *Anjuman-i-Islam* by Tyabji and his Muslim supporters.[81]

WOMEN'S PUBLIC DISCOURSE: FEMINISM AND SISTERHOOD STEPS

By the end of the nineteenth century, the development of reformist literature and social activities gradually offered a public space to women. Indeed, this social discourse became a widening channel for the expression of their cultural experiences and feminist behaviour. Feminism not only led them to fulfil their personal inspirations but further developed a sense of sisterhood for their betterment. Later, these concerns would prove more helpful for South Asian élites, to discover new dimensions in their political and constitutional struggles.

Notably, the achievements of European women (mostly associated with Christian missionaries) can be considered as the early participation of women in public discourse in India. Their social activities led them to work in the field of female education both in schools as well as at homes. The first women's organization, the Juvenile Female Society (1820), managed to establish three girls' schools in Calcutta, Chitpore and Sibpore, where girls were taught reading, spelling, geography and religious education. In 1840, Mr T. Smith of the Free Church Mission proposed a scheme for the home education of upper class women. The local *ashraf*, particularly in Bengal, responded fauourably to this scheme as they were not in favour of their daughters being educated in schools. A large number of women offered their services as governesses for home-to-home education. Thus, they got a chance to exchange their views with local women on different socio-cultural matters. The influence of European women on the lives of respectable families could be found in the social gatherings of the *ashraf* to which they were cordially invited. Later, the life sketches of these ladies were appreciated as symbolic characters in novels and other forms of fiction mostly written by Indian female writers in vernacular languages. For instance, the characters of Miss Thompson and Miss Lily were appreciated by Mrs A.Z. Hasan in her novel *Roshnuk Begum*. These ladies were the governesses of Roshnuk Begum, the daughter of Nawab Sayyed Muzaffar Ali of Delhi.

Note should be taken that during the early twentieth century, European women expanded their social activities in new directions. They wanted to see the emancipation of Indian women not only in terms of their educational progress but also through the acquisition of increased social and political rights. To achieve these objectives, the Women's Indian Association, mentioned earlier, was formed by Mrs Annie Besant in Madras in 1917. The association was warmly welcomed both by many Hindu as well as Muslim women. Women like Sarojini Naidu and Bi Amman (the mother of Muhammad Ali and Shaukat Ali) supported the cause of this Association by demanding the right of enfranchisement for Indian women.

The early social activities of local women, therefore, had started by the closing years of the nineteenth century and Bengal became the first centre of their public discourse. The initial step forward was taken by Hindu women. The first important Indian women's association, the Ladies' Theosophical Society, was founded by Swarnakumari Debi in 1872. After the failure of this society, Swarnakumari established another organization, the *Sakhi Samiti*, in 1886 with the cooperation of women belonging to respectable families. The main aim of the society was to provide financial assistance to poor widows, by selling handicrafts which were made by women for women.[82] This social work was further expanded by her daughter Sarala Debi, who had already expressed her feminist attitude through the editorship of the monthly journal *Bharati* which was published from Calcutta. She founded the *Bharat Satri Mahamandal* in 1910. The association organized women, belonging to different races, creeds and classes, on the basis of their common interests.[83] For the advancement of female education, it made special arrangements in various parts of India. For instance, in its Calcutta branch, six female teachers were engaged to educate eighteen girls of ten families, while in its Lahore branch, free private *zenana* classes were arranged three times a week, in which English, Sanskrit, Hindi, Urdu, arithmetic, needle work and music were taught by six volunteer female teachers.[84]

As far as Muslim women were concerned, they found their public place both in the form of *purdah* clubs and organizations where they had the chance to exchange ideas with each other and formulate their reformist work. Hyderabad, Deccan, became the first centre of these social activities. In 1901 the Ladies' Social Club was started with the cooperation of local and European women who used it as a way of gathering together eastern and western women. In later years two more clubs, the Zenana Recreation Club and the Lady Barton Club were opened for the same purpose.[85] With the formation of the *Anjuman*

Khawateen in 1901, the women of Hyderabad had another channel to exchange their feminist experiences. For instance, a *zenana* departmental store called 'The Deccan Store' was established in 1901 which was run by women of respectable families. It provided the marvellous facility of independent shopping for women in Hyderabad.[86]

Gradually a large number of organizations were established in different parts of India usually run by the women of prominent local families. Families like the Tyabjis in Bombay, Suhrawardys in Bengal and Shafis in the Punjab were actively taking part in the social transformation of the colonial state. For instance, the *Anjuman-i-Khatunan-i-Islam* was founded by Begum Muhammad Shafi in Lahore in 1907 for the development of sisterhood among Muslim women. Through its monthly social meetings Muslim women had a chance to define their religious and social ideas and remove their superstitions. Any woman could become a member and usually the membership fee was spent to fulfil the needs of poor women.[87]

The activities of the Muslim Educational Conference expanded to include developing modern education for Muslim women. Its women's branch, the All-India Muslim Ladies' Conference, was founded by the Begum of Bhopal in 1914, on the occasion of the inauguration ceremony for a new residence hall for Aligarh's girls' school. The several branches of the Conference not only promoted female education by opening girls' schools in different parts of India, but also became meeting places for female social activists.[88] The Government also accepted the several proposals of Muslim Educational Conference, regarding the opening of teacher training schools and reservation of quota in the teaching and inspecting departments.[89] Above all, the formation of the All-India Muslim Ladies Conference further paved the way for the foundation of the Indian Women's Association (1917). But the most active was the All-India Women's Conference founded in 1927 at Poona predominately by Hindu women with the support of Muslim women like Begum Hamid Ali. In Bengal, individual examples were set by Suhrawardiya Begum and Nawabzadi

Sarah Bano Begum. The former opened a *Purdahnasheen Madrasa*, in 1913 for the progress of female education, and the latter founded the organization 'The Servant of Humanity', in 1920, to improve the health condition of *purdah* observing women. In latter years the society opened a Health and Recreation Club for this purpose.[90]

Along with these above mentioned popular Muslim women's organizations, many other associations were opened by local women in these years. For example, the *Anjuman-i-Khawateen-i-Deccan* and Lucknow Women's Organization were working well for the social uplift of women.[91]

* * *

The debate over the status of Muslim women in India pointed to those changes which had taken place among Muslims during the period under discussion. In the early stages of the movement for women's emancipation, social activists, judging from the considerable amount of reforming literature that they produced for and about women, did not all agree about what type of model of reform was suitable in the context of the cultural complexity of South Asian society. The early efforts of the reformers were directed towards defining the domestic role of women. In this, particular attention was paid to combating social evils such as *sati*, child marriage and the customary ban on a widow remarriage. It was only gradually that the reformers went beyond this narrowly-defined agenda to redefine and broaden the appropriate roles for women, extending their spheres of influence and activity beyond the four walls of the house. In a sense, this marks what could be called the beginnings of a distinct feminist perspective.

Rashid-ul-Khairi gave voice to the principles of this new feminism which was growing amongst educated Muslim women, as Muslim women themselves understood it, the feminism for which they were struggling encompassed the following:

(a) *Huquq-e-niswan* (the rights of women), to try to redefine their status according to Islamic teachings and Western inspiration which would lessen the burden of local traditions, superstitions and social evils;

(b) *Azadi-e-niswan* (the liberation of women), to give them opportunities for getting education and increasing social awareness, which would ultimately become the channel for their public discourse;

(c) *Bedari-e-niswan* (the awakening of women), to promote consciousness of their new roles, rights and responsibilities in the light of the changing social conditions

(d) *Faraez-e-niswan* (the duties of women), to fulfil their roles as mothers, wives and individuals so as to properly fulfil the needs of the new scientific culture;

(e) *Islah-e-niswan* (the reformation of women), to work for their moral and material progress by removing ignorance and superstitions in their lives.[92]

NOTES

1. Faisal Fatehali Devji, 'Gender and the Politics of the Space: The Movement for Women's Reforms 1857–1900', in Zoya Hasan (ed.), *Forging Identities: Gender, Communities and the State*, pp. 22–37.
2. Wilfred Cantwell Smith, *Modern Islam in India: A Social Analysis*, (Victor Gollancz, Ltd. London, 1946), p. 11.
3. Barbara D. Metcalf, 'Reading and Writing About Muslim Women', in Zoya Hasan (ed.), *Forging Identities*, pp. 1–21.
4. Radha Kumar, *The History of Doing: An Illustrated Account of Movements for Women's Rights and Feminism in India, 1800–1990*, (Kali for Women, New Delhi, 1993), p. 3.
5. Niaz Husain, 'The Purdah (Veil) System Amongst the Muslim Women in India', *The Islamic Review*, Vol. XVII, No. 9, September 1923, pp. 1–18.
6. Ayesha Jalal, 'The Convenience of Subservience; Women and the State of Pakistan', in Deniz Kandiyot, (ed.), *Women Islam and State*, (Macmillan Press, London, 1991), pp. 77–109.
7. Shahida Lateef, *Muslim Women in India: Political and Private Realities, 1890–1980*, p. 34.

8. K.C. Nag, 'Women and Our Final Emancipation', *The Modern Review*, Vol. XXVII, No. 164, August 1920, p. 188.

9. I. M. Lapidus, *A History of Islamic Societies*, (Cambridge University Press, Cambridge, 1988), p. 893.

10. R.A. Sayyed, 'Muslim Women in India: An Overview', in Anjum Mohani (ed.), *Muslim Women in India*, (Radiant Publishers, Delhi, 1992), pp.1–18.

11. F.C.R. Robinson, *Separatism Among Indian Muslims: The Politics of the United Provinces' Muslims 1860–1923*, Oxford University Press, Delhi, 1993), p. 273.

12. Barbara D. Metcalf, 'The Making of a Muslim Lady: Maulana Ashraf Ali Thanawai's Bihisti Zewar', in Milton Israel and N. K. Wagle, (ed.), *Islamic Society and Culture*, (Manohar Publication, New Delhi, 1983), pp. 17–38.

13. P. Hardy, *The Muslims of British India*, (Cambridge University Press, Cambridge, 1973), p. 171.

14. Barbara D. Metaclf, 'The Making of a Muslim Lady', pp. 17–38.

15. Garcin de Tassy, *La langue et la Litterature Hindoustanies en 1850–69. The Opening lectures on the Hindustani Course of Study*. Translated in Urdu under the title of *Khutbat-e-Garcin de Tassy*, (Anjuman-e-Taraqqi-e-Urdu, Hyderabad Deccan, 1935), p. 484.

16. *The Nineteenth Century Review*, Vol. XXIX, No. 169, March 1891, pp. 359, 66.

17. Raziq-ul-Khairi, 'Savan-e-Umri Allama Rashid-ul-Khairi', *Ismat*, Vol. 113, No. 1, 2, July 1964, p. 465.

18. Marcus B. Fuller, *The Wrongs of Indian Womanhood*, (Oliphant Anderson and Ferri, New York, 1900), p. 241.

19. Ibid.

20. See, Marcus B. Fuller, *The Wrongs of the Indian Womanhood*, G. David, *Women's Seclusion and Men's Honour: Sex role in India, Bangladesh and Pakistan*, (Arizon Press, Tucson, 1982), and Patricia Jeffry, *Frogs in a Well*, (Zed Books, London, 1979).

21. See, Nikki Keddie and Beth Baron (ed.), *Women in Middle Eastern History: Shifting Boundaries in Sex and Gender*, (Yale University Press, New Haven, 1991).

22. I.M. Lapidus, *A History of Islamic Societies*, p. 893.

23. Nazir Ahmed, *Mauizat-e-Hasna. A collection of letters written by author to his son*, (Matbah Ansari, Delhi, 1876), pp. 188–89.

24. Raziq-ul-Khairi, *Savan-e-Umri, Allama Rashid-ul-Khairi*, p. 674.

25. Ibid., p. 674.

26. Ibid., p. 675.

27. Shahida Lateef, *Muslim Women in India: 1890–1980*, p. 79.

28. Barbara D. Metcalf, 'The Making of a Muslim Lady', pp. 17–38.

29. Gail Minault, 'Shaikh Abdullah, Begum Abdullah and Sharif Education for Girls at Aligarh', in Imtiaz Ahmed (ed.), *Modernization and Social Change Among Muslims in India*, (Manhor Publications, New Delhi, 1983), pp. 207–236.

30. Ibid.

31. B. Sorabji, *Changing Status of the Women of the Orient*, (New Art Printing Press, Bombay, 1914), pp. 1–12. The Paper was read in a Conference held in America in 1914.

32. Ibid.

33. Muhammad Jamiluddin, *Arsi Mushaf*, (Agra Educational Press, Agra, 1874), p. 3.

34. Ifthakar Ahmed, *Nazir Ahmed: Ahwal wa Asar*, (Majlis-e-Adab Urdu, Lahore, 1971), p. 319.

35. Rabia Iqbal, *Urdu Adab aur Tabqa-e-Niswan*, (Idara Urdu, Hyderabad, Pakistan, 1990), p. 11.

36. Ibid., p. 18.

37. Sayyed Munir, *Larkiyon ki Talim*, (Matbah Munshi Nawal Kishore, Allahabad, 1869), pp. 2–5.

38. Inayat Husain, Kishore, *Mufid-ul-Khaliaq*, (Matbah Munshi Nawal Kishore, Allahabad, 1869), pp. 14, 23, 25, 28, 35.

39. See, Muhammad Nizar Ahmed, *Mirat-al-Arus*, (Matbah Munshi Nawal Kishore, Lucknow, 1896).

40. See, Muhammad Nazir Ahmed, *Banat-un-Nash*, (Matbah Nawal Kishore, Lucknow, 1877).

41. Muhammad Ahsan, *Zad-ul-Mukhaddarat*, (Matbah Siddiqui, Bareilly, 1871), pp. 2, 5, 18, 28, 32, 62.

42. Muhammad Muslihuddin, *Kuhl-ul-Jawahir*, (Matbah Mufid Amm, Agra, 1873), pp. 10, 16, 22.

43. Muhammad Zahiruddin, *Fawaid-un-nisa*, (Matbah Munshi Nawal Kishore, Lucknow, 1873), pp. 9, 11.

44. Abdul Rahim, *Randho ki Shadi*, (Matbah Nawal Kishore, Allahabad, 1873), p. 3.

45. Gail Minault, 'Hali's Majalis-un-nisa: Purdah and Women Power in Ninteenth century', in Milton Israel and N.K. Wagle (ed.), *Islamic Society and Culture*, pp. 39–40.

46. Altaf Husain Hali, *Majalis-un-nisa*, Vol. 1, (Matbah Muhammadi, Lahore, 1874), pp. 8–9.

47. Ibid.

48. Ibid., p. 91.

49. Ibid.

50. Altaf Husain Hali, *Majalis-un-nisa*, 2nd Part, p. 5.

51. Abdul Rahim Khan, *Chasmah-e-Khirad*, (Matbah Abal Alai, Agra, 1876).

52. Ibid., pp. 25, 26.

53. Ibid., pp. 26, 27.
54. Ibid., p. 29.
55. Shahjahan Begum, *Tehzib-Niswan*, (Matbah Ansari, Delhi, 1889), pp. 10, 35, 132, 144, 195, 238, 480.
56. Altaf Husain Hali, *Ek Bevah ki Munajat*, (Delhi, 1892), pp. 15–25.
57. Barbara D. Metcalf, 'The Making of a Muslim Lady', pp. 17–38.
58. Ashraf Ali Thanawi, *Bihishti Zewar*, 4th Part, (Karkhana Tejarat-e-Kuthab, (Karachi, 1962), p. 36.
59. Ibid., 10th Part, p. 54.
60. *Rafiq-e Niswan*, (Methodist Publishing House, Lucknow, 1884).
61. Barbara D. Metaclf, 'Reading and Writing About Muslim Women in British India', in Zoya Hasan, (ed.), *Forging Identities*, pp. 1–21.
62. Zuhra Begum Faizi, 'Tehzib-e-Niswan ki Bani', *Tehzib-e-Niswan*, Vol. 43, No. 27, 16 July 1940, pp. 633–35.
63. *Khatun*, Vol. 6, No. 8, August 1909, p. 284.
64. In 1905, Altaf Husain Hali wrote his well-known poem, *Chup ki Dad* at Shaikh Abdullah's request and first published in *Khatun* in the same year. In the same way, Sultan Jahan Begum introduced a curriculam in vernacular for girls' schools which was also published in *Khatun*, Vol. 8, No. 12, January 1912.
65. *Khatun*, Vol. 6, No. 2, February 1909, p. 96.
66. Among the prominent women whose writings were published in *Khatun* were Rabia Sultan Jahan Begum, Zuhra Begum Faizi, Sakina Khatun, Nafees Dulhan, Mrs Agha Mahmood, Qasir Dulhan, Sajad Nazar-ul Baqar, Badar-un-nisa, and Miss Naseeruddin.
67. Zuhra Begum Faizi, 'Ap Bite', *Khatun*, Vol. 6, No. 6, June 1910, pp. 278–80.
68. In 1920, Rashid-ul-Khairi, took the initiative for the opening of school for Muslim girls at Delhi. The idea was widely circulated in *Ismat* and was appreciated by the local *ashraf*. After taking into account all considerations, a board was established including Mir Jalib,the editor of *Hamdam*, Lucknow, Mulla Muhammad Wahidi, the editor of *Khatib*, and *Nizam-ul-Mashaikh*, Delhi, Mirza Abdul Qadir, a local social activist and Maulvi Abdul Ghaffar Khairi, the cousin of Rashid-ul-Khairi. In March 1921, the recommendations of the Board were published in *Ismat*'s special issue in the form of an article which was given the name of *Talim-e-Niswan*. It was suggested in these recommendations that a *purdah* observing school, *Tarbiyat ghah-e-Banat*, would open which would be based on kindergarten methods; girls from six to eleven years of age would be admitted in the school. Subjects like Religious Education, English, History, Geography, Mathematics, Physical Education, Household Management and and Needlework would be taught in the

school. The school was started in February 1922 with twenty-one students. Raziq-ul-Khairi, *Savan-e-Umri-Rashid-ul Khairi*, pp. 200–201.

69. Among his books adopted as texts in different parts of India for higher Degree in Urdu were, *Manazil-e-Saerah*, *Subih-e-Zindgi*, *Larkiyon ki Talim*, *Sham-e-Zindigi*, *Tufan-e-Hayat* and *Johar-e-Qadamat*.

70. Raziq-ul-Khairi, *Savan-e-Umri-Rashid-ul-Khairi*, p. 512.

71. *The Modern Review*, Vol. IX, No. 5, March 1909, pp. 107.

72. *The International Reviews of Missions*, Vol. VI, No. 22, April 1917, pp. 295.

73. *Indian Ladies Magazine*, Vol. 11, No. 5 December 1928, pp. 235–37.

74. *Stri Dharma*, Vol. XI, No. 12, October 1912, pp. 312, 315.

75. Garcin de Tassy, *Khutbat-e-Garcin de Tassy*, pp. 685–86.

76. Ibid., pp. 797-99.

77. Ibid., p. 790.

78. Ibid., pp. 790–91.

79. *The Indian Magazine*, No. 205, London, March 1888, p. 192.

80. Garcin de Tassy, *Khutbat-e-Garcin de Tassy*, p. 575.

81. Shahida Lateef, *Muslim Women in India: 1890–1980*, p. 28.

82. Radha Kumar, *The History of Doing*, p. 28.

83. Ibid.

84. *The Modern Review*, Vol. X, No. 58, October 1911, pp. 347–48

85. M.H. Zaidi, *Muslim Womanhood in Revolution*, (Muhammadi Press, Calcutta), 1937, p. 107.

86. *Khatun*, Vol. 7, No. 6, June 1909, p. 141.

87. *Khatun*, Vol. 7, No. 10, October 1909, pp. 371, 75.

88. Gail Minault, 'Sisterhood or Separatism: The All-India Muslim Ladies Conference and the National Movement', in Gail Minault (ed.), *The Extended Family: Women's Political Participation in India and Pakistan*, (South Asia Books, Columbia, 1983), pp. 83–108.

89. Abdul Rashid Khan, 'The Contribution of the All-India Muslim Educational Conference to the Education and Cultural Development of Indian Muslims 1886–1947', (Unpublished Ph.D. Thesis, University of London, 1991), p. 211.

90. M.H. Zaidi, *Muslim Women in Revolution*, p. 107.

91. Ibid.

92. See, Raziq-ul-Khairi, *Savan-e-Umri Rashid-ul-Khairi*, pp. 675–712.

2

OPENING UP A PUBLIC SPACE FOR WOMEN: THE ROLE OF EDUCATION (1920–1947)

The period 1920–47 was one of great significance in the history of Indian education. Dramatic developments took place during this period, including the two world wars and the growth of the nationalist movement in the country. Above all, measures for women's emancipation actually began to be put into practice in this period. The education of women emerged as a major public issue, with a growing realization that educating a woman meant educating the society as a whole. Indeed, this new change in the direction of the lives of women took them out from their houses into schools and colleges. Women now began to move into the public sphere, into the labour force and into public life, and then from these advantageous points they sought a further improvement in their conditions. To analyse this chain of developments, this chapter focuses on the following:

(a) The nature of education as a channel for women's emancipation and the state of Muslim women's education in 1920.
(b) The agencies working for women's education.
(c) Muslim women's attitude towards new educational developments.
(d) The role of educated women in the public sphere.

Before looking at how political change in the second decade of the twentieth century was driving women into public life, it is quite striking to note, that while society was still in the midst of the old debates of nineteenth century vintage which seemed without any hope of resolution, women all of a sudden were sucked into mass movements and into a realm with a totally new discourse of its own. To begin with, their new role related to their growing participation in the national movement and it was only later on that they came to focus on developing an agenda for advancing their interests in the public sphere, particularly in the field of education.

Women burst onto the public stage at a time when Indian Muslims were coming increasingly to engage with the developing democratic system now being sponsored by the colonial state. At the same time they were trying to express their identity through this system. The first major demonstration of this process was the demand for their separate representation under the Morley-Minto Reforms. By and by their involvement in the realm of politics grew. Many of their demands were Pan-Islamic, the most notable of these being the *Khilafat* Movement to protect the Caliphate of the Ottomans in Turkey. These developments had crucial consequences for the way in which the Muslim woman came to be seen. While earlier she was seen as merely a housewife, with hardly any public role to play, she now increasingly began being seen as a major source of encouragement and support to the struggle in which Muslim men were deeply involved.[1]

The first Muslim woman actively to involve herself in the national movement during this period was Abadi Begum, mother of Muhammad Ali and Shaukat Ali, more popularly known as 'Bi Amman'. Her first public appearance came in 1913 on the platform of the *Anjuman-e-Khuddam-e-Kaaba*, an organization set up by her sons and their religious preceptor, Maulana Abdul Bari of Firanghi Mahal in Lucknow. The purpose of the *Anjuman* was to maintain the honour of the *Kaaba* and other holy places of Islam and to save them from the aggression of non-Muslims. Maulana Bari appealed to every Muslim in India, man, woman and child, to participate in this struggle. The *zenana* branch of the *Anjuman* usually held its meetings at Delhi and Lucknow. These were attended by thousands of women, many of whom were so zealous in the cause that they donated their gold ornaments to help the cause of their faith.[2]

Later, the anti-Turkish policy of the British Government helped to spawn the Khilafat Movement and generated a high degree of Hindu-Muslim unity under the leadership of the Ali Brothers and Gandhi. At this point, Muslim women were greatly supported by their Christian and Hindu counterparts; prominent among the latter were Mrs Annie Besant, Sarojini Naidu, Sarala Devi and Basanti Devi who participated in the Khilafat and Non-Cooperation movements alongside 'Bi Amman', Begum Muhammad Ali, Begum Hasrat Mohani and other Muslim women. Female participation in these movements not only provided moral and material support for the development of anti-colonialist politics but also helped in the crystallization of their future identity.

Under the Montagu-Chelmsford reforms of 1919, a small step forward was made in the direction of the development of self-government in India and a system of diarchy was introduced at the provincial level. Under this new system provincial subjects were divided into two parts: the Reserved and the Transferred. The departments of education and health were transferred to the control of provincial governments. This change gave a boost to education as Indian ministers were now made responsible for the spread of education.

THE NATURE OF EDUCATION AS A CHANNEL FOR WOMEN'S EMANCIPATION 1900–1920

During the two decades leading up to 1920 female education came to receive much more attention both from state and society. Progress was made mainly in two directions. Firstly, the range of educational opportunities was expanded and was made more attractive and advantageous for women. Secondly, a growing realization developed of the usefulness of higher education for girls to enable them to enter the job market and to brighten their chances in the marriage market.

The first initiative to make education more attractive for females was taken in the early years of the twentieth century by Lord Curzon, the Viceroy of India (1898–1905). In his view, female education could be promoted by providing suitable teachers and by the setting up of model schools.[3] The 1913 Government Resolution on Educational Policy voiced a similar opinion. It emphasized the social dimensions of the problem of female educational backwardness and pointed out that any great advance in the education of women was not possible unless social prejudice against it was overcome.[4] With the assistance of missionary and non-missionary societies, the Government tried to overcome hindrances and difficulties in this regard. Taking account of *purdah* restrictions, the number of female institutions and teachers was increased. To make female education more practically relevant for women, subjects like physiology, domestic economy, and hygiene were included in the school curriculum. Efforts were also made to make educational facilities available to females from a wider cross-section of society. For instance, scholarships were reserved for girl students at every level. Girls' primary schools under public management usually did not charge fees, except in Madras and Bengal where there was a provision for remitting the fees when required.[5] In the same way, ladies' as well as mixed standing committees were formed to look after the affairs of female institutions. Initially committees were established in the United Provinces (1905), Assam (1908), and Bengal (1913). Later, an increasing number of educated women showed interest in the management of educational institutions. For example, in the United Provinces a local female committee was successful in constructing girls' schools buildings at Lakhimpur and Faizabad in 1914 with the financial assistance of a local benefactor, Babu Dewan Chand.[6]

The Government, Christian missionaries, and Indian social reformers played an important role popularizing collegiate education among women. In 1914, there were sixteen colleges for women, most of them in Madras, Bombay, Calcutta, Lahore and Lucknow, in which 730 women students were enrolled. Their number rapidly increased to 1,263 in later years. Besides these, a small number of women were also receiving their education in colleges meant for men. However,

> They were prevented from taking any part in the corporate life of the college concerned. They sat apart in the class-room, hardly mixed with their fellow men-students and had no opportunities to participate in activities like the gymkhana or the debating society. In short, they formed a small world of their own.[7]

Another step forward for the expansion of women's higher education was taken in the form of a separate university for them. A scheme in this direction was launched by a Hindu social reformer, Professor D.K. Karve, who had already become involved in popularizing the cause of widow remarriage. In 1916 he founded the Shreemati Nathibai Damodher Thackersey University, more commonly known as S.N.D.T. University for Women, at Poona. The institution started its work in the Hindu Widow's Home at Poona and its own campus was set up in 1920. Professor Karve prepared a detailed curriculum for women's education which included a mixture of traditional and modern subjects. He formulated courses of study which he believed suited the special requirements of girls and included subjects such as domestic science, general psychology, hygiene and fine arts. The suggested medium of instruction was the girls' mother tongue while English was included as a compulsory subject in the collegiate course of studies.[8] Above all, candidates staying in remote places were able to appear for the examinations of this university without attending its classes, so that married women in particular could benefit from this scheme.[9] The example of this university was soon followed by other institutions. In 1922, the S.L.U. College of Ahmedabad became the first to secure affiliation with this university.

⌐Alongside the patronage of education in vernacular languages, some Indian parents were also coming to believe in the desirability of modern education for their daughters.⌐Modern, English-medium, European schools were opened in different places. They offered a special curriculum. For example, in the Central Provinces, the European schools introduced English, French, composition, grammar, geography, history and arithmetic.[10]

In the same way, vocational and industrial education was introduced in different parts of India. In 1917, there were six government and two Church Zenana Mission schools in Bombay Presidency, working for poor widows and deserted women.[11] In Bengal, the number of such institutions was eleven. Among them the most prominent was Kalimpong Industrial School under the Church of Scotland Mission in which women learned lace-making and embroidery.[12] In the United Provinces, the Lucknow Industrial School received a Government grant, while in the Punjab, Bihar, Orissa and Central Provinces, mission industrial schools took the initiative by introducing the flower-making, sewing, spinning, *kashida* work and lace-making classes.[13]

⌐The enthusiasm of many Indian parents about the new educational developments and opportunities that were becoming available was particularly noticeable.⌐Indian public opinion gradually, yet noticeably, began to shift away from its former attitude of positive dislike for the education of women and progressed, from apathy to cordial cooperation with the agencies involved in efforts being made in this direction.[14] According to one enthusiastic report 'even in villages and outlying districts the former indifference or even antagonistic attitude towards the improvement of the intelligence and status of women was fading away.'[15]⌐The social barriers of early marriage were also gradually being relaxed, which enabled a growing number of girls to receive primary and secondary education. Educated men increasingly began desiring educated wives for their sons; women who could be in a real sense companions and helpmates. Thus, education was becoming increasingly valued by parents as a way of improving the marriage prospects of daughters.[16] On the other hand, education was also opening up economic opportunities to parents belonging to poorer classes. Some of these parents were actually more interested in the value of education in the subsequent employment of their educated daughters than in its role in a successful marriage for them.[17] Primary school teaching was a popular occupation adopted by the women of such families as, for instance, had been the case in Europe as well. Similar was the case in the field of industrial education, through which several poor widows and deserted wives not only improved their technical skills but also received stipends during the training period.[18]

Another important feature of the widening range of education was the introduction of physical education for women. For this purpose, directresses of physical training were appointed in different provinces who trained teachers for girls' schools. Notably, special training courses were organized under the auspices of the Young Women's Christian Association. In 1914 the association trained forty-one female teachers in Bombay Presidency alone.[19]

THE STATE OF MUSLIM FEMALE EDUCATION 1900–1920

The education of Muslim women was sought to be promoted through the evolution of a creative synthesis between local cultural values, norms and institutions and external influences. Like the social reformers of other communities, education was also seen by Muslim reformers to be the tool which could uplift the social status of Muslim women, which, in itself, was the pressing debate of the times. Taking advantage of this growing receptivity towards Muslim girls' education, the Central Government introduced several measures through various provincial Governments. Thus, separate schools both for Muslim male and female students were set up in many parts of the country.

In 1916, the local district boards of the United Provinces opened special primary *maktab* schools where Muslim students could acquire Islamic as well as secular education. For this purpose, *maktab* committees were established in all districts which started their work under the supervision of the Provincial *Maktab* Committee. Among the prominent functions of these *maktab* committees were preparation or selection of readers for *maktabs*, establishing special normal schools for the secular training of teachers, and appointment of an additional inspector to assist in and advise on various measures to be taken for the extension of Muslim education.[20] In the same way, *purdah* arrangements were made in middle, high, and elementary institutions which were meant for Muslim females. Among such arrangements that were made for encouraging Muslim education were their admission on half the normal fees in all institutions, additional training classes for Muslim women teachers, the conversion of many *maktabs* into recognized primary schools with secular classes and the appointment of Muslim inspecting staff for Muslim schools.[21]

Urdu and the Question of Muslim Education

The Urdu-Hindi controversy of the late nineteenth century played a vital role in further crystallizing and then hardening separate communal identities. Urdu became an increasingly significant marker which separated Muslims from Hindus, it being increasingly identified as a part of the religious and cultural heritage of Indian Muslims. Even though generally they spoke their own local languages at home, such as Bengali and Punjabi, many Muslims preferred to receive their education through the medium of Urdu. Early efforts to promote education in Urdu came from the Muhammadan Educational Conference founded by Sayyed Ahmed Khan in 1886. The Conference followed Muslim wishes and their sentiments in this respect. In 1903, the Conference formed an Urdu section known as *Anjuman Taraqqi-e-Urdu*. Its aim was to preserve Muslim cultural heritage through translation of Oriental literature into Urdu and to make the language into a suitable vehicle for the transmission of modern European sciences to the community.[22] At the same time, the Conference tried to urge the Government to adopt Urdu as a medium of instruction in those schools where Muslim students were receiving their education, particularly at the primary stage. Apart from textbooks and the curriculum, the Conference also made efforts to convince the Governments of various provinces either to open Urdu schools or to arrange Urdu classes in provincial institutions.[23]

The patronage of Urdu by the Government may be seen as a part of the special measures which were taken up for the progress of Muslim education. For instance, in the Bombay Presidency, a committee was appointed to consider special recommendations for the promotion of education in Urdu in educational institutions meant for Muslim students. The Committee suggested the setting up of a training school at Ahmedabad for Urdu teachers. For this purpose, Mr I. Farooqui, Assistant Headmaster at the Thana High School, was appointed as instructor. The Committee suggested that students be allowed to take their Vernacular Final Examination in Urdu and recommended that a new and revised syllabus for Muslim boys' and girls' schools in all divisions of the Presidency be introduced.[24] Female education in Urdu was given particular impetus through the efforts of the Director of Public Instruction of Bombay, Mr Sharp. With the assistance of local men like Maulvi Rafiuddin Ahmed, he was able to start, on an experimental basis, an Urdu school for girls. Another major step forward was the appointment of a Muslim woman, Halimannisa Begum, the Honorary Secretary of Muhammadan Ladies Educational Conference, as inspectress of Urdu girls' schools in the Presidency, the first of which was opened at Poona in 1913.[25]

AGENCIES WHICH WIDENED THE CHANNEL FOR WOMEN'S EDUCATION FROM 1921–1947

The three main agencies of women's education, as of men's education, in British India were the Government, Christian missionaries and social reformers, all of whose efforts were directed largely in the same direction. Their early efforts in the twentieth century were made mainly within the traditional framework of Indian society. However, in later years, several measures were introduced which made education more modern and functionally relevant for women. The progress of Muslim women's education in this period was not the consequence only of the general arrangements that were made for the uplift of Indian women but also of the special measures that were taken for the betterment of the condition of the Indian Muslims. This section discusses Government educational policies, the achievements of missionaries especially in the field of women's higher education and, finally, the attitudes of and important contributions made by social reformers.

THE ROLE OF THE STATE

By the end of the second decade of the twentieth century, state provision for education steadily increased even though financial constraints resulting from the First World War led to cuts in the budget. This development came about mainly due to growing public interest in the sphere of women's education.

The first achievement in this regard was the increasing number of female students enrolled in educational institutions all over the country.[26] It should be noted that in spite of the general backwardness of the Muslim community the percentage of Muslim students was 0.1 per cent higher than the percentage of all students to the total population in India.[27] Likewise, with regard to Muslim girls, in spite of different kinds of obstacles such as *purdah* and early marriage, the percentage of Muslim girls under instruction to the total Muslim female population in four provinces was more than the other girls of all communities taken together.[28] Though the great majority of Muslim pupils were still studying in primary schools, the progress made here had proved to be quite satisfactory.[29]

During this period the Government continued to provide further facilities for the development of Muslim female education. For instance, in the Bombay Presidency Muslim girls students were admitted without the payment of fee into all district local board and municipal primary schools. In addition to the fees concession, a number of special scholarships were reserved for Muslim girls who were studying in primary schools.[30] In Bengal, the number of recognized *madrasas* increased from 1,500 to 2,100 and a revised curriculum was introduced for *maktabs* which brought many schools more into line with the Government primary schools in the provinces.[31] The same was done in the United Provinces. With grants-in-aid from the Government, the number of maktabs increased considerably.[32] In Bihar and Orissa, too, a Madrasa Examination Board was formed to introduce a new syllabus and supervise examinations introduced in all recognized *madrasas*.[33] In the Central Provinces, the number of special Anglo-Urdu and Urdu schools for Muslims increased from 233 to 280.[34] In Assam the Second Muhammadan Conference was held at Shillong in 1926. The Conference passed numerous resolutions for the development of Muslim education in the province, including one for the improvement of the junior *madrasa* course with a view to bringing it into line with the middle school course, another for the revision of textbooks and yet another, for the appointment of special inspecting staff.[35]

The end of the second decade of the twentieth century saw the passing of an increasing number of social reform legislations related to girls and women. In the context of constitutional reforms, education played a crucial role both as a symbol of political power as well as in the construction of community identity. On the part of many women's associations and individual feminists, education became a vital campaigning tool for the political enfranchisement of Indian women. By opposing the property qualification for voters, many of them now began demanding an educational qualification.

In this situation the Government, with the full concurrence of legislative councils, granted large sums of money for the progress of education and introduced several new educational schemes. One such measure was the formation of the Auxiliary Committee of the Indian Statutory Commission charged with the responsibility to analyse the previous educational developments and to make suitable suggestions for the future. The Committee was appointed in 1927 under the chairmanship of Sir Philip Hartog. In his memorandum entitled *The Growth of Women's Education in India in 1929,* Hartog appreciated the keen desire for education and knowledge on the part of Indian women even in provinces where the observance of *purdah* was widespread, such as the Punjab, the United Provinces, Bengal and Assam.[36] In the same way, the Quinquennial Report of Mr Jalaluddin Kadri, the Educational Inspector of Bombay, highlighted the advancement which had been taking place in the field of women's education. As he observed:

The wide and rapid awakening in regard to female education is not found only among the advanced classes but also among the backward classes. Even Muslim girls are now coming out of their seclusion and trying for their emancipation. These are the signs of a growing appreciation of female education in the country brought about by improved social and political conditions and the large scope of rights and privileges and freedom enjoyed by women in recent years. So women's activities have spread of late into educational, social, economic and political spheres of life.[37]

An important suggestion for the growth and expansion of female education made by the Hartog Committee was the removal of the disparity between the education of boys and girls through provision of equal opportunities and granting more funds for girls' education. It also recommended the appointment of women officers of high standing at the educational headquarters of different provinces, increasing the number of women inspecting staff and the nomination of women's representatives in local bodies and educational committees.[38] The Committee also emphasized the need to remove the shortage of women teachers by opening more training institutions in order to fulfil the growing requirements of primary schools.[39]

In the light of these suggestions, further educational reforms were made by the Government. The reforms were not only welcomed in relatively developed areas of the country but also in those provinces where traditional educational systems were still popular, particularly among the Muslims. In the United Provinces, the growing demand for additional girls' secondary schools and an active desire to raise educational standards was seen as a clear sign that parents wanted to prolong the school life of their daughters.[40] In Bengal, too, *purdah* relaxation and the enforcement of the Child Marriage Constraint Act (Sarda Act) enabled Muslim women to be gradually relieved from the bonds of social fetters.[41] The passing of the Marriage Reforms Act and the general climate of political awakening proved to be potent factors in promoting the cause of female education and emancipation of Indian girls and women.[42]

By 1932, the total number of female students in British India stood at 24,64,684. The number of Muslim female students on the rolls was 6,47,713, among whom 5,66,359 were studying in recognized institutions and 81,354 were receiving their education in unrecognized schools.[43] The progress of education among Muslim females becomes clear from the following Table 1:

Table 1
Percentage of Muslim female students as compared to total female and Muslim female population to total number of female students in 1932

Province	% of Total Female Population	% of Muslim Female Population	% of Total Female Population
Madras	7.5	5.1	11.5
Bombay	8.4	2.9	19.8
Bengal	55.2	2.3	55.4
U.P.	14.9	0.8	15.7
Punjab	56.9	1.6	47.2
Bihar	12.9	1.1	19.7
C.P. Berar	4.2	2.8	13.6
Assam	33.0	1.5	22.0
N.W.F.P	92.9	0.5	38.5
Sindh	72.7	N.A.	N.A.
Orissa	1.6	N.A.	N.A.
Coorg	6.6	0.9	1.4
Delhi	32.4	2.6	.3
Ajmer & Merwara	16.8	1.6	16.5
Baluchistan	91.6	0.4	31.4
Bangalore	20.4	6.1	12.4
Other areas	21.6	5.1	9.4

Source: See note 44

This trend continued in the period from 1932 to 1937, when the overall situation became more favourable for the Muslims. There was a corresponding increase in the percentage of Muslim students to the Muslim population, from 3.3 in 1921–22 to 4.7 in 1926–27 to 5.2 in 1931–32 and then to 5.5 in 1937. Despite these increasing numbers of Muslim students, however, there were certain sections of the Muslim community which still hesitated to accept the idea of modern education, justifying this reluctance on their part with arguments emphasizing the absence of any provision for religious instruction in, and the non-Islamic character of, the ordinary schools. The best solution to this problem, suggested by the Hartog Committee, was the provision of religious instruction in those ordinary schools which had a majority of Muslim students.[45]

EDUCATION UNDER PROVINCIAL AUTONOMY
1938–1947

The Government of India Act of 1935 marked a further step in India's onward march to complete independence. It put an end to the diarchical system of administration, abolished the distinction between reserved and transferred departments and placed the whole field of provincial administration under a ministry responsible to a legislature which had an overwhelming majority of elected members. With the beginning of provincial autonomy, earnest hopes of great educational advance were at once raised. Most of the constraints which had hampered the work of the Indian ministries between 1921–37 were no longer present.[46] The achievements of this period in the field of education can be divided into two categories: (i), educational reforms administered by the Central Government and (ii), educational activities of local governments in different provinces.

The efforts of the Central Government during this period were largely reflected in the various activities of the Central Advisory Board of Education. The Board appointed the Wardha Education Committee in 1937 which dealt with self-supporting basic education. It advocated a system of compulsory education for all boys and girls between the ages of 7 and 14. However, girls could be withdrawn after the age of 12 if their guardians so desired.[47] In the matter of female secondary education the Committee suggested the introduction of such courses as cookery, laundry work, needle work, home-crafts and first-aid.[48] In 1944, another attempt to plan a national system of education for India was made by the Central Advisory Board of Education. The Board submitted a detailed report, commonly known as the Sargent

Report after the name of John Sargent, the Educational Advisor to the Government of India. The report suggested the introduction of free basic compulsory (primary and middle) education for all boys and girls between the ages of six and fourteen years.[49] It also recommended a vast increase in the number of women teachers and the adoption of a certain minimum standard of training, as well as specific recruitment and service conditions. For this purpose it was suggested that kindergarten classes should be conducted by women and, in case there were insufficient children, such classes should be affiliated with primary schools.[50]

For the Muslims, the period from 1937 to 1947 was a decade of great social and political challenges. It was in this period that Muslim women's right to a share in property was legally recognized (The Muslim Shariat Application Bill of 1937) as well as their right to get a divorce (The Dissolution of Muslim Marriages Act of 1939). It was in this period that the demand for a separate Muslim state of Pakistan began to gather momentum. The use of education to get the right of a vote both for men and women was considered as helping to consolidate the Pakistan cause. The progress of Muslim female education, however, varied from one province to another.

In the Madras Presidency, which was, in terms of education, considerably better off than, say, the north of the country, the new educational opportunities for girls were increasingly taken advantage of by Muslims. In 1940, the number of Muslim girls under instruction stood at 1,14,237. They were receiving education in Government as well as in European schools.[51] Besides this, ten secondary girls' schools were reserved for Muslim female pupils who observed *purdah*. College education was also becoming popular among them; girls generally preferred to seek admission at the Queen Mary's College and Islamia College.[52]

In the Bombay Presidency the number of Muslim female students had increased to 72,760 in 1945 from 51,234 in 1938. In the period 1944–45 there were 2,503 Muslim female students in the secondary stage while 113 were receiving their education in different colleges at Bombay, Poona, Ahmedabad and Baroda affiliated with the S.N.D.T. University for Women.[53]

When Sindh became a separate province in 1936, further developments were made in the region, particularly in the field of female education. The number of Muslim female students registered a significant increase in all kinds of educational institutions, especially in secondary and higher schools. To encourage Muslim female education the Government sanctioned four scholarships of Rs.20 per mensem each for Muslim girls tenable for four years.[54]

Striking progress in the field of female education was also made in the Punjab. A forward step in this regard was the appointment of additional female inspecting staff, including one Circle Inspectress, nine District Inspectresses and three Domestic Science Supervisors.[55] Along with these arrangements, special attention was also now being paid to raising the standards of female training institutions. In 1942 new junior and senior vernacular courses began to be offered at the Girls' High School, Jullunder, and the Government Middle Girls' School, Lyallpur. The first batch consisted of twenty women teachers who completed their training during the same year.[56]

Another prominent feature of the progress of female education in the province was the growing demand for co-education at different levels: owing to the absence of the required courses in women's colleges, female students were compelled to join men's colleges.[57] As for Muslim females, considerable progress was made in this period. In 1941–42 the total number of Muslim female students was 1,43,035, a significant increase from 1,12,502 in 1938. The number of Muslim female students saw a remarkable increase in the field of higher education. There were 405 Muslim female students in Intermediate, 231 in Degree and sixteen in postgraduate classes, while 938 female students received special education.[58]

One important aspect of the work carried out during these years was the spread of female education in the educationally-backward N.W.F.P. In 1938–39, the number of recognized female institutions rose to 167. Among these, 134 were primary, including one Agency School at Parachinar, nineteen vernacular, ten Anglo-Vernacular Middle, three high schools and one normal school. Urdu was adopted as medium of instruction in 100 schools while Hindi, Gurmukhi and other languages were taught in another sixty-seven institutions.[59] The total number of Muslim girls under instruction was 8,734, which was 9 per cent of all local female students. The Lady Griffith Government High School and C.E.Z.M.S. Elizabeth High School, Peshawar, were particularly popular among Muslim girls. The former also offered Intermediate-level classes. In this year, eleven girls appeared for the intermediate examinations at this school. Among them five were Muslim, four Hindu and two Sikh. During the same period seven girls passed the Matriculation Examination; five were Muslim, one was Hindu and one Sikh. The latter school had a well-equipped laboratory and offered Physics and Chemistry to girls who wished to study these subjects.[60]

As in other areas, the Muslims of the Central Provinces were taking part in the transformation of society, and many had been convinced of the need to educate their women. To fulfil the growing demand for Urdu teachers, the Government introduced several measures. It set up the Urdu Normal School for women at Jubbulpur in 1941 which offered fifteen stipends for women first and second year trainees.[61] In 1943 the Director of Public Instruction took steps to reorganize women's education. To make the scheme more practical, an officer on special duty submitted a report prepared on the lines recommended by the conference on women's education held in 1944 in the province which was attended by educationalists from all parts of India.[62]

In the United Provinces, too, there was a rapidly increasing demand for more high schools and colleges for women. In order to make female education more effective, a general scheme was introduced under the supervision of the local Ministry of Education. In 1946, a woman Officer on Special Duty was appointed to conduct a survey for the progress of female education in the province.[63]

It is interesting to note that Muslims of this province seemed more keen to educate their daughters than their sons. For instance, in the district of Agra, Muslims were mainly self-employed traders, artisans and small industrialists, using the young boys of their families in their businesses or work-places. In contrast, their girls, not required to work in this way, usually had a chance to educate themselves, and in the case of wealthy families, some of them were even able to study uptil the secondary and intermediate level, sometimes even being allowed to continue their education after marriage.[64]

CHRISTIAN MISSIONS AND MUSLIM WOMEN'S EDUCATION

Christian missions played a major role in the education of women in India. They not only organized a large number of primary girls' schools but secondary schools, industrial homes and teachers' training institutions were also in their hands. Their close contacts with Indians stemmed from their missionary zeal and religious enthusiasm, which led them not only to study Indian customs and languages but also to work for general social uplift. They firmly believed that for the re-building of society it was necessary for women to be educated in order to take their legitimate place in the home and society. The lead given by the Christian missionaries in this field inspired Indians, too, to take similar steps. Among Hindu organizations such as the *Arya Samaj*, the *Ramakrishna Mission* of Bengal and the Educational Society of Poona emulated the missionaries by starting girls' schools and colleges as well as hospitals of their own.

In northern India, where Muslims were found in greater numbers, the missionaries did pioneering work in the field of girls' education. The Isabella Thoburn College for Women was started in Lucknow by the Methodist Mission in 1887. In later years it also went on to offer teachers' training classes. After passing the matriculation examination, girls could get admission in training classes for two years; during this period they were also granted scholarships of eight rupees per month.[65]

One of the major achievements of the missions in the second decade of the twentieth century was the establishment of the United Women's Christian College at Madras. The idea came up for discussion for the first time in 1909 by some missionary societies working in Madras.[66] Since there were no facilities for collegiate education for girls, they had to attend classes in men's colleges, which not many people looked upon with favour. An all-women's college was seen as the only answer. In support of this, a memorandum was submitted by the Rev. George Pittendrigh (a professor at the Madras Christian College for Men and secretary of a committee formed by some Madras-based missionaries to promote the cause of female education), to the European Section of the Special Committee on Education and the Education Section of the Continuation Committee in 1909. It was strongly supported by Sir Andrew Fraser and the Rev. T.R.W. Lunt, Chairman and Secretary respectively of the Education Committee, and J.H. Oldham, the Secretary of the Continuation Committee.[67] Lunt played an especially active role in obtaining the support of various missionary societies for the proposed college. His correspondence in connection with the opening of a female college highlighted his deep concern for the promotion of the cause of women's education in India. For instance, in one of his letters to Mr H.P. Napier Clavering, Secretary of the Church of England Zenana Missionary Society, London, he emphasized that higher education for Indian women had to be planned with the mutual cooperation of missionary societies.[68] To make this scheme more practical, a special meeting of the representatives of different missionary societies was held at London in October 1913 in which the proposal was fully considered and members were asked to collect an initial amount of £200. The first principal of the proposed college was Miss Eleanor McDougall whose name was unanimously recommended by the Madras Committee. She was appointed in 1914 and the college received its first batch of students in 1915.[69] The United Christian College for Women was in every way a cooperative venture enjoying the support of bodies such as the Church of England Zenana Missionary Society, the Church of

Scotland, the Church Missionary Society, the London Missionary Society and similar societies in the United States and Canada. It not only played an important role in promoting female education but also emerged as a major training centre for Christian women teachers. The two-year training project was sponsored by different missionary societies.[70]

The establishment of the United Christian College for Women led to an increasing number of women graduates. As a result, the natural corollary was the need to provide these women graduates with professional training. In 1921 the Women's Christian College, Madras, was asked by the Missionary Educational Council of South India to undertake the establishment of a teacher's training college. Eventually, the St. Christopher Training College for Women was set up in Nungambakam, near Madras, in 1923. The college had its own Council and Association as well as British and American Sections of the Board of Governors, including representatives of supporting societies. In subsequent years, other institutions amalgamated with this college. For instance, the Bentinck Girls High School became part of the college in 1935 while in 1944 further training institutions in the city moved in the same direction.[71]

Besides these important colleges for women's higher education, several other institutions were established by missions. Prominent among these were St. Joseph's Training College for Women and St. Theresa's College for Women (United Provinces), St. Mary's College (Assam), Patna Women's College (Bihar), St. Bede's College (Simla), Hawabagh Women's Training College for Women (Jabalpur), Holy Cross College, Nirmala College, Sarah Tucker College, St. Ignatius Training College, Stella Maris College, Y.M.C.A. College for Physical Education (Madras) and Nirmala Niketan College (Bombay), Kinnaird College (Lahore), and Women's Christian College (Bengal).[72]

Another remarkable feature of the work of Christian missionaries was the individual efforts of women who were associated with the missions. The close social contacts of these women with many Indian families and female students enabled them to chalk out new directions for the progress of female education in India. A notable example was Winifred Edith Wenger, the wife of the Rev. Edward Leslie Wenger, teacher at the Calcutta College.[73]

The Muslims' response to the missions' efforts for female education was perhaps not as enthusiastic as that of other Indian communities. However, any analysis of the situation cannot ignore particular socio-religious factors that were at play. Muslim women came into the broader field of education at a time when almost two generations of their men had already gone through this process. To add to this was the conservatism of the community in general as regards modern female education, many seeing it as un-Islamic in a way. Despite all these obstacles and socio-religious prejudices the efforts of Christian missions for the education of Muslim girls were not totally ignored by the Muslims.[74] In the Punjab and Madras, for instance, a large number of Muslim girls did enrol in the Christian schools.[75] In 1937 there were eight mission institutions in Madras meant specially for Muslim girls in which 277 students were under instruction.[76] There were three other such schools, working in Ajmer and Merwara in which ninety-four girls were receiving their education in 1932.[77]

Women's Education and Social Reforms

The third agency for Muslim women's education was the social reformers who were either affiliated with an organization or worked independently. In the latter half of the nineteenth century, two distinct movements for educational reform arose among Indian Muslims. Both were cultural but potentially political.

To begin with, the education of Muslim women was not a priority on the agenda of these reformers, stemming as this did from the then generally held belief that education was of but little use to women. The first step forward in the direction of Muslim girls' education was taken by the Muhammadan Educational Conference, founded in 1886. The occasion was the annual meeting of the Conference, held at Bombay in 1903. For the first time women participants were invited to attend the meeting and the first voice raised at the forum was that of Chand Begum, a Muslim woman from Madras. She, however, did not attend the Conference herself but her paper was read out by a Parsi woman. Chand Begum called upon Muslim women to take to education in a big way and to bid farewell to the incorrigible *maulvis*.[78]

The activities of the Muhammadan Educational Conference for the spread of women's education were further extended after the formation of the All-India Muslim Ladies Conference in 1914. The early participation of women in this forum such as Begum Sayyed Mahmood, the daughter-in-law of Sir Sayyed Ahmed Khan; Begum Abdullah, the wife of Shaikh Abdullah; Abru Begum, the sister of Maulana Abul Kalam Azad; and Nafees Dulhan, the Honorary Secretary of the Ladies Conference, proved that even Muslim women could become involved in the social betterment of their sisters. The Conference expressed a keen desire to spread modern education among ordinary Muslim women. In this regard a resolution was passed at its fourth meeting held at Delhi in 1917. Begum Qazi Ghulam Ahmed, the wife of the Municipal Commissioner of Panipat, proposed opening schools for Muslim girls in different villages of the country where Muslim girls could learn English along with traditional religious education.[79] Further development in this direction was made by providing financial assistance in the forms of grants and scholarships. An initial grant of Rs.50 was sanctioned to the Aligarh Muslim School in 1917. A grant of Rs.100 was provided to the Muslim Girls' School at Delhi and a sum of Rs.300 was sanctioned to Sagheer Fatima School, Agra.[80] In the same way, stipends were given for the spreading of education among the Muslim girls.

To ensure the satisfactory progress of education in particular, the standard of Islamic teaching, the Conference conducted a survey of all recognized institutions in which Muslim girls were studying. Initially, three girls' schools, the Karamat Husain Girls' School, the Saeeda Ihsan-ul-Haq Girls' School at

Lucknow, and the Sakhawat Memorial Girls' School, Calcutta, were inspected under this scheme.[81] Another remarkable achievement was the foundation of Muslim Anglo-Oriental Girls' School at Calcutta in 1927 with the financial assistance of the Conference.[82]

Noteworthy efforts for the spreading of Muslim female education were made by Afzal-ud-Daula, the fifth Nizam of Hyderabad. He opened several *maktabs* and schools at various district headquarters, prominent of which were the Nampalli Girls' High School, Mahboobia High School, Stanley Girls' High School, and St. George Grammar High School. However, his most remarkable achievement was the foundation of the Osmania University in 1919 in Hyderabad, where almost every subject was taught in Urdu. Among its affilitated colleges, the Hyderabad Zenana College offered higher degrees both in the sciences and the arts in Urdu. The college was opened in 1924, beginning with intermediate classes. Degree classes were started in 1926 and MA courses in 1936. The female teaching staff of the college worked under the supervision of Dr Amina Pop, an English woman who had converted to Islam in 1901. After receiving her degree from the Royal College of Music, London, she was first invited by Justice Karamat Husain and the Raja of Mahmoodabad, both prominent Muslim social activists, to run the Muslim girls' school at Lucknow. However, later, at the request of Akbar Hyderi, the Chief Inspector of Education of Hyderabad, she accepted the principalship of the Zenana School at Hyderabad in 1912. In 1924 this school was upgraded to become the first Zenana College in the state. The establishment of the Department of Science in the college where Mathematics, Physics, Chemistry, Botany, and Zoology were taught was one of the achievements of Dr Amina Pop. It should be noted that all these subjects were taught in Urdu. The majority of the female students were Muslims, who were receiving their education in *purdah*.[83]

The example of the Nizam was also followed by local social reformers. Many Muslim women of Hyderabad took an active interest in the expansion of female education. Prominent among those were Lady Hyderi, the wife of Akbar Hyderi, Sughra Humayun Asghar, a famous writer and member of the All-India Muslim Ladies Conference and Ashraf-un-nisa Begum, a local social worker. These women opened several institutions for the advancement of women's education in Hyderabad.[84]

Similar work was being done in neighbouring Madras. Educationalists like Maulvi Abdul Haq, Principal of Islamia College, Madras, Professor Abdul Wahab and Dr Burhan-un-nisa had a keen desire to educate local Muslim girls. Mention must be made of the great achievements in this direction of Begum Amiruddin, daughter of Agha Jalaluddin Husain, editor of *Akhbar-e-Jablul-Mateen,* Calcutta. After her marriage, she settled down in Madras with her husband, Justice Sayyed Amiruddin, where she actively participated in the campaign to advance Muslim female education.[85] She not only succeeded in establishing several middle and secondary schools for Muslim girls but, through her efforts, several Muslim girls were able to get admission in the prestigious Queen Mary's College, Madras.[86] Along with Maulvi Abdul Haq she later made efforts to establish a college and boarding house for Muslim women in 1946.[87]

In the Bombay Presidency, the Muslim population consisted, among others, of the Halai, Memon, Sulemani Bohra, Daudi Bohra, Kohkni and Gujrati communities. Although they had different cultures and languages, Urdu was the common medium of communication. Several Urdu schools were opened in different parts of the presidency by the *Anjuman-e-Islam*. With the efforts of one Mr Usman Sobani the *Anjuman-e-Islam* opened a girls' high school in Bombay. Another such school was established in the District of Poona by Mr Rafiuddin Ahmed, a former Minister of education.[88]

The history of Muslim women's education in Bengal cannot be completed without reference to Rokeya Sakhawat Husain, a local female activist of the early twentieth century. In 1911, Rokeya opened the Sakhawat Husain Girls' School in Calcutta with only eight girls in a small building. By the end of 1915, four years after the opening of the school, the number of students had increased from eight to eighty-four and the school was shifted to a larger building. By 1930 the school had become a high school, including all ten grades. The curriculum included physical education, handicrafts, sewing, cooking, nursing, home economics, and gardening, in addition to regular courses such as Bengali, English, Urdu, Persian and Arabic.[89]

In the United Provinces, much work for the uplift of Muslim women was done by Shaikh Abdullah and Justice Sayyed Karamat Husain. Shaikh Abdullah founded the Aligarh Girls' School in 1906 which ultimately became an Intermediate college in 1925 and started Degree classes in 1937. The curricula included Urdu reading and writing, basic arithmetic, needle work and the teaching of the Quran. Sayyed Karamat Husain established the Muslim Girls' School at Lucknow which was renamed after him following his death in 1917. The school was founded in 1912 and occupied rented quarters in the city, with a boarding house for girls in *purdah*. In 1920 the school was moved to a new building built on land donated by the Raja of Mahmoodabad.[90]

Among the important Muslim women's associations working in the province were the Lucknow Women's Association and the Muslim Ladies Conference, Agra. The latter organization started industrial classes for local Muslim girls and arranged zenana industrial exhibitions. In 1932 an exhibition was held at Agra in which 400 Muslim girls participated by sending different samples of their embroidery, knitting, and sewing.[91]

In the Punjab, the *Anjuman-e-Himayat-i-Islam* did much by way of propagating the cause of female education. The preservation of traditional Islamic values remained the main objective of the *Anjuman's* educational programme. The *Anjuman* went on to found the Anglo-Vernacular Islamia Girls' Middle School in 1925. In the same way, the *Anjuman*, was able to start a Degree college for women in 1939.[92] Alongside the remarkable efforts of the *Anjuman*, some reformist work was also done by certain individuals in the field of Muslim women's education. One such example was Fatima Begum, the former educational superintendent of Municipal Schools, Bombay, and the daughter of Munshi Mahboob Alim, editor of the *Paisa Akbhar*, Lahore. She opened a women's college at Lahore in 1939. Special arrangements for *purdah* and religious education were made in the college under her supervision. The college had female staff, including one European teacher. It also provided residential facilities for Muslim female students.[93]

Amritsar was the second biggest city in the Punjab, and here, too, increasing numbers of Muslim girls were taking to education. The Islamia Girls' Middle School was opened by the *Anjuman Islamia* in the city. The school was upgraded in later years. Some Muslim women of the city had been involved in educational activities through associations such as the *Anjuman Dar-ul-Khawateen* and the *Anjuman-Ittihad-e-Khawateen*. The former Anjuman ran an industrial school and granted scholarships to poor women, while the latter managed a night school and orphan house for Muslim women and girls.[94]

In the Province of Bihar and Orissa, too, efforts were made to spread education among local Muslim women. The Badshah Nawab Rizvi Girls' High School was founded at Patna by Nawab Rizvi. The school provided senior training classes for female matriculate students and junior training classes for middle-pass female students. Women from poor families and young widows were awarded scholarships during the course of their training. Among local Muslim female activists, Lady Imam, the wife of Sir Hasan Imam, M.L.A., was well known for her educational work for women. In 1924, she represented India at the India Day at Wembley (England) and was also nominated as an official member of the Provincial Franchise Committee.[95]

WOMEN'S ATTITUDE TOWARDS NEW EDUCATIONAL DEVELOPMENTS

A salient feature of the growing movement for spearheading female education among the Muslims was the increasing participation by women themselves in the field of education. Some women even went abroad for higher education. The changing attitude of Muslims towards female education can be seen by comparing the period from 1917 to 1947. During the period 1917–22 there were only thirty Muslim female students receiving their education at the college or university levels. By 1927 the number had increased to 537; among them most of the students belonged to rather backward provinces like the United Provinces and the Punjab. In later years, the situation was further improved in these provinces. In the Punjab, by 1946, 651 Muslim female students were receiving higher education; among them 405 were in the Intermediate, 231 were in the degree classes and fifteen were in the postgraduate classes.[96] One, Miss Khadija Firozuddin, the Principal of Women's College, Amritsar, was even awarded a doctorate degree by the University of Punjab in 1940.[97]

In more advanced provinces like Madras, although the number of Muslim female students was less, they were active in obtaining modern and professional education. By 1946 several Muslim women had entered the medical profession. Prominent among them were Dr Noshaba Malkar, Dr Afzal-un-nisa, Dr Burhan-un-nisa, Dr Humaira Saeed, Dr Karima Begum, Dr Amina Ghori and Dr Abdia Lateef. These women worked at different hospitals in Madras. Besides these career women, there were a growing number of women who were receiving their education in colleges and universities.[98]

Among the Indian states, Hyderabad was particularly advanced, and here there were many Muslim female students. College education, too, was becoming popular among them. The Zenana College at Hyderabad attracted many students because of its facilities for research up to the MA and M.Ed. levels. By 1945 many dissertations had been submitted in Urdu for the MA and M.Ed. degrees by Muslim female students. The subjects of some of the following dissertations illustrate the nature of their research work:

1. *Maulana Muhammad Husain Azad* was written by Jahan Bano Naqvi, for the degree of MA in Urdu.
2. *Tasawwuf aur Urdu Shairi* (Mysticism and Urdu Poetry), presented by Lateef-un-nisa Begum, for MA degree in Urdu.

3. *Maulana Shibli aur unki Nasar Nigari* (Maulana Shibli and his Prose Writings), by Naeem-un-nisa Begum, for MA degree in Urdu.
4. *Bahadur Shah Zafar aur unki Shairi* (Bahadur Shah Zafar and his Poetry), presented by Tasnim Yazdani, for MA degree in Urdu.
5. *Sir Sayyed Ahmed Khan aur unki Nasar Nigari* (Sir Sayyed Ahmed Khan and his Prose Writings), written by Najum-un-nisa Begum, for MA degree in Urdu.
6. *Nizam Ganjwi* by Razia Begum, for MA degree in Persian.
7. *Hyderabad main Anjuman hai Imdad-e-Bahami ka Qiyam aur Irtiqa* (The Emergence and Development of Cooperative Societies in Hyderabad), by Salamat-un-nisa Begum, for MA degree in Economics.
8. *Berkeley ka Falsafah-e-Tasawwurat* (Imagination of Berkeley's Philosophy), by Qamar Abbasi Begum, for MA degree in Philosophy.
9. *Sir Sayyed Ahmed Khan aur unki Samaji aur Siyasi Takhaiyyulat* (Sir Sayyed Khan and his Social and Political Ideology), by Balqees Begum, for MA degree in History.
10. *Hyderabad ki Talim-e-Niswan (Sanwi)* (Secondary Education of Women in Hyderabad), by Naeem-un-nisa, for M.Ed.[99]

MUSLIM WOMEN'S EDUCATION ABROAD

A keen desire to avail of the increasing educational opportunities led many Indian women to go abroad for higher education. Indeed, this represented a great revolution in South Asian society in which women were often secluded within the four walls of the house and treated as subordinate creatures in a male-dominated system.

In the early twentieth century the government started a scheme of special scholarships for women's higher education abroad, in particular in Britain. To provide better boarding facilities, a hostel for women from India was started in July

1920 at Highbury in north London. Another hostel was also opened with the cooperation of the London School of Medicine for Women: eight rooms were reserved for Indian students of the School. The Secretary of State for India made a loan of £1,000 towards the initial expenses of these boarding houses.[100]

As in the case of other communities, Muslim female students began going abroad to study. The earliest example was the Faizi sisters, Attiya, Zuhra and Nazli. Many Muslim female students succeeded in getting government scholarships in later years. For instance, in 1923, Miss S. Khan and Miss G.M. Ali received such scholarships. The former got a degree in higher education from the Maria Grey Training College, London, while the latter did her specialization in medicine from the Lock Hospital, London.[101] In the 1924–25 session Miss M.A. Shah Gilani was awarded a degree in Veterinary Science from the Royal Veterinary College, London.[102]

To encourage more female students to be educated abroad, the provincial governments of British India began sanctioning grant-in-aid scholarships in 1926. Under this scheme the first Muslim woman who was awarded a scholarship from the Government of Madras was Miss J.M. Sirajuddin, who received a diploma in teachers' training from the Maria Grey Training College, London.[103] In 1929, Miss Fazilit-un-nisa and Miss K.J. Abdullah succeeded in getting the grant-in-aid scholarships from the governments of Bengal and the United Provinces respectively. The former was awarded a higher degree in education from the Maria Grey Training College, London, and the latter also got her degree in education from the University of Leeds.[104]

In later years, the scheme of grant-in-aid scholarships was also extended by different Indian states such as Bahawalpur, Baroda, Junagadh, Kashmir, Mysore, and Hyderabad. In particular, the State of Hyderabad took an initiative by sending some Muslim women to Britain for higher education. Prominent among them were Begum Nawab Yar Jung, Begum Sayyed Jamiluddin and Miss Ashraf-ul-Haq.[105] This scheme was also encouraged by the private sector. In particular, several trusts and generous persons in India as well as in Britain showed great interest in this regard. In India, however, such kinds of funds were usually distributed on a communal basis. Among Muslims, for instance, the Haji Muhammad Suliman Botowala and Fatima Bibi Rogay Trusts allocated scholarships for those Muslim students who wanted to go abroad for higher education. The King Edward Memorial and the Sussex Trusts however gave their scholarships on the basis of merit.[106]

The Indian Education Department at London was quite satisfied with the educational progress of Indian female students as well as their social adjustment in a new society. According to one of its reports published in 1935–36 these women had organized themselves through their Indian Women's Education Association (established in 1921) and had arranged some trips to European countries. The Department also showed great interest in the activities of female students. It arranged dinners and social gatherings from time to time, usually held at the Office of the High Commission for India in London.[107]

It appears that the experiences of these female students became an important source of information for ordinary Indian women who were curious to know about foreign culture and society. Sometimes their letters and daily dairies were published in the form of books and articles. For instance, the experiences of Attiya Faizi were published in 1932 in the form of a book entitled *Zamana-e-Tahsil* (The Period of Education). Another prominent example was Muhammadi Begum, the great-granddaughter of Muhammad Nazir Ahmed, the famous Urdu novelist. Muhammadi Begum was sent for higher education to Oxford from the State of Hyderabad. She regularly wrote letters to her mother, which were occasionally published in *Ismat*. In one of her letters she wrote of her appreciation of the hard work of English women by citing the example of her landlord's daughter-in-law who was running the household as well as dairy and poultry farms in the countryside thirteen miles away from Oxford. As compared to Indian women, she noted, English women were more industrious. In the end Muhammadi Begum advises her Indian sisters to follow this particular example of English womanhood.[108]

THE ROLE OF EDUCATED WOMEN IN
PUBLIC LIFE

The most important aspect of the feminist movement in India was the emergence of a public sphere for women. In particular, modern education enabled many women to play a role in the rebuilding of Indian society. Although this trend was slow in process, it caused a far-reaching impact on their social and economic life. This section discusses the nature of their extended role and their entry into different professions, in particular those which were previously reserved for men.

WOMEN AND EXTRA-CURRICULAR ACTIVITIES

Extra-curricular activities for female students were started in their educational institutions either with the help of the government or by different social agencies. One such example was the introduction of physical education in these institutions. Under the new arrangements, several colleges for physical training were opened in different parts of the country. Among these were the Government College of Physical Education for Women, Calcutta, the Y.M.C.A. College for Physical Education, Madras, St. Mary Training College, Poona, the Physical Training College, Nani Tal, and the Zenana Physical Training College, Hyderabad. Above all, arrangements for sports competitions between different women's educational institutions increased the interest of women in this field. Inter-School and Inter-Collegiate tournaments were arranged and games like netball and badminton became increasingly popular among women. It was because of these kinds of activities that many Indian women began to feel that the standard of traditional Indian beauty—pale complexioned and slim, with a thin body structure—was no longer acceptable to them. Instead, they wished to become as healthy as British women by participating in different kinds of sports.[09]

Increasing numbers of educated women now began to take to social service. Associations like the Girl Guides and the Blue Birds were introduced in schools after the second decade of the twentieth century. In all provinces, girls responded positively to these associations. In particular, in the United Provinces, Bihar, Sindh, and N.W.F.P., their participation was clothed in a nationalist garb.[110] Hindu and Muslim girls studying in *purdah* schools who had never left their cities before, after joining these associations went out to camps in the forests for at least three weeks at a stretch.[111] In 1938, another step was taken by introducing the All-India Girl Guides Training Scheme. It was under this scheme that Miss Baker, the Training Inspectress of Schools of Sindh, trained 200 girls as Blue Birds with a grant of Rs.1,000 sanctioned by the Government.[112] In the Punjab, Girl Guides were started under the supervision of Miss Thomas, the Deputy Directress of Education, Punjab. The girls took an active interest in extramural activities such as educational campaigns, visiting villages and helping in women's welfare leagues working in different provinces. In 1942, this scheme was further extended by appointing the Girl Guides advisers for the Multan and Ambala divisions where it was becoming popular among the girls of local schools.[113] The same was done in the N.W.F.P. where the Girl Guides were becoming increasingly popular under the supervision of Miss Littleward, the Inspectress of Schools, who received a special grant of Rs.1,056 for this purpose. There were thirty-five Girl Guides companies and Blue Birds Flocks in the province; the movement was flourishing chiefly in the districts of Peshawar, Abbottabad, and Dera Ismail Khan. The Girl Guides and the Blue Birds made their first major public appearance on 25 March 1939, when a big rally was held at St. John's Church, Peshawar, and was greatly appreciated by the local people.[114]

These associations played an active part during the Second World War period by supporting the cause of the WACI (The Women's Auxiliary Corps India) and other military organizations. In the same way, the War Fund and War Comforts Schemes were successfully run by these associations. For example, in the

N.W.F.P., they collected Rs.1,056 for the Red Cross and War Fund while articles such as mufflers, pullovers and gloves were knitted for soldiers.[115]

WOMEN AND THE WIDER EXPANSION OF SOCIAL ACTIVITIES

Educated women now began taking to writing in a big way in the form of books, both poetry and prose, as well as journalism. As for Muslim women, there had been several poets among them in the late nineteenth century who were associated with *Dabistan-e-Delhi* or *Dabistan-e-Lucknow*. However, most of their poetic work was confined to romanticism and entertainment, and not particularly expressive of feminist concerns.[116] This, however, began to change in the twentieth century, with their poetry now becoming increasingly concerned with social issues. A good example of this kind of literature was the poetic work of Noshaba Khatun Qurashi of Hyderabad, Deccan. Her poems became popular among Muslim women during the period of *Khilafat* movement in India. Later, a collection of her poems was published from Hyderabad under the title, *Mauj-e-Takhaiyyal* (The Surge of the Imagination) in 1938.[117] Another poetic work, the *Firdaus-e-Takhaiyyal* (The Paradise of Imagination), was published by Miss Z.K.S. of Lahore in 1945.[118]

Compared to poetry, the works in prose produced by women writers were more concerned with religious, social, and historical issues. Early examples of this were works by the Begums of Bhopal. Women like Muhammadi Begum, (editor of *Tehzib-e-Niswan*), Tayyaba Begum Bilgrami, (novelist), and Khajasta Sultan Begum Suhrwardi (historian) went on to make valuable contributions in this field. The further expansion of this literature, in particular after the second decade of the twentieth century, led many educated women from middle class families to write about their social experiences. Prominent among them were Sughra Begum, Sayyeda Zamiruddin, Khawar Durrani, Riffat Jahan, Rihat Ara Begum, Dr Rashid Jahan Begum and Ismat Chughtai.

As for journalism, women had been fairly active participants from the closing years of the nineteenth century through editing magazines and writing articles. The trend became more popular during the early twentieth century and onwards. Several women's magazines in Urdu began being published under the editorship of modern educated women. For instance, the *Haya*, the *Zeb-un-nisa*, the *Irim* and the *Subras* were published under the editorship of Sughra Begum, Bilqees Begum, Miss Shakila and Sakina Begum respectively.[119]

In the same way, the radio became another powerful media which helped educated women to communicate with their female listeners. A major step forward was taken in 1944, when a women's section was formed in the Department of Information and Broadcasting under the supervision of Begum Shah Nawaz. Increasingly, special programmes, features, debates, and cooking recipes were broadcast by women for women. The different centres of All-India Radio such as at Delhi, Lahore, Lucknow, Peshawar, Bombay, Madras and Hyderabad, broadcast special programmes for women in Urdu, usually, presented by educated Muslim women.[120]

WOMEN AND ORGANIZED SOCIAL ACTIVITIES

Women's organized activities which were also started during the last decades of the nineteenth century further developed at the national and international levels in the twentieth century. Many educated women from all social classes and backgrounds took part in organizing women's social activities in different parts of India. The National Council of Women in India was founded in Bombay in 1925 in order to federate the other women's associations with the aim to advance the education of Indian women and to forge links with international women's movements. Under its auspices, the first All-India Women's Conference on Educational Reforms was held at Poona in 1927 and from that year the Conference regularly conducted its annual meetings in different parts of the country. It also formed various standing committees to undertake practical schemes of work. For instance, one of its standing committees, the All-India Fund Association, collected Rs.80,000 and it was decided to devote all this money for the formation of a central teaching college for women.[121]

In 1929 another initiative was taken by the All-India Teachers' Federation. The federation nominated Mrs Kamala Chattopadhyaya to represent Indian women at the meeting of the World Federation of Educational Associations at Geneva. During her visit to Europe she also had a chance to attend the International Women's Congress at Berlin on behalf of her Indian sisters.[122] Another example of this growing activism at the international level was the first International Conference of Women which was arranged at the Town Hall, Calcutta, in 1936. Women from Britain, France, Holland, Switzerland, Belguim, Australia and China represented their countries. In its opening session, presided over by the Maharani of Baroda, the Conference emphasized the importance of the educational advancement of Indian women. It further suggested the removal of social disabilities of women by giving them equal rights and equal opportunities in different fields of life.[123] It seems that the matter of female education in India had, by this time, become so important for its promoters that they tried to avail of every single chance to discuss it.

PROFESSIONAL STATUS AND OPPORTUNITY

The scope for women in different professions, in particular in teaching, considerably expanded over the time. This was given a big boost by the establishment of the Women's Indian Educational Services by the Royal Commission on Public Service in India in 1917. The Commission recommended the creation of forty-six class I and class II posts for women in the Department of Education as inspectresses, sub-inspectresses and principals in different provinces of India.[124] In 1920 a further step was taken by creating a new post of Deputy Directress of Public Instruction and the first post was created in the Madras Presidency. In taking this initiative, Dewan Bahadur

Ramachandra, Secretary to the Government of Madras, argued that for the advancement of female education in the presidency it was necessary to attach a senior woman officer to his office who would not only deal with routine educational matters but would also have special powers for the appointment of female teachers. Above all, she would be able to handle those problems which were peculiarly feminine in character.[125] In later years similar posts were created in the Bombay Presidency and in the Punjab. Several women's inspectresses were also appointed in different provinces in 1938–39. They were responsible for matters relating to female education in their assigned areas. Table 2 illustrates their designations and number of posts.

Table 2
The number of women's higher posts in the department of education in the year 1938–39

PROVINCE	DESIGNATION	NO. OF POSTS	DESIGNATION	NO. OF POSTS
Madras	Inspectress	6	Assistants & Sub-Assistant	53
Bombay	do	3	do	Nil
Bengal	do	2	do	12
U.P.	Chief Inspectress	1	do	11
Punjab	Deputy Inspectress	1	Circle & Assistant Inspectress	18
Bihar	Inspectress	1	District Inspectress	7
C.P. & Berar	do	2	Assistant Inspectress	4

Assam	Nil		do	1
N.W.F.P.	Inspectress	1	do	1
Sindh	do	1	do	Nil
Orissa	do	1	District & Assistant Inspectress	2

Source: See note 126

Besides these above-mentioned posts for women there were some other special posts created in different provinces. For example, in the Punjab there was a female Supervisor of Domestic Science as well as a Physical Training Supervisor for Girls. Likewise, to look after the educational affairs of Muslim female students, a special post of a Lady Superintendent was created in the Province of Bihar.[127]

The main purpose behind these new developments was the wider expansion of female education under the direct supervision of women. This led to a considerable increase in the number of female teachers and the setting up of a number of centres to train such teachers, particularly in Bengal, the Punjab and the United Provinces.

MUSLIM WOMEN AND PROFESSIONAL TRAINING

As in the case of their other Indian sisters, educated Muslim women seem to have been initially attracted to teaching as a profession before they began to enter other professions, including those previously reserved for men, such as medicine, law, and even banking. Women who took the initiative in this regard included Miss Shareen, the first Indian Muslim M.B.B.S. lady doctor who received her degree in 1934, Begum Sakina Moidzada, the first Indian Muslim lady advocate who started her practice at the Bombay high court in 1941 and Zubadia Mansoor Ahmed, the first Indian Muslim woman banker who received her higher education in 1944 from the U.S.A. In the same way, the number of Muslim women in different professional and technical institutions also rose considerably with the passage of time. Table three shows the number of educated Muslim women in different professional and educational institutions.

Table 3
Number of Muslim women in professional education

PROFESSION	1921–22	1922–27	1927–32	1932–37	1938–39
Medical	14	26	36	144	104
Medicines		7	20	40	43
Teaching training	303	303	657	759	871
Technical & Industrial	85	127	313	568	760
Commercial	Nil	3	Nil	3	3
Schools for Adults	Nil	140	156	104	211
Law	Nil	Nil	Nil	Nil	1
Others Schools	899	257	1,090	2,817	5,513

Source: See note 128

In some provinces the growth in the number of Muslim women in professional educational institutions was particularly impressive. For instance, in Madras 3,138 Muslim women were receiving professional education during the above-mentioned period. The majority being in training and industrial schools. In Bombay and Punjab the number of such women was 1,660 and 1,080 respectively.[129] The number of Muslim women who were receiving professional education in other parts of the country during this period is not available; educational reports for the last years were usually published by either the Indian or Pakistani Governments.

Interestingly, a number of women went on actively to participate in the military services during the Second World War. The Women Auxiliary Corps India (WACI) and Women's Royal Indian Navy Services (WRINS) were constituted in India under the Ordinance No. XIII of 1942 for the formation of women's corps in various capacities. In 1944, Miss Shanthi Ranga Rao, the Second Deputy Chief Commander of the WACI, became the first Indian woman to be granted a direct commission as colonel.[130] In 1945, thirty-one WACI officers completed their course at the WACI Staff College, Quetta. Their course of training was the same as that for men.[131] Some Indian women were even sent abroad for military training. The first Indian woman to complete her military training from Britain was Second Officer Kalyani Sen of the WRINS. She had earlier done an MA in English Literature from the University of Punjab, Lahore.[132] It is interesting to note that women from all communities took an interest in these national services. Table 4 shows the number of women at various posts in the WACI and WRINS

Table 4
Number of women on different posts according to community in 1945

COMMUNITY	OFFICERS	AUXILIARIES
Europeans	767	1,405
Hindus	147	3,918
Muslims	5	92
Sikhs	1	78
Parsi	27	296
Indian Christians	39	2,182
Jews	1	102
Others	8	160

Source: See note 133

When the war ended, the women's corps were made to engage in civil duties. For this purpose, a women's section was set up under the charge of fully trained personnel at employment exchanges at Delhi, Calcutta, Bombay, Madras, Nagpur, Patna,

Lucknow, Karachi and Lahore. Trainees were provided with free boarding, lodging, medical facilities and transportation, in addition to a monthly stipend of Rs.101. Subjects offered at these centres included typing, stenography, commercial practice, clerical work, commercial arts, hairdressing and beauty culture, as well as the more traditional subjects such as tailoring, cookery and confectionary.[134]

* * *

In conclusion, the gradual spread of modern education among Muslim women led slowly, though surely, to the opening up of new public spaces for them, hitherto unthought of. Undeniably, the degree of change among them was not as considerable as it was in the case of their Hindu sisters. Their relatively late entry into modern education, two generations after their menfolk, was one reason for this. Another seems to have been the great role that traditional *madrasas* continued to play in the life of the community. Yet, keeping in mind the initial disabilities that they started off with, what is undeniable is that Muslim women made impressive use of the new public spaces made available for them through education.

NOTES

1. Gail Minault, 'The Extended family as Metaphor and the Expansion of Women's Realm', in Gail Minault (ed.), *The Extended family: Women and Political Participation in India and Pakistan*, pp. 3–18.
2. Ibid.
3. S. Nurullah and J.P. Naik, *A History of Education in India During the British Period*, 2nd edition, (Macmillan, London, 1951), p. 493.
4. Ibid.
5. *Abolition of Fees in Primary Schools*, Selection from the Record of the Government of India, No. ccc XLV, (Home Department Printing Press, Calcutta, 1910), p. 3.
6. *General Report on Public Instruction in the United Provinces of Agra and Oudh, 1912–13*, (Government Printing United Provinces, Allahabad, 1914), p. 19.

7. S. Nurullah and J.P. Naik, *A History of Education in India During the British Period*, p. 574.

8. N. Desai and K. Bhansali, 'A Struggle for Identity Retention: A Case Study of S.N.D.T. Women's University', in P.R. Panchamukhi (ed.), *Reforms Towards Equality and Relevances: Studies in Educational Reforms in India*, Vol. III, (Indian Institute of Education, Puna, 1989), pp. 20–50.

9. Ibid.

10. *The Educational Manual of the Central Provinces and Berar, European Schools*, Vol. 2, (Government Press, Nagpur, 1911), p. 11.

11. *Progress of Education in India, 1917–22*, Seventh Quinquennial Review, Vol. 1, (His Majesty's Stationery Office, London, 1919), p. 175.

12. Ibid.

13. Ibid.

14. *Progress of Education in India, 1917–22*, Eighth Quinquennial Review, Vol. 1, (His Majesty's Stationery Office, London, 1924), p. 129.

15. Ibid.

16. Ibid.

17. Ibid., p. 130.

18. Ibid.

19. Ibid., p. 179.

20. *Memorandum on the Progress of Education in British India Between 1916–26*, (Government Printing Calcutta), 1927), p. 59.

21. Ibid., p. 57.

22. Abdul Rashid Khan, 'The Contribution of the All-India Muslim Educational Conference to the Educational and Cultural Development of Indian Muslims 1886–1947', (Unpublished Ph.D. thesis, University of London, 1991), p. 256.

23. Ibid.

24. *The Problems of Urdu Training in the Bombay Presidency*, (Government of Bombay, Department of Public Instruction), p. 7.

25. *Muhammadan Education Recent Development in the Bombay Presidency*, Government of Bombay, Department of Public Instruction), p. 4.

26. See, *Progress of Education in India*, Eighth Quinquennial Review, p. 28, and *Progress of Education in India 1922–27*, Ninth Quinquennial Review, Vol. 2 (Government of India, Central Publication Branch, Calcutta, 1929), p. 11.

27. *Progress of Education In India*, Ninth Quinquennial Review, p. 11.

28. Ibid., p. 238.

29. Ibid., p. 237.

30. Ibid., p. 241.

31. Ibid., p. 242.

32. Ibid.

33. Ibid., p. 243.
34. Ibid., p. 243.
35. Ibid.
36. Sir Philip Hartog, 'Notes and Memoranda on the Growth of Women's Education in India in 1929', MSS. Eur. E. 221, p. 2, IOL.
37. Ibid., p. 3.
38. *Progress of Education In India 1927–32*, Tenth Quinquennial Review, (Government of India, Central Publication Branch, Calcutta, 1934), p. 3.
39. Ibid.
40. Ibid., p. 164.
41. Ibid.
42. Ibid., p. 169.
43. *Progress of Education in India*, Eleventh Quinquennial Review, (Government of India, Press, Simla, 1938), p. 241.
44. Ibid., p. 243.
45. Ibid., pp. 247–48.
46. S. Nurullah and Naik, *History of Education in India During the British Period*, p. 748.
47. *Report of the Second Wardha Education Committee*, Central Advisory Board of Education, (Government of India Press, New Delhi, 1941), p. 1.
48. Ibid.
49. *Report by the Central Advisory Board of Education on the Post-War Educational Development (Sargent Report)*, (Manager of Publication, Delhi, 1945), p. 15.
50. Ibid.
51. *General Report on Public Instruction in the Madras Presidency in 1939–40*, (Government Press, Madras, 1941), pp. 31–34.
52. Naseeruddin Hashmi, 'Madras ki Ala Talim yaftah Khawateen', *Ismat*, Vol. 76, No. 3, March 1946, pp. 194–95.
53. *Annual Report on Public Instruction in the Presidency of Bombay for 1944–45*, (Government Central Press, Bombay, 1946), p. 39.
54. *Annual Report on Public Instruction in Sind, 1939–40*, (Government Press, Karachi, 1943), p. 5.
55. *Report on the Progress of Education in the Punjab in 1941–42*, (Government Printing Punjab, Lahore, 1943), p. 4.
56. Ibid.
57. Ibid., p. 37.
58. *Report on the Progress of Education in the Punjab for 1945–46*, (Government Printing West Punjab, Lahore, 1948), p. 13.
59. *Annual Report on the Public Instruction in the N.W.F.P. for the Year 1938–39*, (Government of the N.W.F.P., Peshawar, 1940), p. 63.
60. Ibid., p. 66.

61. *Report on the State and Progress of Education in the Central Provinces and Berar for 1941–42*, (Government Printing Press, Nagpur, 1942), p. 43.
62. Ibid., p. 44.
63. *General Report on Public Instruction in the United Provinces for 1947*, (Superintendent Printing Press Allahabad, 1949), p. 36
64. *Ismat*, Vol. 63, No. 1, July 1939, p. 138.
65. 'Papers and Correspondences Relating to the Foundation and Early Years of the Women Christian College, Madras', MSS. Eur. F. 220, n.p., IOL.
66. Ibid.
67. Ibid.
68. Ibid., p. 88.
69. Ibid.
70. Ibid.
71. Ibid.
72. See, Richard Dickinson and Nancy Dickinson, (ed.), *Directory of Information for Christian College in India*, (The Christian Literary Society, Madras, 1967).
73. Abstracts are taken from a tape recorder interview with Mrs Wenger, 1976, MSS. Eur. F. 219, IOL
74. H. Kraemer, 'Islam in India Today', *Muslim World*, Vol. XXI, (New Jersey, 1931), pp. 151–76.
75. *Progress of Education in India*, Tenth Quinquennial Review, pp. 208–209.
76. Ibid., p. 211.
77. Ibid., p. 212.
78. Sarfaraz Husain Mirza, *Muslim Women's Role in the Pakistan Movement*, (Research Society of Pakistan, University of the Punjab, Lahore, 1969), p. 12.
79. Abstracts are taken from the *Salana Report: All-India Muslim Ladies Conference*, held at Delhi in 1917, MEC., Report, n.d., pp. 62–63.
80. Ibid.
81. Ibid.
82. M.H. Zaidi, *Muslim Womanhood in Revolution*, p. 106.
83. Naseeruddin Hashmi, 'Hyderabad ka Zenana College', *Ismat*, Vol. 66, No. 1, January 1941, pp. 46–48.
84. Ibid.
85. Naseeruddin Hashmi, 'Madras ki Ala Talim Yaftha Muslim Khawateen', *Ismat*, March 1946, pp. 194–95.
86. Ibid.
87. Ibid.
88. *Ismat*, Vol. 62, No. 2, February 1939, pp. 42–43.
89. See, Roushan Jahan (ed. and trans.), *Sultana's Dream: and Selections from the Secluded Ones*, (The Feminist Press, New York, 1988), pp. 41–42.

90. Gail Minault, 'Sayyed Karamat Husain and Education for Women' in Violette Graff, (ed.), *Memories of a City: Lucknow 1772–1991*, (Oxford University Press, New Delhi, Forthcoming).

91. Fatima Begum, 'Muslim Ladies Conference aur Zenana Sanati Numaish', *Ismat*, Vol. 48, No. 2, February 1932, pp. 144–45.

92. Sarfaraz Husain Mirza, *Muslim Women's Role in the Pakistan Movement*, p. 19.

93. *Ismat*, August 1939, p. 209.

94. *Ismat*, Vol. 62, No. 2, February 1939, p. 126.

95. Razia Abdul Qadir, 'Khawateen-e-Bihar', *Ismat*, Vol. 64, No. 4, October 1941, p. 251.

96. *Report on the Progress of Education in the Punjab 1945* (Government Printing Press, Punjab, Lahore, 1947), pp. 13, 46.

97. *Ismat*, Vol. 66, No. 1, January 1941, p. 70.

98. Naseeruddin Hashmi, 'Madras ki Ala Talim Yaftah Khawateen', *Ismat*, pp. 194–95.

99. Naseeruddin Hashmi, 'Osmania University ki Niswani Maqalat' *Ismat*, Vol. 74, No. 1, January 1945, pp. 43–44.

100. *Report of the Indian Students Department*, for April 1920 to March 1921, Office of the Commission for India, (His Majesty's Stationery Office, London, 1922) p. 33.

101. *Report of the Indian Students Department*, for April 1922 to March 1923, Office for the High Commission for India, (His Majesty's Stationery Office, London, 1923), p. 19.

102. *Report on the Work of Education Department*, London, for April 1924, to March 1925, Office for the High Commission for India, (His Majesty's Stationery Office, London, 1925), p. 18

103. *Report on the Work of Education Department*, London, for April 1925 to March 1926, Office for the High Commissionfor India, (His Majesty's Stationery Office, London, 1926), p. 22.

104. *Report on the Work of Education Department*, London, for April 1928 to March 1929, Office for the High Commission for India, (His Majesty's Stationery Office, London, 1928), p. 15.

105. Naseeruddin Hashmi, 'Hyderabad ki European Talim Yafth Khawateen', *Ismat*, Vol. 74, No. 4, September 1945, pp. 243–44.

106. *Report on the Work of Education Department*, London for April 1933 to March 1934, Office for the High Commission for India, (His Majesty's Stationery Office, London, 1934), p. 32.

107. *Report on the Work of Education Department*, London, for April 1935 to March 1936, Office for the High Commission for India, (His Majesty's Stationery Office, London, 1935), p. 18.

108. *Ismat*, Vol. 55, No. 3, September 1935, pp. 255–56.

109. Begum Abdul Rashid, 'Nazakat aur Chusti ki Jung,' *Ismat*, Vol. 51, No. 6, December 1933, pp. 471–72.

110. *Education in India in 1938–39*, Bureau of Education, (Manager of Publication, Delhi, 1941), p. 90.

111. A.R. Caton and Martelli, 'Home and Marriage' in A.R. Caton (ed.), *The Key Progress of Women: A Survey of the Status and Condition of Women in India*, (Oxford University Press, London, 1930), pp. 101–30.

112. *Annual Report on Public Instruction in Sindh*, (Government Press, Karachi, 1943), p. 93.

113. *Report on the Progress of Education in the Punjab in 1941–42*, p. 4.

114. *Report on the Public Instruction in N.W.F.P. in 1938–39*, p. 93.

115. Ibid., p. 76.

116. Among the prominent Muslim poetesses associated with Delhi and Lucknow schools were, Akhtar, Hatim, Naz, Nazuk, Yad, Parsa, Hijab, Dulhan, Zuhra, Mahboob,Yasmine and Zia. The above-mentioned names are taken from Naseeruddin Hashmi, 'Urdu ki Nuashv-o-noma main Auratho ka Hisa', *Ismat*, Vol. 71, No. 1 July, 1943, pp. 37–40.

117. Ibid.

118. *Tehzib-e-Niswan*, Advertisement Section, Vol. 49, No. 14, 16 April 1946, p. 22.

119. Naseeruddin Hashmi, 'Hyderabad ki European Talim Yaftah Khawateen', *Ismat*, July, 1943, pp. 37–40

120. Ibid.

121. A.R. Caton, 'Women in Public Life', pp. 80–100.

122. *Stri Dharma*, Vol. XIX, No. 4, May 1936, p. 126.

123. *Indian Ladies Magazine*, Vol. 2, No. 6, January 1936, p. 332.

124. *Royal Commission on the Public Services in India*, (His Majesty's Stationery Office, London, 1917), pp. 119–20.

125. Abstracts are taken from the *Proceedings of Madras Goverment: Education including, Confidential*, Letter No. 994, dated 31 August 1920, n.p., IOL.

126. *The Progress of Education in India in 1938–39*, Eleventh Quinquennial Review, pp. 251–53.

127. Ibid.

128. Figures are derived from the *Progress of Education In India*, Eighth Quinquennial Review, p. 165, Ninth Quinquennial Review, p. 30, Tenth Quinquennial Review, p. 32, Eleventh Quinquennial Review, p. 34 and *Education in India*, p. 51.

129. Ibid.

130. *Official Handout*, 28 December 1944 (Public Relations Directorate General Headquarter, New Delhi, 1944, File No. 462/78, L/1/1/1020, n.p., IOL.

131. Ibid.

132. *Official Handout*, 1 August 1945, ibid.
133. *Press Release*, 5 June 1945, ibid.
134. Press Information Bureau, Government of India, 28 November 1946, ibid.

3

OPENING UP A PUBLIC SPACE FOR WOMEN: THE ROLE OF HEALTH CARE ARRANGEMENTS

In the late nineteenth century medico-scientific concerns about the female body began to develop in the West. It increasingly led people to see through the rational and scientific disguises of power, and enabled them to recognize that women's suppression was socially, not biologically, ordained.

In India, too, the impact of this new Western medical discourse began to be felt. It pushed people, in particular the newly emerged educated middle class, to embrace the subject of women's health status and their reproductive role in society. For Muslim women, it opened up a space not only socially but economically as well. For instance, the emergence of new health care arrangement, in particular the beginning of the maternity and child welfare work, preventative campaigns against maternal mortality and the enactment of various items of medical legislation encouraged more and more Indian women to go to hospitals and maternity centres, and to take advantage of western biomedicine. Both directly and indirectly, these changes reduced the impact of social restrictions such as *purdah*. Similarly, it provided new opportunities for women to attain greater economic independence, as they entered in larger numbers into different health care professions. Even women belonging to prosperous families abandoning earlier prejudices, chose to become doctors, health visitors, and midwives.

The drive to open up more space for women's health was further strengthened after the realization of the existence of medical and social problems which were caused by the institutions of *purdah* and child-marriage. It aroused widespread interest throughout the society and produced support for the urgent need to provide medical facilities considered more fit to mitigate the consequences of these customs. One of the first steps taken in this direction was the starting of maternity and child welfare work in the second half of the nineteenth century, following closely on the establishment of women's hospitals by missions and by the Government. Medical work among women quickly led to the recognition of the poor conditions surrounding childbirth in the country; because the *dai*—the traditional Indian midwife—seemed to be the basic problem. The earliest efforts to raise the standard of midwifery were directed towards improving her methods. Later on, further developments were made by training health visitors, nurses and female doctors all over the country and appointing them at *zenana* dispensaries and hospitals. Alongside the wide expansion of medical work, new means of preventive action for adequate health protection of mother and child were introduced over time.

At the same time, the status of women's health was further considered after the realization that, besides their maternity and labour experiences necessary for the fulfilment of their reproductive role, it was their fundamental right to keep themselves physically fit and to try to look more healthy and attractive. Thus another facet of the introduction of new approaches towards women's health was the emergence of a women's 'beauty culture' which somewhat paradoxically drew on the overlapping sphere of 'traditional health care. New pharmaceutical companies marketed products which incorporated *unani tibb*, thus expanding the range of 'traditional' prescriptions to include these very female concerns. The contents of women's journals highlighted the extent to which women themselves were involved in the communication and exchange of these ideas with articles on the subjects to be found in leading publications fairly regularly. Women also challenged the disparity between the upbringing of boys and girls as they were convinced that equal diet and equal treatment were the only way to regenerate society as a whole. In this way the idea of happy and healthy life was promoted alongside the insurance of safe motherhood.

In order to study the status of women's health in the context of this evolving medical process, the present chapter discusses the following:

(a) Muslim women's traditional health status *vis-à-vis* maternity and child welfare work 1920–1947.
(b) The beginning of preventative campaigns.
(c) Legislation and improvement of maternity welfare work.
(d) Women and medical education.
(e) Muslim women and new trends in health behaviour.

MUSLIM WOMEN'S TRADITIONAL HEALTH STATUS *VIS-À-VIS* MATERNITY AND CHILD WELFARE WORK 1920–1947

Sex differentials in India between the situation of boys and girls made an important impact on their lives, chances, and opportunities. As compared to boys, girls were more exposed to hazards because they tended to be neglected in matters of nutrition and health care. According to the ideal image of Indian womanhood, a woman was supposed to eat only after the rest of the family had eaten, and often she was given just the left-overs. Girls and women were not encouraged to participate in activities outside the home and were even also discouraged from talking and laughing aloud. Above all, the sufferings of early marriage and maternity were likely to cause them to lose their physical and mental vigour. 'Her life was a long, lingering misery; she was a sacrifice at the altar of custom'.[1]

Given this, it was hardly surprising that women were prohibited from discussing details of their health and medical problems with other members, especially with male relatives.[2] For instance, due to *purdah* restrictions, particularly among the Muslims, no male doctor would ever under normal circumstances be allowed into the *zenana*; he would only be admitted at the last extremity and would never get a chance of making a real examination of the patient's state. He could through a hole in the curtain check her temperature, feel her pulse or see her tongue, and this would most likely be the last moments of her life. However, at the time of labour no male doctor would ever be called and for all female diseases and chronic ailments, women were most likely to be left without any practical medical aid. This left women in labour at the mercy of the local *dai* (midwife), usually an elderly woman with no medical training who relied on traditional lore passed down from her maternal forebears. Her typical 'tools of the trade' carried in an old cloth bag included a rubber enema syringe, lumps of dirty cotton, bottles with no labels, a Vaseline jar without a top, a bundle of country drugs, a loose, dirty hank of surgical silk that was used as a bandage.[3] The *dais* were unaware of even the basics of hygiene. In the district of Chhatisgarh, after the birth of the child, the navel string was cut by the *dai* with broken pieces of a *handi* (a mud pot) or a sharp tin and after that it was buried with other dirt in the corner of the labour room. This was then set on fire as it was believed that by doing this the mother and child would escape from evil spirits.[4] Usually, after giving birth to a child, a mother was not allowed to drink any liquid for three days except bitter drugs and condiments. As a result, especially in summer, many women actually died of thirst. In Rajputana, for instance, in the case of the child's death, the proper diet of the mother during the first three days was a decoction of copper coins and bamboo. Rice and pepper water was what mothers were usually given for the first few days after delivery.[5]

The room chosen for labour was usually separated from the rest of the house with the smallest possible doors and windows, which were always kept tightly shut. Even in hot weather every breath of fresh air was prohibited for the mother and the child as it was believed that, whether cold or hot, it was dangerously harmful for both. In these circumstances, the Indian *dai*, dirty in habit, careless in work, bold in treatment and often callous to sufferings, appeared to be the problem which was in most urgent need of reform.

The first initiative in this direction was taken by Christian missionaries. They did remarkable work for the extension of medical aid in India, setting up hospitals and training medical men and women. Medical women from the Mission came into *zenanas* to treat women who lived in seclusion. However, while their motive was to relieve human sufferings, mission hospitals at that time were regarded as an adjunct to mission work rather than an object in themselves.[6]

It should be noted that Christian missionaries were also pioneers in starting the first training classes for *dais*. In 1866, Dr Aitchinson succeeded in opening a special class for *dais* at Amritsar under the auspices of the Church of England Missionary Society. Later, it became well-known as the Amritsar *Dai* School under the supervision of Miss Hewlett. In 1917 a class for training women as sub-assistant surgeon was also started in the school. With a grant of Rs.3,000 from the Government, its building was expanded to include quarters for sisters and nurses.[7]

Over time, the Government emerged as the major agency working for the medical relief of Indian women. Most health centres and hospitals in the country were opened either by the authorities or with official government grants-in-aid. The earliest such instance was the establishment of the Government Hospital for Women and Children at Egmore (Madras) in 1844. In 1885 another step forward was taken by the wife of Lord Dufferin, the Viceroy of India. She founded the National Association for Supplying Female Medical Aid for the Women of India, generally known after her name, the Lady Dufferin Fund, which aimed at alleviating women's sufferings caused by various ailments. This Association opened several women's hospitals and women's wards in general hospitals.

During the first decade of the twentieth century, the long-established tradition of Indian midwifery was further challenged by the antenatal movement at work in many parts of the world. In India the earliest example of this was the foundation of Victoria Memorial Fund in 1903, which followed closely upon the passing of the first Midwives Act in Britain in 1902. The

Fund, which was formed by Lady Curzon, had as its main objective the improvement of traditional methods of indigenous midwifery in the light of modern sanitary and medical knowledge. A large number of *dai* training classes, aided by grants from the Victoria Memorial Fund, were started in different parts of the country.

The example set by Lady Curzon was followed by the wives of later Viceroys. For instance, in 1906 the Lady Minto's Nursing Association was founded and, ten years later, the Lady Hardinge Hospital and Medical College was opened at Delhi, both of which were staffed entirely by women. In 1918 Lady Chelmsford interested herself in the welfare of women and children of the country. She first sought the help of provincial Governments but could not get the promise of such financial aid from local authorities. A public appeal was, therefore, launched in 1919, and the Lady Chelmsford All-India League for Maternity and Child Welfare was formed the following year. The objects of the League were to give grants-in-aid to welfare centres, to produce propaganda material, to publish a quarterly journal, to stimulate interest in maternity and child welfare work and to give technical advice to the voluntary committees already at work in different parts of India.[8]

The maintenance of central offices and staff made a heavy demand on the relatively small income of the Lady Chelmsford League and, to generate additional funds for field work, the office of the League and Dufferin funds started their work jointly under the supervision of the Secretary of the Dufferin Fund. In later years, the Victoria Memorial Scholarship Fund as well as the Association for the Provision of Health Visitors and Maternity Supervisors were also administered from the Dufferin Office.[9] In 1920 the cause of maternity welfare was further encouraged by the Indian Red Cross Society which aimed to arouse interest in all kind of medical work in India. In order to avoid overlapping, the Maternity and Child Welfare Bureau was established under the auspices of the Society which took over the charge of all activities concerned with the maternity and child welfare movement in India.[10]

The work for maternity and child welfare was further encouraged through different kinds of demonstrations and exhibitions such as the All-India Maternity and Child Welfare Exhibition, which was held in Delhi in 1920. This exhibition was organized by the Office of the Dufferin Fund, although the idea was first mooted by the Association of Medical Women in India. The success of the exhibition led to a marked improvement in the functioning of these organizations and the working of the existing welfare centres.[11]

Medical aid to the women of India was also extended by generous individuals. In 1878 for instance, Sir Salar Jung of Hyderabad opened a *zenana* dispensary with the assistance of an American lady doctor. However, due to opposition by local women towards European methods of treatment, the dispensary was closed in 1880. In the same year, Dora White, another European female doctor, was summoned to Hyderabad to take charge of the *zenana* consulting room in Afzal Jung Hospital. The female portion was built in the form of quadrangle enclosing a large courtyard with a fountain in the centre. This arrangement enabled *purdah*-observing women to come to the hospital frequently. By 1881 the daily average of the out-patient was between forty and fifty, which gradually increased in later years. This medical work was further expanded in the form of home visits, usually at the time of labour.[12]

In 1886 another dispensary with suitable buildings and well-planned arrangements was opened for women and children as a result of the efforts of Jaffer Suleiman, a Muslim from Bombay.[13] The most noteworthy example was the founding of the Cama Hospital (1886) at Bombay by a well-known Parsi lady, Bhikaiji Cama. It was the first women and children's hospital in India to be staffed exclusively by medically-trained women.[14]

These examples were followed by several others during the first two decades of the twentieth century. In 1909, efforts to improve the traditional methods of traditional midwifery were made by Hakim Ajmal Khan, a well-known Muslim physician who founded a training centre for *dais* at Delhi. Lady Dane, the wife of the Lieutenant-Governor of the Punjab, was in the chair on the occasion of its inaugural ceremony when she expressed her appreciation of his efforts and emphasized the need for further examples to be set in this particular field.[15] In 1912, Seth Brij Boshan Das Atma Ram opened the Rukmani Bhai Maternity Home at Bombay under the supervision of his son, Dr Mungal Das. During the first year after its foundation, sixty-six women were admitted for delivery while the number of out-patients was 13,471.[16]

Note should be taken that to increase women's awareness about health issues, some literary work was also done in vernacular languages, mostly based on western methods of treatment. Most significant in this regard was the publication of *Sehat-un-Nisa* (The Health of Women) and *Muhafiz-ul Sibyan* (The Protection of the Health of Children) written in Urdu by Dr Azizuddin, a Medical Officer of a local hospital in the district of Rohtak, in the Punjab. The first book contained a list of all possible diseases that females were vulnerable to and their simple treatment, while the second work mostly concentrated on childcare.[17]

The work was continued during the period from 1920 to 1947. The concerted efforts for the progress of maternity and child welfare work were made by the Government and its associated agencies working in different parts of India. A major step forward was taken by introducing new measures through the Government of India Act of 1919. The Act encouraged greater initiative in health policy and facilitated its implementation all over the country. Under this Act, responsibility for medical administration, including hospitals, dispensaries, and provision for medical education, public health, sanitation and vital statistics, with certain reservations in respect of legislation by the Indian Legislature, were transferred to the provinces. As a result of these changes the Indian ministries were motivated to work towards promoting the growth of medical relief and preventive health measures as far as funds permitted. Indeed, these changes brought far greater public health activity in the provinces than ever before, particularly in the field of maternity and child welfare work.

The work was further harmonized under the Government of India Act of 1935, which provided a common platform both for the Central and Provincial Governments to discuss important health matters jointly. For this purpose a Central Advisory Board of Health was established under the chairmanship of the member in charge of health in the Viceroy's Executive Council, and with other members consisting of the health ministers in the provinces and the representatives of the Indian states. Among the official representatives of the Government of India a woman member was also included, generally nominated by the Government. The Board emphasized the improvement of health services for women and children. Among its recommendations was the appointment of an ad hoc committee to review the whole maternity and child welfare situation in India. This committee was finally set up in 1938. The Committee suggested further reforms for the progress of maternity work in different parts of India which can be seen through various arrangments made both by central and provincial Governments. The progress of maternity welfare work, however varied from one province to another.

Among the Indian provinces, Madras was the most advanced. Where *purdah* hardly existed, and women went out to hospitals freely for their confinements. Many educated girls had also taken up midwifery and nursing as a profession. Owing to the growing demand of trained medical women, efforts were made by starting training classes at municipal hospitals. In 1931 a special section of maternity and child welfare was set up in the Department of Public Health under the supervision of Assistant Directress of Public Health. The Department arranged refresher courses for health visitors working with local bodies. The first course was started at the Poonamallee Health Unit during the same year.[18] In the Bombay Presidency much attention was paid to the development of maternity work by increasing the number of maternity centres in different parts of the presidency. These centres were also facilitated with the services of the touring nurses whose duties were to educate mothers with regard to safe midwifery; to give lectures to local *dais* and to attend midwifery cases in their distributed areas.[19] Another major advancment in this period was the training of health visitors at advanced level under the auspices of the Bombay Mofussil Maternity and Child Welfare Council. It helped to improve the quality of maternity work both in urban and rural areas.[20]

The maternity service in the United Provinces was one of the most extensive in India. Due to *purdah* restrictions, domiciliary midwifery was more acceptable for Muslim women. To make it more secure and scientific, special attention was paid to the training of indigenous *dais*. For this purpose, training centres were opened in different parts of the provinces and trained women were appointed at different localities to visit the homes of expectant mothers and conduct their labour cases. In the same way antenatal cases were visited and supervised by these trained medical women.[21] In the provinces of Punjab the maternity welfare work was further extended with the establishment of training schools for health visitors under the supervision of the Delhi Training Centre. Similarly, refresher and diploma courses for trained *dais* were started under the supervision of Inspectress and Assistant Inspectress of Health Centres.[22]

In the province of Bengal, maternity and child welfare work was extended under the auspices of the Indian Red Cross Society. With the help of the certain grant from the Government, the Society was able to establish maternity and child welfare centres with the minimum standard of qualified female staff, equipment and buildings. Initially, five centres were started. They rendered domiciliary midwifery services through trained *dais*.[23] In the Central Provinces too, most of the attention was paid on the training of local *dais*. Biweekly classes of eight to twelve each according to the standard syllabus were started at various centres. The general response of local women was quite positive. Expectant mothers visited the maternity clinic while labour cases were conducted by health visitors. In fact it represented a great achievement gained with the cooperation of local people, especially women, and this was highlighted by the Honorary Secretary of the Provincial Red Cross society who mentioned that the future of the maternity welfare work in the province was radiant with hope to fulfil the noblest cause of the world—to build up a nation.[24] In the province of N.W.F.P., maternity welfare work was started under the auspices of Lady Chelmsford League and attention was paid to improve the standard of domiciliary midwifery. Two training centres were opened at Peshawar and Dera Ismail Khan. Gradually all the district welfare centres and agencies had benefited from the training courses of these centres. *Dais* were sent for training, and after the course they were attached to small civil hospitals and dispensaries.[25]

In general, the progress of maternity and child welfare work was quite satisfactory in India although the measures introduced in this regard remained inadequate to fulfil growing needs. The reasons for this were the lack of proper planning and the fact gender prejudices still prevailed in society. However, efforts were continued by Government and other agencies.

THE BEGINNING OF PREVENTATIVE CAMPAIGNS

Those involved in the maternity and child welfare movement in India, began, over time, paying increasing attention to the development of measures for adequate health protection to mothers and children. One reason for this was the very high rate of maternal mortality in the country. The several findings of enquiries which were conducted between 1930 and 1936 in different parts of India suggested that the maternal mortality rate was approximately 18.5 per 1,000 live births.[26] However, the number of recorded live births in 1936 in British India totalled (A nearly 10 million per annum; among them the rate of maternal mortality was 2,00,000 or 20 per 1,000 live births.[66] It should be noted that this was a very conservative estimate. Along with this wastage of life a very serious wastage of health was taking place in the form of maternal ill-health. The percentage of women disabled as a result of pregnancy and labour was estimated to be not less than 30 per cent, which was a very shocking fact and highlighted the magnitude of the problem to be faced in planning a campaign for healthy motherhood in India.[27]

THE CAUSES OF MATERNAL MORTALITY

To improve this situation and to enquire into the diseases related to childbearing and childbirth, a number of special enquiries were made in different parts of India. The definition of maternal mortality adopted during these enquiries covered those deaths which occurred during pregnancy or within four weeks after the termination of pregnancy or later if illness originated during pregnancy, childbirth or the puerperium. The causes of maternal mortality were classified as (i) deaths due directly to childbearing and (ii) deaths due to associated diseases during childbearing.

The first study of maternal mortality was made by Dr A.L. Mudaliyar in 1931–32. The survey was financed by the Indian Research Fund Association and the Madras Corporation. Dr Mudaliyar carried out an investigation in Madras city in the following year and produced a report in 1933. He investigated 436 death cases; among them 317 deaths occurred due to childbearing while 119 deaths occurred due to associated diseases during pregnancy.[28] In 1935 the Association decided that the study of this pressing problem should be undertaken both in rural and urban areas. An important and comprehensive enquiry was conducted in Calcutta by Dr M.I. Neal Edward, a Professor of Maternity and Child Welfare at the All-India Institute of Hygiene and the Public Health, Calcutta. The period covered by the survey was 15 June 1936 to June 1937 while the area chosen was under the control of the Health Officer of the Calcutta Corporation.

Different methods were adopted during the investigation. Firstly, all maternal deaths were followed up within a few days after receiving the duplicate registration cards from different hospitals and maternity homes of Calcutta. Secondly, visits to the homes were made for the collection of information regarding past history, living conditions, health in pregnancy, the place of delivery and names of attendants. In the case of deaths which occurred in hospitals or maternity homes, these particulars were collected from the concerned doctor, midwives and *dais*. Besides these, efforts were made to collect information about home conditions and general surroundings which included the number of rooms, the number of people occupying them and their cleanliness, ventilation and drainage. A weekly meeting between the investigators and the officers in charge of the enquiry was held for the purpose of reaching conclusions regarding the causes of deaths. In this way each case was discussed while the circumstances were fresh in the mind of the investigator. The total number of registered births which occurred during the period was 28,714 and, in addition, 2,889 still births were registered. There were 887 maternal deaths investigated during the enquiry. Among them 701 deaths which occurred due to childbearing while 186 occurred as a result of independent diseases concurrent with pregnancy or childbearing. The number of deaths due to the causes mentioned by the enquiry, however, varied from one community to another. For example, among the 701 deaths which were due directly to childbearing, there were 533 Hindus, 146 Muslims, eleven Indian Christians and eleven Anglo-Indians, while among the 186 deaths due to associated diseases 124 were of Hindus, fifty-seven of Muslims and five of Indian Christians.[29]

The third enquiry was made by Dr Jhirad, of the Cama and Albess Hospitals, Bombay. The investigation was started in Bombay City in July 1937 and lasted for one year. It was based on the duplicate forms of deaths of those women who died between the ages of 10 to 50 and which stated whether the woman was pregnant or not at the time of death. Five hundred and twenty-five cases were investigated during the enquiry. Among the death cases investigated during the enquiry, 340 deaths occurred due to childbearing, and 175 deaths were due to associated diseases during pregnancy.[30]

Note should be taken that among the more common causes of maternal mortality found during these enquiries were

Puerperal sepsis (Infection during puerperium), Puerperal albuminuria, (High blood pressure in pregnancy), anaemia in pregnancy and tuberculosis. Among the other diseases were Septic abortions, Ectopic gestation (Pregnancy in other than the uterus), Accident of pregnancy and Toxaemia of pregnancy. Table 1 shows the comparative distribution of maternal deaths due to direct child bearing in three of these important enquiries.

Table 1
Comparative distribution of maternal deaths in different enquiries

Causes	Madras 1933	Calcutta 1936–37	Bombay 1937–38
Abortion septic	14	33	10
Abortion non Septic	22	4	4
Accidents of pregnancy	Nil	7	1
Puerperal sepsis	115	224	113
Puerperal albuminuria	42	126	36
Toxaemia of pregnancy	38	15	8
Embolism	8	11	23
Accident of childbirth	25	224	18
Unspecified condition	Nil	126	3
Anaemia	50	15	58
Acute Yellow fever	1	11	10
Ectopic gestation	2	6	6

Source: see note 31

As the figures above show, sepsis deaths were very common and usually took place after spontaneous delivery at homes. The main reasons for such deaths were ill health, malnutrition, overcrowded and dirty homes and female seclusion. Dr Edward noted that 55.26 per cent deaths examined during the enquiry occurred in families living in one room, 25.28 per cent in two rooms and 16.08 per cent in more than two rooms.[32] Similar findings were made by the Bombay enquiry. There, 340 deaths occurred due to over crowding; among them 242 in families living in one room, forty-one in two rooms and twelve in more than two rooms.[33] As far as home conditions were concerned it was found during the Calcutta investigation that 40 per cent of the houses were found dirty, ventilation was described as 65 per cent bad. while 57 per cent of the houses reported bad drainage.[34] In Bombay among the 155 houses ninety-four were found to be dirty. However, the ventilation and drainage systems were comparatively better than in Calcutta.[35]

After puerperal sepsis the second most common disease was anaemia. Attention towards anaemia first began to be paid in 1930. The initiative was taken by the Indian Research Fund Association and by independent workers. In 1933 an enquiry was conducted by the School of Tropical Medicine, Calcutta, under the auspices of the Indian Research Fund Association. During the period there were 2,517 hospital deaths due to childbearing; among them 422 or 17 per cent were due to anaemia. A further fact demonstrated by this enquiry was that in case of diseases like sepsis, toxaemia of pregnancy and the accidents of labour, anaemia was probably the most important cause of death.[36] While, Dr Mudaliyar, during his Madras enquiry, assigned 50 or 11.5 per cent deaths in a sample of 436 to anaemia of pregnancy and drew attention to two forms of disease, one a macrocytic type and another secondary to hookworm infection.[37] The macrocytic anaemia, in particular, appeared to be associated with the observance of *purdah*. The pallor and debility which resulted from close confinement within the four walls of the house and the consequent lack of fresh air and sunlight was probably similar to the chlorosis of a previous generation in England.[38] Dr Neal Edward found out that among the 701 deaths due to direct childbearing there were 165 or 23 per cent cases attributed to anaemia. It is striking to note that the proportion of these sufferings from anaemia was higher among Muslims and Hindus than among other communities: of the 701 deaths, the proportion was 43 per cent and 41 per cent among Hindu and Muslim women respectively.[39] In contrast, according to the report of the *Indian Journal of Medical*

Research which was prepared after the examination of maternity cases admitted to the Eden Hospital, Calcutta during 1928–30, the proportion was 8.09 per cent and 19.09 per cent among Hindus and Muslims respectively.[40]

Tuberculosis was the most frequent cause of maternal deaths due to diseases associated with childbearing. Again, the proportion was very high among Hindu and Muslim women. Poverty, lack of cleanliness, bad ventilation and improper drainage were all responsible. For instance, carelessness regarding cleanliness at surgical operation resulted in blood-poisoning. The fatal form of fever following child-birth which was so often regarded as due to chill was nothing other than blood-poisoning or germ infection closely connected with tuberculosis.[41]

NEONATAL CARE WORK

Neonatal care work was considered as the first priority of the preventive campaign. During different enquiries it was noticed that a very large number of Indian women did not even know about specific health measurements of weight, blood pressure and urine examination. For example, during the Calcutta investigation it was found that only 16 per cent women had ever had even a single urine test. If this was the position in Calcutta, where intensive maternity care was available in the form of qualified doctors, certainly the conditions were even worse in other parts of India.

To overcome these problems several proposals and suggestions were made by the Special Committee on Maternity and Child Welfare Work in India. Institutional midwifery and the provision of prenatal clinics and prenatal beds in public and maternity institutions were considered as the first priority in this regard. The Committee was of the opinion that sound training of medical students and midwives should be provided in every medical institution, while the provision of prenatal clinics was suggested in the form of consultative and treatment facilities. These facilities included the promotion of health

through the education of mothers in the hygiene of pregnancy
and the diagnosis of minor degrees of ill-health to be provided
by hospital's prenatal departments or maternity welfare centres.[42]
The Committee also emphasised the setting up of two types of
prenatal clinics; central or consultative clinics were proposed
for the investigation or treatment of diseases, and subsidiary
clinics for the promotion of health through the education of
mothers in the hygiene of pregnancy and in the diagnosis of
minor degrees of ill health.[43]

For the supervision of expectant mothers lady doctors and
medical women were attached to the civil hospitals and
dispensaries, touring maternity and child welfare offices. The
initiative was taken by the Inspector-General of Civil Hospitals,
Punjab. In 1938 a circular was issued laying down the attendance
of prenatal sessions held at welfare centres as one of the duties
of medical women, attached to institutions working under the
supervision of a medical department. Under these new
arrangements sixty prenatal clinics were organized at different
health centres in 1940, mostly by lady doctors employed at civil
hospitals and dispensaries. In these clinics 6,940 cases were
examined and the total number of home visits paid by health
visitors was 4,20,697.[44] In the same way, in the United Provinces
there were twenty-two lady doctors, twenty-one health visitors,
and 119 assistant midwives whose services were used for
domiciliary midwifery.[45]

INTRA-NATAL CARE

Arrangements for intra-natal care were suggested in the form of
institutional and domiciliary midwifery. It was pointed out by the
Special Committee that the number of beds required varied from
area to area in accordance with the customs, habits and education
of the people.[46] The information supplied by different hospitals
and maternity centres about the number of maternity beds varied
widely, ranging from thirteen beds in rural areas to forty-eight in
urban areas. The standard of one bed per 100 births was quite
reasonable according to the general standard of Western countries.

However, in India the provision of these facilities was heavily skewed in favour of urban areas.

Compared to institutional midwifery, domiciliary midwifery was relatively easy to provide, cheaper to maintain and to meet the requirements of normal confinements even where home conditions were not satisfactory. In this situation the midwife or indigenous *dai* played a central role in domiciliary midwifery. According to the enquiry of the Special Committee, in 1936 almost 70 per cent cases took place without any skilled attention for mothers in different parts of the country. Most of the trained *dais* were incapable of diagnosing septic cases and referring them to hospitals. The situation was summed up by the Committee in the following words:

> Many women who develop fever during the puerperium are never seen by a doctor and the midwife gives simultaneous attendance on septic and normal cases without taking any precautions. Records are very inadequately kept even by literate midwives, and where records are demanded, the illiterate keep the data in their memories until some relative who can write is available to do the recording. In many areas no record is kept of the puerperium except a list of the names and address of the women confined. No scheme for domiciliary midwifery can be safe under these conditions.[47]

It was suggested by the Committee that there should be a supervisor appointed to guide the midwife on all technical matters affecting the well-being of her patients. The duties of the supervisor were not confined just to the inspection of records but were also supposed to include paying unexpected visits during confinement and puerperium in order to check the method of diagnosis and treatment given by the midwife.[48]

MEDICAL LEGISLATION AND THE ENACTMENT OF MATERNITY BENEFIT ACTS

Several legislative measures in connection with maternity and child welfare work were introduced during this period. The initiative was taken during the last decade of the nineteenth century. The Births, Deaths and Marriage Registration Act was the first legislative measure enforced in a number of provinces in 1886. Later on, much of the legislation was framed by local municipalities. For example, in the United Provinces local municipalities framed by-laws under which all births and deaths had to be reported to the medical officer of health within three days of their occurrence.

The acts for the registration of nurses, midwives and health visitors came into forces in different provinces at different times. These included:

1. The Madras Nurses and Midwives Act, 1926 (as amended by Act VII of 1934).
2. The Punjab Nurses Registration Act, 1932.
3. The United Provinces Nurses, Midwives, Assistant Midwives and Health Visitors Registration Act, 1934.
4. The Bengal Nurses, Midwives and Health Visitors.
5. The Bombay Nurses, Midwives ad Health Visitors Act, 1935.
6. The Bihar and Orissa Nurses Registration Act, 1935; and
7. The Central Provinces Nurses Registration Act, 1936.

In the same way, to prohibit unrecognized practices by *dais*, special powers were given to provincial Governments to frame rules for the supervision of these women. The Bengal Act, for instance, gave the provincial Government power to make rules for the regulation, supervision and restriction, within limits, of the practice of nursing, midwives, and health visitors and to lay down the powers and duties of a Supervisory Board to be framed in every district. The municipal and local board acts also gave these local bodies the power to incur expenditure on maternity and child welfare work. However, due to lack of sufficient funds from their ordinary revenues, special grants-in-aid were sanctioned by provincial Governemts on the condition that certain standards had to be maintained.

A major achievement in this regard was the enforcement of the Bombay Maternity Benefit Act 1929 (As modified by Act VII of 1935) and the Mines Maternity Benefit Act of 1941 (as modified by Act XIX of 1946). The former Act dealt with every married woman employed in factories in Bombay Presidency. Under this Act, married female workers became entitled to get maternity benefit payment at the rate of eight *annas* a day in the cities of Bombay, Karachi and Ahmedabad. In other parts of the province, the benefit was available at the rate of the average daily wage calculated to the nearest quarter of an *anna* on the total wages earned during a period of three months immediately preceding the date on which she gave notice for the four weeks leave immediately before her confinement and the four weeks' immediately following it. According to the Act, such women were not to do any work elsewhere during the period for which they were receiving maternity benefits. To get medical benefits a woman would have to submit a certificate signed by a registered medical practitioner certifying that she was expected to be confined within the following month for which she was entitled to maternity benefit. During the absence of an expectant mother from the or, it was not lawful, according to this Act, for her employer to give her notice of dismissal on the grounds of her taking maternity leave.[49]

Unlike the Bombay Act, the Mines Maternity Benefits Act was enforced throughout British India. According to this Act any married woman employed in a mine, who had been continuously employed in that mine or mines belonging to the owner of that mine for a period of not less than six months proceeding the a date of her delivery, was entitled to receive maternity benefit at the rate of twelve *annas* a day during the four weeks immediately preceding and including the day of her delivery. To get the benefit she had to give notice in writing in the prescribed form signed by a registrated medical practitioner to the manager of the mine that she expected to deliver a child within one month of the date of the notice. Such absence would be treated as a period of authorised absence on leave. As far as the payment of bonus was concerned, section 15 of the Act provided that if a woman who was entitled to maternity benefits utilised the services of a qualified midwife or other trained person, then she was entitled to receive an extra bonus not exceeding three rupees.[50]

WOMEN AND THE MEDICAL PROFESSION

Note should be taken that in India medical education for women was started before any other kind of professional education. Christian missionaries who went into *zenanas* grew increasingly aware of the amount of the suffering endured by women on account of their seclusion. This led different missionary societies to send medical women to relieve the suffering of Indian women. However, the number of such workers was small in comparison with the need of the country. To fulfil the growing needs of the *zenana*, necessary arrangements were made to train local women both for institutional as well as domiciliary midwifery. For this purpose a large number of training centres, nursing training institutions, medical schools and colleges were opened in different parts of India. Besides these, certain training classes were attached with women's hospitals and maternity homes. By passing an Act to constitute a Medical Council in India, a uniform standard of higher medical education for the whole of British India was adopted. Under the Act the Council was given powers to inspect the courses of instruction and examinations. Under these new arrangements the period of study for higher medical education was defined as not less than five academic years from the commencement of a student's study of the subjects. The first two years were to be spent in the study of the professional scientific subjects like the dissection of the entire body, Histology, elements of Human Embryology, General Physiology, Pathology, Bacteriology and Pharmacology. The last three years were to be spent on clinical studies in which special subjects like Midwifery, Gynaecology, Infant Hygiene, Applied Anatomy, Physiology of Pregnancy and Labour were taught.[51] Besides, special lectures and demonstrations in Clinical

Midwifery, Gynaecology and Infant Hygiene were also arranged. During this clinical work each student was supposed to personally conduct twenty cases of labour either in hospitals or in domiciliary practice.[52] A further suggestion was made in this regard in a report which was published by the Health Survey and Development Committee in 1946. The Committee suggested an increase in the clinical work to at least six months, with twenty delivery cases at hospitals or maternity homes.[53] While the practice of domiciliary midwifery was considered invaluable by the Committee, it was believed that it did not give the student an insight into different causes of abnormal cases. In contrast, attendance at antenatal clinics and working at gynaecological out-patient clinics and wards would prove to be more profitable.[54]

Women responded positively towards higher medical education even in co-educational institutions. While their number was much less than male doctors, it was indeed a bold step taken by women. During 1937–38 there were eleven medical colleges; among them two were meant for women. The Lady Hardinge Medical College, Delhi, was founded in 1916 which offered the M.B.B.S. degree. Eight female medical officers employed as members of the teaching staff. Among the pupils under instruction, who came from every part of the country, were girls belonging to different communities of India. For example, in 1930–31 the total number of students in residence was 129, among whom forty-five were Hindus, twenty-seven Indian Christians, thirteen Europeans, thirteen Anglo-Indians, thirteen Muslims, ten Sikhs and seven members of other communities.[55]

The Christian Medical College and Hospital for Women was founded by Dr Idas Scudder, a daughter of a well-established American missionary family in India. She returned to India in 1900, after receiving her medical training in the United States. In 1902, she established a Mary Taber Schell Hospital for women at Vellore. The shortage of female doctors led her to set up a medical college to train those local Indian women who were interested in the medical profession. In 1918, she founded the medical college at Vellore which was financed by different missionary societies of America and Great Britain. Later, the college proved a major source of medical education for the women of Southern India. Note should be taken that the college not only provided maternity and antenatal care facilities but the services of its women doctors were also utilized voluntarily, in different maternity centres of the area.[56]

TRAINING OF HEALTH VISITORS

By 1938 seven schools in India were training health visitors. They were located at Delhi, Lahore, Madras, Nagpur, Poona, Bombay and Calcutta. The preliminary educational qualifications required for admission were similar in all the schools. Students had to be not less than twenty-one years of age, with a matriculation degree, a good knowledge of English and possessing a recognized midwifery certificate. However, in the Nagpur and Poona schools a lower standard was accepted. The initial period of training was nine months, which was later extended to eighteen months. The medium of instruction was English as well as vernacular languages. The final examination was held by the Provincial Nursing Councils and by authorities appointed by the Provincial Governments, while the course for health visitors was midwifery with some elementary training in general hygiene and preventive work.[57] Their duties, in general, were to be the supervision of domiciliary work of midwives and of trained *dais* and participation in preventive work. However, it was realized that, without proper training in general nursing, it was not possible for health visitors to take part in the extension of preventive health work to the homes of people. To combat these difficulties, a scheme was drawn up by Dr Ruth Young, Director of the Indian Red Cross Bureau, for a four year training course for health visitors. The first two years were to be spent on basic science, including biology, chemistry, physiology, anatomy, with general nursing practical training arranged by affiliated hospitals. The third year's course would include training in midwifery and in prenatal and post-natal care while the fourth year would correspond more or less with the existing syllabus of the health schools.[58] It was further suggested by the Special Committee that a period of residence and practical training in rural areas should be made a compulsory part of the curriculum in all health schools. For this purpose every student was to spend a period of two to three weeks in rural maternity and child welfare centres already operating in the United Provinces, Madras and Delhi.[59]

TRAINING OF MIDWIVES

As far as the training of midwives was concerned, the majority of the *dais'* training classes were held in conjunction with welfare centres and instruction was given by the health visitors working there. There was no uniformity in the course of training prescribed for *dais* in the various provinces. After one year's training both in institutional and domiciliary methods, the *dais* became eligible for their certificates. While the past attempts to train the *dai* in modern methods met with little success, the Special Committee recommended that efforts in this direction should be expanded. The best way of supervising the *dais*, suggested the Committee, was through prenatal clinics managed by a travelling woman doctor or health visitor.[60]

WOMEN AND NEW TRENDS IN HEALTH BEHAVIOUR

The idea of safe motherhood not only attacked traditional social behaviour of Indian women towards women, but also became helpful in inspiring many women to improve their health status in general. The major task in this regard was the realization of the importance of women's role not just as mothers or wives, but as persons. Early efforts in this regard can be seen through those forms of literature and books which were written to redefine women's social status. For social reformers, certain positive changes including the western method of midwifery could be adopted as it was more safe and hygienic as compared to indigenous Indian *dai* system. Thus, for Muslim women in

India, there was a coming together of new ideas about how to take care of themselves. More traditional approaches towards medicine, in particular *unani tibb* (Greco-Arabic medical system) were also harnessed to the cause of improving the health of women.

Many Muslim social reformers in this period turned their attention to issues related to women's health. One such person was Macho Khan, publisher of the *Mufid-ul-Madaras*, a monthly journal launched in 1872 from Agra. The magazine was strongly supported by the Government as it stridently advocated the spread of general education among women. In his writings, Khan emphasized the removal of the 'evil' practices of traditional midwifery by adopting the modern and scientific methods of Europe.[61]

In the same way, Sultan Jahan Begum, the ruler of Bhopal, focused on the importance of physical fitness in women's lives in her remarkable book, the *Hifz-e-Sehat* (The Protection of Health). Here she emphasized the ways to achieve this fitness by exercise, balanced diet, fresh air, clean surroundings, and, above all, a positive approach towards life and its problems. In this context she cited the example of Professor William, a teacher of King Edward VII, whom she met during her voyage from India to Europe. Professor William told her that he used to walk at least one mile a day, while his daily diet included one slice of bread, some boiled meat and potatoes.[62]

The reformist *ulama*, on the other hand, particularly those from the *Dar-ul-Ulum* Deoband, were tempted to play down the education of women in favour of the fulfilment of their religious obligations and social relationships. This, they argued, could be achieved through the revival of religion rather than by adopting the Western agenda of social reforms. Yet, they did not turn a completely blind eye to matters related to health. In fact, they patronized *unani tibb* which was taught as an ancillary subject at Deoband. This system of medicine was considered as equivalent or even superior to the Western medical system.[63]

From *fatawa* to the writing for amulets, the writings of the *ulama* were considered as authorities, even in such matters as the social and spiritual well-being of women. In this regard, the ninth part of Maulana Ashraf Ali Thanawi's *Bihisthi Zewar*, highlighted the role of women in keeping their family healthy and cheerful. As Thanawi stated in the introduction to this section:

> There is a statement of some methods of cares in this part that should be adopted by women for the maintenance of their health as well as their children. The women who do not know about all these cannot prove themselves as good mothers as their children suffer due to their ignorance. Their action also creates trouble for their husbands and sometimes they have to spend money on such petty problems that can be resolved easily by adopting the method of health care and medicine as it was also appreciated by our Prophet Muhammad (PBUH).[64]

Thanawi described two types of diseases and their *unani* prescriptions: (i) general diseases and (ii) specifically 'female' diseases. In the context of general diseases, the Maulana provided a list of illnesses like headaches, eye infections, nasal problems, toothache, throat and chest infections, heart disease and stomach problems. In connection with preventive treatment against smallpox, eruptions and plague, he prescribed several *unani* medicines. For instance, for plague he suggested taking tablets made from pearls, *zahr mohrah* (an antidote to poison), *sandal* (sandal wood), *jawadar* (zedoary), *kafur* (camphor), *waraq-e-nuqrai* (a leaf made of silver) and *isaphghol* (seeds of fleawort).[65]

With regard to' female' disease he discussed two types of problems. Firstly, problems and diseases which generally follow menstruation. Prominent among these was irregularity in menstrual course, *sailan-e-rahim* (leucorrhea), and *ikhtank-ul-rahim* (a sort of swooning due to severe pain in the womb). It is interesting to note that Thanawi pointed out that the latter problem was sometimes due to psychological stress and frustration, usually among young widows and unmarried girls. However, in case of other reasons, he suggested consulting a *hakim*.[66]

As far as the use of amulets and incantations was concerned, interestingly for a *Deobandi* who would normally be opposed to all forms of superstitions, Thanawi did not deny their importance in removing the different types of problems and sicknesses in daily life. As he stated:

> Alongside medicinal treatment, the method of amulets is also useful during the treatment of different diseases. Usually, illiterate women believe in superstitions. Particularly during the sickness of their children or in case of barrenness they are used to going to fortunetellers, visiting shrines or making a vow. In this way they not only waste their money but also act against their religion. To overcome these superstitions, it is necessary to tell them some incantation which is not against Quran and religion.[67]

Thanawi suggested various Quranic words and verses which could be used either through written amulets or incantation. This sort of treatment, according to Thanawi, could be very effective in cases of stomach ache, cholera, plague, fever, snake or insect-bite as well as in abortion and small pox.[68]

Thanawi's advice relied on his knowledge of *unani tibb* alone. By the early decades of the twentieth century, however, an increasing number of both men and women began writing health manuals which blended traditional knowledge with a greater awareness of western scientific approaches, thus enabling their readers to pick and choose between the two medical systems. On the part of many Muslim women a major role was played by women's journals and many individuals. One such manual was *Kamil dai* (The Perfect Midwife) published by Ihsan and Company, Punjab in 1934. It enabled many women to acquire western and *unani* knowledge about the different stages of pregnancy and childbirth.[69] Another important work in this direction was done by Dr Nasiruddin Ahmed, a Medical Officer of Delhi. In 1934 he wrote *Zachchah Khanah* (A Maternity Home) in two *volumes*. The book mostly dealt with female diseases and their treatment by western methods of midwifery.[70]

In the same way, certain books were also written to raise the standard of women's general health status. Prominent among these were *Tandrushti Hazar Niamat* (Health is Wealth) and *Mufid-e-Niswan* (Of Benefit to Women). The former work was published in 1934 by Zuhra Begum Faizi a younger sister of Attiya Faizi. A noteworthy feature of the book was the narration of the experiences of its writer during her stay in America and England. The health care methods of women of these countries were highlighted in very simple Urdu.[71] The latter book (1934) was based on *unani* prescriptions, and dealt mostly with eye diseases, small pox, constipation and heart diseases.[72] The main theme of these writings was the importance of the stability of the woman's body. Fresh air, different kinds of exercises and balanced diet were suggested by these health care manuals.

One distinctive way in which we can see the emergence of women in their own right is the development of beauty care advice. Few other developments could be regarded so calculated to enhance the self-regard of the individual. At this stage, women had depended largely on homemade prescriptions or pharmaceutical products usually advertized in women's journals and magazines. Among the women's magazines, *Ismat* became a major channel for the exchange of ideas on physical fitness and health care arrangements among women. It had a permanent column arranged by Maulvi Muhammad Zafar, a local advocate. The column was called *Khanah Dari* (Domestic Work). It contained health and beauty care prescriptions which could be made at home or bought from the market. For skin care, Muhammad Zafar advised that women who played tennis or went for long walks should use home-made facial creams made of wax, spermaceti, Vaseline, sweet almonds, rose water and egg.[73] As for the selection and designing of dresses, he suggested that it should be made according to income, personality, need, height and weight.[74]

With the rising demand from women for beauty products, and also the need for traditional preparation of *Unani* medicines to find new ways of making money, many companies became actively involved in this field. The Dilkushah Perfumery Company, based in the Punjab, became famous for its hair tonic, *Dilkushah hair oil*.[75] Another company, the Baharistan Nazar

Bagah, was a big supplier of hair tonic and perfumes in North India. Its popular products were *Roghan-e-Bahar*, *Jamal-e-Tail* and *Mothi*.[76] Saeed Brothers and Company, Delhi, manufactured Flower Scent, Flower Snow, *Shahi Manjun* (Tooth Powder) and *Rukhsaroun-ki-Surkhee* (Blush-on). These products were popular particularly among the *sharif* women of Delhi.[77] The Facrine Pharmacy in the Punjab was producing several products which were very popular among women.[78]

It is interesting to note that some individual efforts were also made by *hakims* who included both men and women. Among male practitioners, Hakim Muhammad Yakub Khan ran the *Dawa Khanah Noratun* at Delhi. He was actively involved in making products like *Pari Jamal Sabun* (Beauty soap), *Zenana Singar Box* (a female beauty box including soap, hair oil, eye liner and lipstick), Paris powder (Face Powder) and *Lali* (blush on).[79] The same was done by some female *hakims* who made *unani* medicines and their beauty care products for women. Among them was Wahida Begum, daughter of Hakim Zia-ul-Hasan, the grandson of Sir Sayyed Ahmed Khan. She established her own clinic, the Wahida Begum Unani Medical Hall, in Delhi in 1933. In 1938 she renamed it the Indian Medical Hall. Some of the products of her 'Medical Hall' were *Raughan-e-Snoon wa Dandan-e-Mukamil* (Medicine for Pioariya), *Farhat Buksh Sharbit Nafees Afza* (A Tonic for Hair Care), *Jarob-e-Dimagh* and *Khamirah-e-Rehan* (A Tonic for the Strengthening of the Brain) and *Mahsalah-e-Gesu-e-Daraz* (A Hair Tonic).[80] H.K. Begum was another big name for products used in the case of 'female' diseases. She ran a *Dawa Khanah* called the *Unani Pharmacy* at Ambala in the Punjab.

* * *

The most important feature of the new medical discourse that marked this period was that it persuaded growing number of Muslim women like their non-Muslim counterparts to raise their health standards in changing circumstances. Despite the difficulties owing to shortage of funds, ignorance, superstition, social customs and apathy, this discourse progressed in every sphere. It forced women from the middle and lower classes to turn in increasing numbers to midwifery as a profession and a means of a livelihood. This was all to the good both because it meant the gradual replacement of the old indigenous type of midwife by a superior one and because it ensured that a larger pool of skilled personnel would be available.[81] In the same way, the emergence of preventative campaigns enquiring into the causes of maternal mortality and antenatal care movement sought to provide a framework within which they could define women's bodies in terms of 'biological behaviour'. Though the number of women who took advantage of this new medicalization was limited, this labelling at least became a part of women's medical culture in India.

Particularly telling is the way in which women took this new attitude to the female body. It is manifest by their growing concern for their physical fitness.[82] It is manifest, too, in their public interest in beauty care. These are potent expressions of a new sense of a female individuality.

Thus, attempts to introduce biomedical approaches towards healthcare on government and individual level, combined with the revival of and expansion into new realms of *unani tibb* helped Muslim women to open up another public space, on the one hand, through the promotion of safe motherhood, and, on the other hand, through the encouragement of female physical fitness and proper considerations of health status.

NOTES

1. *Report of the Age of Consent Committee 1928–29*, (Govrnment of India, Central Publication Branch Calcutta, 1929), p. 102.
2. Maithreyi Krishnraj, and Karuna Chanana, *Gender and the Household Domain: Social and Cultural Dimensions*, (Sage Publication, New Delhi, 1989), p. 158.
3. Pat Bar, *The Dust in the Balance: British Women in India 1905–45*, (Hamish Hamilton, London, 1989), p. 87.
4. *Ismat*, Vol. 50, No. 6 June 1932, p. 521.

5. A. Lankertar, *The Responsibility of Men in Matter Relating to Maternity*. A lecture delivered at the Maternity and Child Wefare Exhibition, held at Delhi, in 1920, (Government of India Press, Simla, 1924), pp. 1–12.

6. Margaret, I. Balfour and Ruth Young, *The Work of the Medical Women in India*, (Oxford University Press Bombay, 1929), p. 76.

7. *Annual Report of the Sanitary Commission with the Government of India for 1917*, (Superintendent Government Printing Press, India, Calcutta, 1919), p. 128.

8. *Report on Maternity and Child Welfare Work in India*, by Special Committee (1938), (Manager, Government of India Press, Simla, 1939), p. 2.

9. Ibid., p. 3.

10. Ibid.

11. Ibid., p. 2.

12. Dora White, 'A Sketch of Zenana Medical Work in Hyderabad', *The Indian Magazine*, No. 14, February, 1887, pp. 66–71.

13. Ibid., No. 186, June 1886, p. 301.

14. Ibid., No. 190, October 1886, p. 15.

15. *Khatun*, Vol. 6, No. 2, February 1909, p. 90.

16. Ibid., Vol. 8, No. 3, March 1912, p. 48.

17. Ibid, Vol. 8, No. 5, May 1912, p. 47.

18. *Indian Medical Review*, (Manager of Publication, Government of India Press, Delhi, 1938, p. 185.

19. *Report on Maternity and Child Welfare Work in India*, p. 6.

20. *Annual Report of the Public Health Commissioner with the Government of India for 1946*, (Manager of Publication, Delhi 1948), p. 51.

21. *Annual Report of the Public Health Commissioner with the Government of India for 1928*, p. 102.

22. *Annual Report of the Public Health Commissioner with the Government of India for 1946*, p. 65.

23. *Bengal Public Health Report for the Year 1939*, (Government of Bengal Public Health Department, Superintendent Government Printing Press, Alipore, 1941), p. 113.

24. *Annual Report of the Public Health Department, Central Provinces and Berar for the Year 1940*, (Government Printing Press, Nagpur, 1941), p. 27.

25. *Report on Maternity and Child Welfare Work in India*, p. 9.

26. Ibid., pp. 25, 32.

27. Ibid.

28. Ibid.

29. *Report of an Enquiry into the Causes of Maternal Mortality in Calcutta*, Health Bulletin No. 27, (Manager of Publication, Government of India Press, Delhi, 1940), p. 20.

30. *Report on an Investigation into the Causes of Maternal Mortality in the City of Bombay*, Health Bulletin No. 29, (Manager of Publication, Government of India Press, Delhi, 1941), p. 1.

31. Ibid., p. 12.

32. *Report of an Enquiry into the Causes of Maternal Mortality in Calcutta*, p. 26.

33. *Report on an Investigation into the Causes of Maternal Mortality in the City of Bombay*, p. 66.

34. *Report of an Enquiry into the Causes of Maternal Mortality in Calcutta*, p. 26.

35. *Report on an Investigation into the Causes of Maternal Mortality in the City of Bombay*, p. 67.

36. 'Anaemia in Pregnancy in Calcutta, an Enquiry under the Indian Research Fund Association', *Medical Research Memoirs* No. 33, (Thacker Spink Calcutta,1941), pp. 2–95.

37. *Report on the Maternity and Child Welfare Work in India*, p. 32.

38. 'Anaemia in Pregnancy in Calcutta', *Medical Research Memoirs* No. 33, pp. 2–95.

39. *Report of an Enquiry into Causes of Maternal Mortality in Calcutta*, p. 26.

40. L.E. Napier, 'Anaemia in Pregnancy in India: the present position', *The Indian Journal of Medical Research*, Vol. XXVII, No. 4, April 1940, pp. 1009–1040.

41. A. Lankertar, *A Responsibility of Men in Matters Relating to Maternity*, pp. 1–12.

42. *Report on Maternity and Child Wefare Work in India*, pp. 40–42.

43. Ibid., pp. 41–42.

44. *Punjab Health Department: Report on the Public Health Administration of Punjab for the Year 1940*, p. 79.

45. *Report on Maternity and Child Welfare Work in India*, p. 44.

46. Ibid., p. 43.

47. Ibid., p. 49.

48. Ibid.

49. *The Bombay Maternity Benefit Act of 1929*, No. VII, modified up to the 1st May, 1935, (Government Press, Bombay, 1935), pp. 1–4.

50. *The Mines Maternity Benefit Act of 1942*, No. XIX, modified in 1946, (Government of India Legislative Department, 1946), pp. 1–3.

51. *Indian Medical Review*, (Manager of Publication, Government of India Press, Delhi, 1938), p. 61.

52. Ibid., p. 84.

53. *Report of the Health Survey and Development Committee*, Vol. 1, (Manager of Publication, Delhi, Government of India Press, Calcutta, 1946), p. 69.

54. Ibid., p. 70.
55. *Moral and Material Progress and Condition of India during the Year 1930–31*, (His Majesty's Stationary Office, London, 1932), p. 449.
56. For deatil see, *Friends of Vellore Papers*, MSS. Eur. F. 219, IOL.
57. *Report on Maternity and Child Welfare Work in India*, pp. 63–65.
58. Ibid., pp. 66–67.
59. Ibid., p. 67.
60. Ibid., pp. 73–74.
61. *Mafud-ul-Madaras*, Vol. 2, No. 1, January 1873, pp. 23–4.
62. Sultan Jahan Begum, *Hifz-e-Sehat wa Khanah Dari*, (Matbah Sultan Bhopal, 1916), p. 4.
63. Barbara D. Metcalf (trans. and ed.), *Perfecting Women: Maulana Ashraf Ali Thanawi's Bihisthi Zewar*, (Berkeley University of California Press, 1982), p. 10.
64. Ashraf Ali Thanawi, *Bihisthi Zewar*, (Karkhana Tajarat-e-Kutub, Karachi, 1962), p. 520.
65. Ibid., p. 595.
66. Ibid., p. 555.
67. Ibid., p. 608.
68. Ibid., p. 109.
69. *Ismat*, Vol. 52, No. 1, January 1934, p. 18.
70. Ibid., Vol. 70, No. 2, February 1943, p. 140.
71. Ibid.,Vol. 52, No. 6, June 1934, p. 16.
72. Ibid.
73. Ibid., Vol. 61, No. 3, October 1941, p. 341.
74. Ibid., Vol. 55, No. 6, December 1935, p. 526.
75. Ibid., Vol. 50, No. 3, October 1941, p. 254.
76. Ibid., Vol. 67, No. 4, October 1941, p. 376.
77. Ibid., Vol. 66, No. 5, May 1941, p. 376.
78. Ibid., Vol. 55, No. 6, December 1935, p. 540.
79. Ibid., Vol. 58, No. 1, January 1937, p. 84.
80. Ibid., Vol. 61, No. 5, November 1938, p. 438.
81. *India in 1934–35*, (The Manager of Publication, Delhi, Government of India Press, Simla, 1937), p. 123.
82. See in this context, Chapter 6, pp. 214–54.

4

OPENING UP A PUBLIC SPACE FOR WOMEN: THE ROLE OF SOCIAL LEGISLATION

Raising the social status of Indian women was a major concern of early Indian social reformers. The nineteenth century campaigns in British India against *sati* and in favour of the re-marriage of widows led Indian reformers to develop a broader legislative agenda which would strengthen the forces of social change. One campaign included in this programme for reform was the movement against child marriage which helped to pave the way for further legislation in the twentieth century. Arguments emphasized the need to remove age-old traditions, customary practices and social taboos which were sapping the vitality of women's role as equal sharers in and contributors towards national life.

However, there were different views on the manner in which social change should be implemented in India. Community interests and the importance of group cohesion strengthened the argument that changes should take place within individual communities. The enforcement of Muslim Personal Law and the realization of women's divorce rights can be cited as a part of the process of the reconstruction of community identity. It was argued that the interests of Muslim women would be best served with the restoration of the rights given to them by Islam, and which, with the passage of time, had been superseded by local customs and traditions. Specially after the Montagu-Chelmsford Reforms of 1919, Muslims felt that they were now in a position to do so without suffering political and economic loss, particularly in the context of a situation in which the Government did not have any intention of interfering in socio-religious matters. The subsequent constitutional discourse became a vehicle to express the numerical strength of the Muslim community as well as highlighting issues concerning the rights of Muslim women.

Indeed, it was not an easy task: the debate between conservatives and progressive reformers politicized the entire affair. Arguments emphasizing the importance of community interests, rather than women's rights specifically, were freely employed to counter the demand for a legislative change.[1] The whole agenda of the restoration of women's social rights revolved around the numerical strength of the community, the attitude of reformers who emphasized specific social changes, the government's approach towards the issue of reform and the magnitude of political support which official remedies would attract.

Above all, pressure from women now carried weight with it. Their growing participation in public life led to the realization that their acquired qualifications would make them fit for the service of the nation. The main question which attracted their attention was the condition of their sex and the means by which they could be improved. Though the number of such women was very small, they exercised considerable influence in shaping reformist legislation that would benefit their counterparts.[2]

To analyse the process of the growth of legislation concerning women's social rights, the present chapter discusses the following issues:

(a)   The practice of child marriage in India.
(b)   The formation of the Age of Consent Committee.
(c)   Muslims and the Age of Consent Committee.
(d)   Women and the Sarda legislation.
(e)   The enforcement of Muslim Personal Law.
(f)   Dissolution of Muslim Marriages Act 1939.

THE PRACTICE OF CHILD MARRIAGE IN INDIA

The practice of early marriage prevailed to a very large extent in several parts of India. Arguments emphasized that the onset of puberty was a natural indication of a girl's fitness for cohabitation and maternity; that consummation soon after puberty was also necessary to satisfy sexual craving in girls, and that, in the cases where there was lack of such satisfaction, girls could resort to 'abnormal' sexual practices. In this way, the institution of early marriage in India was considered a vehicle to save and preserve social order. In some places the practice was so deeply-rooted that often marriages took place even before the onset of the girl's puberty itself. Particularly among Hindus, the custom of 'baby' marriage was performed as a religious duty, for the *Dharma Shastras* (Hindu religious texts) sternly condemned the marriage of a girl after puberty.[3] The best time for a marriage of a girl in the opinion of orthodox Hindu religious leaders (*dharamacharyas*) was in the eighth year from conception; the ninth and tenth years were the next best; after that, up to puberty, and after puberty, it was absolutely reprehensible.[4] According to a more 'liberal' point of view, the maximum age for a girl to marry could be extended upto twelve years or within three years of puberty, although in general the best marriage was the one which occurred before puberty.[5]

Like Hindus, many Muslims practised child marriage. This could be seen as (i) the cultural influence of one community on another, (ii) particular community behaviour, and (iii) as a common practice in Indian society.

CHILD MARRIAGE AS THE CULTURAL INFLUENCE OF ONE COMMUNITY ON ANOTHER

The custom of child marriage was very common in those areas of India where Hindus were in a majority. The influence of Hindu culture also led Muslims to develop similar practices. In the Punjab, which accounted for one-fifth of the total Muslim population in India, the proportion of married girls between the ages of five and ten were 70 per 1,000 among Hindus, 26 per 1,000 among Muslims and 25 per 1,000 among Sikhs. On the other hand, in the Himalayan areas where there were thirty Muslims as compared to 642 Hindus per 1,000 of the population, the proportion of married girls in the same age group were much higher among Muslims than Hindus, the proportions being 415 and 390 respectively.[6] In the Central Provinces and Berar, where Hindus represented the vast majority of the local population, the custom of child marriage was quite common both among Hindus and Muslims. The Census Report of 1921 pointed out that the number of married girls per 1,000 between the ages of five and ten was 173 among Hindus as compared to 51 among Muslims. Between the ages of ten and fifteen, this difference widened slightly, with the proportions being 572 and 304 among Hindus and Muslims respectively.[7] Alongside this, the customs of pre-puberty marriage and consummation prevailed to a large extent among the depressed classes of both communities.

CHILD MARRIAGE: THE PRACTICE OF SOME SOCIAL GROUPS

In the Muslim-majority N.W.F.P., the practice of child marriage was least prevalent: no baby girls less than five years were married both by Hindus as well as Muslims, whereas the proportion of child marriage between the ages from five to ten years was only eleven and two per 1000 among Hindus and Muslims respectively.[8]

Despite this general trend, at times the individual customs of particular communities appeared to outweigh any kind of common behaviour. For example, in the districts of Kohat and Dera Ismail Khan a few sects and castes among local Muslims observed this custom. It prevailed more extensively among the *Rangrez* (the dyer caste of Muslims) who married their girls off at an early age.[9] The same standard was adopted by Muslims in Sindh: among those who lived in cities, marriages occurred at the age of sixteen years or upwards, while those living in rural areas generally married off their girls between the ages of twelve to fifteen years.[10] In the province of Delhi, which was inhabited by various communities, while child marriage was not uncommon, like the other parts of India, the proportion was slightly less among high class Hindus and Muslims, while the lower classes extensively practised the custom. Note should be taken that the practice was also shared both by certain high class Hindus as well as Muslims—Brahmins, Rajputs (Hindu and Muslim), and Sayyids—all of whom considered it as a symbol of honour.[11]

CHILD MARRIAGE AS A COMMON PRACTICE

Child marriage as a common practice, therefore, could be found across Indian society without discrimination of caste and creed. The practice of child marriage was widely prevalent in Bombay and Bengal. In the Bombay Presidency, girls were married more frequently than elsewhere at a very low age. According to the Census of 1921, there were 1,666 girls married or widowed less than one year of age, 1,671 baby girls married or widowed between one and two years of age, 4,378 girls married or widowed between two and three years of age, 7,219 girls married or widowed between three and four years of age, 12,834 between four and five, 1,93,582 between five and ten and 4,98,706 between ten and fifteen years of age.[12] While the position of Muslims was somewhat better compared to that of Hindus, yet early marriage was also quite common among them too.

In the province of Bengal, both Hindus and Muslims, with only a very slight difference between them, practised child marriage. According to the Census Report of 1921, the proportion of child marriage was 62.04 per cent and 52.03 per cent among Hindus and Muslims respectively. Pre-puberty consummation was also very common and violation of the law of 1890 which dealt with the consent of marriage was rampant.[13]

In general, we can say that everywhere in India the practice of child marriage was common among all castes and communities. On such grounds reformers could argue that Indians were 'inhuman', citing, in particular, the case of marriages which were performed at a very early age and sometimes resulted in the widowhood of baby girls who were never allowed to remarry in their life. The magnitude of the problem can be seen from the following two tables of the civil status of little girls in various provinces of India.

Table 1
Female population under the age 5 and their civil status in different provinces in 1921

PROVINCE	MARRIED	UNMARRIED	WIDOWED	TOTAL
Assam	81	5,32,013	12	5,32,106
Bengal	23,246	30,57,696	2,819	30,83,761
Bihar & Orissa	40,665	20,13,142	2,510	20,56,317
Bombay	26,287	11,80,148	1,501	12,07,938
C.P. & Berar	17,514	9,09,125	547	9,27,186
Madras	20,192	6,36,933	2,298	26,59,423
N.W.F.P.	Nil	1,53,595	Nil	1,53,595
Punjab	18,882	13,98,665	Nil	14,00,547
U.P.	18,663	27,53,446	1,202	27,73,311

Source: See note 14

Table 2
Female population between the ages 5 and 10 and their civil status in different provinces in 1921

PROVINCE	MARRIED	UNMARRIED	WIDOWED	TOTAL
Assam	11,256	6,10,35	578	6,22,469
Bengal	2,46,462	33,35,493	16,086	36,16,041
Bihar & Orissa	4,26,830	21,98,747	22,561	26,48,138
Bombay	1,84,025	11,86,269	9,557	13,79,851
C.P. & Berar	1,72,665	9,27,815	6,649	11,07,129
Madras	1,22,991	27,66,058	7,101	28,96,150
N.W.F.P.	324	1,63,825	13	1,64,189
Punjab	50,960	13,95,526	1,717	14,48,203
U.P.	3,06,618	27,21,133	12,223	30,39,974

Source: See note 15

Child Marriage as a Moral and Physical Disability

The 'evil' practice of child marriage caused great dissatisfaction among educated Indians. The issue was repeatedly discussed and several demands were made to improve the situation by the enforcement of the law. In the midst of the debate the question of child marriage was suddenly stirred emotionally by the publication of Katherine Mayo's book *Mother India* in 1927. In her book Mayo tried to highlight the condition of Indian society through reference to child brides and mothers.[16] The title of the book was taken from one of the chapters which described in terrible detail the ministrations of the *dais* or midwives who attended Indian mothers during childbirth. The conditions that the mothers of Indian children had to endure while giving birth invoked Mayo's greatest indignation and sympathy. The rhetorical strategy adopted by Mayo in *Mother India* depicted child marriage as one of those many evils which degraded the lives of Indian women. Mayo focused directly on Hindu child wives and mothers. She demonstrated the cruel and barbaric custom of pre-maturity sexuality as a 'Hindu phenomenon.'[17] Because of these direct attacks on Hinduism, and its perceived anti-Hindu bias, the book was banned in India. Several books and reviews were written in response to the book, prominent among which was 'The Review of Drain Inspector's Report' written by M.K. Gandhi. In the opinion of Mrinalini Sinha, 'Gandhi himself admitted that though the isolated facts in the book were "true" the book as a whole was untrue but he felt that Indians could nevertheless use *Mother India* to address some of the problems within Indian society'.[18]

Compared to many Indians, Western critics considered the book as a way of addressing the real historical and material foundations of women's subordination in Indian society. For instance, the *Daily News* suggested that Indian leaders should not confine their criticism to 'mere vituperation', but, instead, consider those truths pointed out by Mayo about the miserable conditions of child wives and mothers in India.[19] The noteworthy feature of the book, in the view of The *Statesman*, was the foreful style in which Mayo had tried to pass on details about the condition of Indian (Hindu) women and their mistreatment by the male population as beasts unworthy of any consideration. She simply stated what were undeniable facts and allowed readers the freedom to form their own conclusions.[20] Mayo herself was of the opinion, as she stated in one of her letters to Cornelia Sorabji,[21] an Indian social activist, that she never intended to make a rounded picture of India. On the other hand, she wanted only to highlight certain basic facts.[22] The matter of child marriage was frequently discussed in the context of women's health. Apart from localized physical injuries, early cohabitation sometimes was a shocking experience that could seriously impair the nervous system, the effects of which were felt throughout life, often leading to pronounced general debility. In the case of early pregnancy, there was also the high risk of maternal mortality.[23] The death rate, in particular, was very high in the first delivery and in ages less than fifteen. A report published in 1929 by Dr R. Adiseshan, Assistant Director of Public Health, Madras, showed that the proportion of maternal deaths were 51.28 per 1,000 for females less than fifteen years of age compared with 33.04 per 1,000 for those between the ages of fifteen and nineteen years.[24] In the same way, there was a high risk of high neonatal mortality in the case of females below the age of fifteen, the figure being 186.05 per 1,000 as compared to 123.17 per 1,000 for females between the ages of fifteen and nineteen years.[25]

Great misery was experienced by young child brides who fell victim to the bestial passions of their older husbands, and cases of injury were never reported to or examined by doctors.[26] On the other hand, such sorrows and pains were considered merely a biologically ordained path through which every woman had to pass. Consulting male doctors for treatment was unthinkable, being considered a gross violation of social norms that rigidly kept women apart from 'strange' men. In the case of the Bengal juvenile courts (established under the Bengal Children Act No. 111 of 1922), the absence of a female doctor to conduct medical examinations created a great deal of complication. The matter was heatedly discussed by different associations and social organizations and several memorandums were sent to the Government, including by the Bar Association and the Public Service Group of Calcutta, stressing the need to appoint lady doctors in these courts.[27]

Gradually the educated Indians came to realize the need to address the problem of child marriage. Some even went so far as to say that it was still a great mistake to assume that the physical signs of the attainment of puberty alone were sufficient indication of the actual maturity of the girl to enable her to consummate her marriage. In the opinion of Dr Miss. I. Balfour, a local medical officer from Bombay, at least the first couple of years after monthly sickness (puberty) was not sufficient evidence that a girl had proved herself strong enough to stand the strain, both physical and emotional, of sexual intercourse.[28]

Another argument that opponents of child marriage employed was that after marriage, young girls were forced to incur the heavy responsibility of a married life for which both their minds and bodies were utterly unprepared. In many ways, it was true that in India there was no girlhood: they were either children or women.[29] Arguments stressed the way in which the morals of girls could suffer by being married too 'late.' The custom was very common among those classes where social depression and economic misfortune appeared as a problem and moral degradation. In a written statement given before the Age of Consent Committee, Haji Ismail Choudhury, M.L.A. from the District of Barisal, made this remark about the cultivator class in Bengal:

In the case of such people to further raise the age of consent in the cases of married wives will mean leaving the girl wife to various sorts of temptation by refusing to allow her to satisfy her sexual appetite legitimately. Among people of the lower class (cultivators) giving away a girl in marriage means giving her protection against allurements of illicit intercourse. The husband jealously guards the girl wife's morals and the men of loose morals in the neighbourhood do not dare to approach a girl after she is married.[30]

These fears about the morals of girls were not necessarily shared by all Indians. In the light of the evidence that it had been able to gather, the Age of Consent Committee concluded that post puberty marriages and consummation among different communities, particularly among Muslims, was a clear sign that there was no danger to the morals of girls. Many young widows who had no prospect of marriage were free from scandals. Above all, the traditional care that Indian parents took of their unmarried daughters was enough to dispel any reasonable apprehensions of such girls going astray.[31]

THE FORMATION OF THE AGE OF CONSENT COMMITTEE

From the nineteenth century onwards legal efforts were made to raise the age of marriage. The Government India Act of 1919 took the initiative to widen the scope of legislative measures in British India. In this context the question of raising the age of consent was again brought up by some Indian witnesses who put forward their views before the Joint Parliamentary Committee. In 1922, Rai Bahadur Bakshi Sohanlal, M.L.A., introduced a bill in the Assembly to amend Section 375 of the Indian Penal Code by raising the age of consent in both marital and extra-marital cases.

The Assembly subsequently circulated the Bill for the purpose of eliciting public opinion through various provincial governments. The government of Bihar and Orissa noted that such legislation would lead to public agitation and discontent by forcing social reforms in advance of public opinion. A similar fear was expressed by the governments of Bengal and Madras. The Central Provinces declined to hazard an opinion while the Government of the Punjab felt it should be left to public demand. Only the Governments of Bombay, the United Provinces and Assam supported the move. The Bill was referred to a Select Committee. The motion was rejected by forty-one votes to twenty-nine, the government remaining neutral. While early attempts to introduce the bill therefore proved abortive, the question itself still remained and, with the passage of time, agitation for the modification of the law grew steadily.

During the life of the second Legislative Assembly, many bills and proposals associated with the issue of child marriage came under discussion. Prominent among the movers of such bills were Dr Hari Singh Gour, Sir Alexander Muddiman and Dr S.K. Datta. After several debates and efforts by the Government, the members of Assembly and different social agencies, the Act of 1925 was passed. This was accepted as a step in the right direction though further efforts continued in this regard. When the third Assembly met, a bill was again presented by Dr Hari Singh Gour for the raising of the age of consent. In the same year, another similar bill was introduced by Rai Sahib Har Bilas Sarda, called the Hindu Child Marriage Bill. Both the bills were relegated to a committee which was appointed by the Government of India on 25 June 1928, consisting of a chairman and five members: four members from the Legislative Assembly were subsequently added on 25 September. The Committee was appointed under the chairmanship of Sir Moropant Vishwanath Joshi, Home Member of the Executive Council of the Governor of the Central Provinces. Among its other members were Rai Bahadur Pundit Kanhaiya Lal, Judge of the Allahabad High Court (Vice Chairman), Mr A. Ramaswami Mudaliyar, Member of the Madras Legislative Council, Khan Bahadur Mahbub Mian, Imam Baksh Kadri, Session Judge in the Bombay Presidency, Satyendra Chandra Mitra, M.L.A., Advocate High Court, Calcutta, Pundit Thakur Das Bhargava, M.L.A., Advocate High Court Lahore, Maulvi Muhammad Yakub, M.L.A., Deputy President of Legislative Assembly and Mian Muhammad Shah Nawaz, Bar-at-Law, Lahore, M.L.A., Lahore. The Committee also included two female members, Mrs O'Brien Beadon, Superintendent at Victoria Government Hospital Madras and Mrs Brijlal Nehru.

The terms of reference of the Age of the Consent Committee were:

(i) To examine the state of the law relating to the age of consent as contained in sections 375 and 376 of the Indian Penal Code 1860 and its suitability to conditions in India.

(ii) To enquire into the effect of those amendments which came after the enforcement of the Act of 1925 and to report whether any further amendment of the law was necessary and, if so, the changes that should be undertaken.[32]

The Committee started its work by issuing a questionnaire, aimed at about 8,000 persons. About 900 written statements were received by the end of August 1928 and the rest arrived within the extension of time granted later. At the beginning of September, the Committee started the examination of different witnesses. From 15 September, the Committee arranged tours and recorded evidence at Lahore, Peshawar, Karachi, Delhi, Ahmedabad, Madurai, Vizagapatanam, Dacca, Shillong, Calcutta, Patna, Benaras, Allahabad, Lucknow and Nagpur. The people who gave evidence included medical men and women, social workers, leading representatives of different classes and communities and exponents of both orthodox and 'advanced' opinions. The Committee also recorded the statements of a large number of lady witnesses in different parts of the country. It is interesting to note that at some places *purdah* parties were organized to ascertain the opinions of orthodox women. In addition, special visits were arranged to selected villages. The committee also benefited from the views of different social reformers and religious associations and received resolutions passed at meetings and conferences.

The evidence of the respondents opposing the proposed legislation was divided into two classes: those who were not in favour of social advancement through legislation, and those who were in favour of raising the age at marriage by social propaganda and not by social legislation.

OPPOSITION TO THE LAW OF CONSENT AND TO THE LAW OF MARRIAGE

Opposition to legislation on the age of consent and a law of marriage was based on various arguments brought before the Committee. Some of them concerned the nature of this social problem and the limitations of the powers of the legislature in this regard. In the first place the question was raised as to whether legislation was the real remedy for this social problem. Arguments emphasizing the very personal nature of this practice were put forward by many people. Unlike *sati*, for instance, the practice of child marriage was based purely on the most personal and intimate relations between human beings which were far above legal enforcement, it was claimed. Secondly, it was argued that due to the limited extent of popular franchises the Assembly could not act as the representative of the entire population. A few representatives from various communities were not competent to enact measures concerning social rights or religious customs. Under these circumstances, some of the witnesses demanded that the function of the Assembly should be confined to secular matters alone.

In answering these objections the Committee came to the conclusion that in every civilized country legislation had been used as a remedy to remove social injustices, including in matters affecting marriage and consent. In the same way, in several Indian states like Baroda and Indore, the Committee mentioned, such sort of legislation had already been enacted.[33]

The Committee classified the evidence and statements which it received from both the Hindu as well as Muslim religious scholars. The existence of various Hindu religious texts (Vedic, Shastras and Smritis) and their different interpretations given by *pundits*, illustrated that Hindu society was involved in a range of practices. For instance, although some sects of Brahmins, like Nambudris and Kulins, observed the practice of post-puberty marriage, there were other Brahmins who observed the custom of pre-puberty marriages. Despite the diversity of opinion amongst theologians themselves regarding the interpretation of texts, the permissibility of marriage in the case of an available suitable match even before eight years of age was not looked upon with disapproval by orthodox Hindus. However, the ideal age of marriage in general was considered to be up to twelve years or within three years after puberty.

As far as the sources of Muslim Law including the Quran, *Hadith*, *Ijma* and *Qiyas* were concerned, marriage amongst Muslims was not merely a civil contract but a particular act, enjoined by religion, the object of which was the procreation of *aulade saleh* (dutiful children) fit to serve God and His creation. To achieve this great mission, however, the particular age of marriage and consummation was not suggested by the Quran, although the second source (*Hadith*) was in favour of post-puberty marriage. The third source of Islamic law (*Ijma*) was not applicable as learned Indian Muslims did not agree on whether or not the proposed legislation was interfering with religion. The fourth source, (*Qiyas*), however, was certainly in favour of such legislation which would advance the interests of the community.[34]

In the light of these arguments, the Committee reached some conclusions that there were various reasons for the advancement of the age of consent. The fixing of the age of marriage was considered vital for safe motherhood and healthy progeny as well for conjugal happiness. At the same time, it opened the way for better educational and economical opportunities for women by raising the age of consent.

MUSLIMS AND THE AGE OF CONSENT COMMITTEE

It has been on numerous occasions suggested that Muslims strongly opposed both the bills on the grounds of their general belief that their law of marriage had already been ordained by Islam and could not be made or changed by the State. To understand this response, we should keep in mind that both the bills, especially the Sarda Bill, were introduced to remove the social disabilities of Hindu girls, though, later, the latter was amended and given the name of the Child Marriage Restraint Act. The communal nature of the bill cannot be attributed to Muslims, particularly in view of the fact that the marriage of girls before the age of puberty hardly existed among them. In the case of *nikah* at an early age, the situation was entirely different as a Muslim girl received the right of consent to her marriage after the attainment of puberty.

There were 166 Muslims, including some women, who came to give evidence before the Committee. Their opinion may be divided into three classes:

1. Those who held that early marriage was not evil and had no effect either on the mother or her progeny. It was also permitted by Muslim Law and was sanctioned by the practice of the Holy Prophet and other eminent personages. Thus, any legislation fixing a minimum age of marriage would be an interference in Islam.

2. Those who held that, though early marriage was to a certain extent an 'evil', it was not such a great 'evil' as to justify interference on the part of the Government. In their opinion the custom would automatically die out with the gradual growth of education, social awareness and better economic conditions.

3. The third category of witnesses comprised those who held early marriage to be a great evil, ruinous to the health and the progress of the community and against the principles and teachings of Islam. They did not believe in relying merely upon social reform and progress of education but were in favour of taking a bold step by legislation in the best interest of the community. They did not agree with *ulama* and *maulvis* who emphasized that marriage legislation or raising the age of consent would not be within the principles of Islam and its teachings.[35]

A MUSLIM'S RELIGIOUS STANDPOINT

The Bill was strongly opposed by *Jamiat-ul-Ulama-i-Hind*, a leading organization when it was discussed in the Legislative Assembly. Among its members who represented the community in the Legislative Assembly were Maulvi Muhammad Yakub, Muhammad Yamin Khan, Nominated Non-Official Member of the Assembly, Maulvi Muhammad Shafi, M.L.A. from Meerut, M.I. Kadri and Muhammad Ghuznavi, M.L.A. from the Deccan. Besides these Members of the Assembly, evidence also came from other Muslims belonging to different classes and professions. They argued that Islam was a self-contained and self-sufficient religion with a complete set of codified laws, and that in socio-religious matters like marriage, divorce, and inheritance, Muslims had to be governed by their laws or the *Shariat*. Any change in this regard, these witnesses warned, would be considered as an interference with religion.

Raising the matter during the fifth session of the Legislative Assembly in 1929, Maulvi Muhammad Yakub criticized those Muslims who intended to impose this legislation in the presence of Muslim Personal Law. By doing so, they were, he alleged, lightly brushing aside the weighty pronouncements of *ulama* like Maulana Mufti Kifayatullah, President of the *Jamiat-ul-Ulama-i-Hind*, Ahmed Saeed and Maulana Husain Ahmed, President of the Dar-ul-Ulum of Deoband.[36] He further highlighted the matter by referring to the resolutions and telegrams which he had received from different religious bodies on this issue.

An important resolution was moved by Maulana Qutbuddin and Muhammad Abdul Wali of Farangi Mahal of Lucknow in a meeting which was held under Muhammad Yakub's presidentship on 18 September 1929 at Delhi. The resolution was strongly supported by important religious leaders like Maulana Nasir Husain and Maulana Inayatullah of Farangi Mahal. It was declared that the Bill to fix the age of marriage and consummation was against Islamic Law and constituted a direct interference with religion and asked the Muslim members of the Assembly to oppose the passing of the Bill.[37] A similar view was expressed by Mr Muhammad Ghuznavi during the same Session of the Assembly. He was of the opinion that the life of a Muslim from the cradle to the grave was a series of religious performances and, therefore, any foreign element which interrupted or put a limitation on these performances could not be tolerated.

Shah Alam, the Emperor of India, had, through a treaty, delegated to the East India Company the responsibility for the civil administration of this country, with the latter guaranteeing the right of the Muslims to be governed according to the laws of their own religion. The British Government, as the successor to the East India Company, was bound by that treaty.[38] Maulvi Muhammad Shafi Daoodi argued that any measure to change the Personal Law of the Muslims of India should be voted upon only by the Muslims in the legislature. He emphasized that the Government should start the convention of not voting for or against a change unless it was sure that the side on which it was voting represented the view of a majority of the Muslims belonging to that legislature.[39]

Another important point raised in this regard was that the problem of early marriage anyway hardly existed among Muslims as Islam was not in favour of such marriages. However, in particular cases, the situation could be different, as Maulvi Muhammad Yakub observed in his note to the Age of Consent Committee. He stated that Islam generally seemed to be in favour of marriage after the age of discretion, but it sometimes happened that special circumstances and the well-being of a girl herself made it imperative to perform it at an early age. Being a practical religion, Islamic law was based on principles that had taken full account of the moral and other frailties of human nature.[40] He sought to elaborate upon his point by citing following the verse from the Quran in which Almighty Allah says:

And keep a vigilant eye on the orphans until they reach the age of marriage, and if you find that they are capable of managing their affairs entrust them with the management of their property.[41]

The conditional clause—'if you find that they are capable of managing their affairs'—underlined, he said, that the phrase 'reach the age of marriage' does not signify the age of puberty but relates to the age of *rushid* (a capacity to manage one's own affairs). In this context, the classical schools of Islamic Law were also in favour of *rushid*, something more than the mere physical indication of the onset of puberty. It should be added, though, that in connection with some *Hadith*, particularly those from *Shia* sources, the marriage of minor girls was condoned to fulfil the requirements of virtue and chastity. For instance, a specific *Hadith* with reference to Imam Jafar Sadiq cited by Maulvi Muhammad Yakub stated that the 'virtuous is one whose daughter does not start menses at her father's house.'[42] However, we should keep in mind, as many Muslim scholars pointed out, that such types of marriages were not favoured by Islam. Although, under special circumstances, the marriage of a minor girl could be conducted by her father or guardian if this was in her best interests. The case cited by Maulvi Muhammad Yakub was that of a young girl whose old father was on his death-bed and there was no one else to safeguard and manage her person and property after his death. It would certainly have been detrimental to the best interests of the girl if in such a case the legislation restrained the father from selecting a suitable husband for his daughter.[43]

Arguments emphasized that it was to secure the consolidation of the institution of marriage that the ceremony of *nikah* was performed. It came into being for the protection of society and to help men and women stay within the bounds of morality. Thus, it had become not only a civil contract but also a sacrament and act of piety for which people were to be rewarded in the next life. There were several authentic *Hadith* which these witnesses used to highlight the importance of *nikah* in the lives of Muslims. Among those cited by Maulvi Muhammad Yakub in his note was the *Hadith* from Imam Bukhari that 'there is no other act of worship except marriage and belief in Almighty God, which have continued from the days of Adam and which would continue in paradise as well'.[44]

Soon after the enactment of the Bill in 1929, the *Jamiat-ul-Ulama-i-Hind* decided to protest against it throughout the country. At its ninth annual session held in May 1929 at Amroha the *Jamiat* passed a resolution moved by Maulana Hifzur Rahman condemning the Sarda Act as an unjustified interference with Muslim Personal Law and urging the Muslims to overthrow the British administration by cooperating with the Indian National Congress in the independence struggle.[45]

MARRIAGE AS A SOCIO-RELIGIOUSLY ORDAINED INSTITUTION

All these points raised on religious grounds were vigorously refuted by liberals and reformist-minded individuals. In this way the Bill was well received by a number of Muslims who either gave evidence in person or in statements. The Bill was particularly warmly welcomed by such people in provinces in which Muslims represented the highest percentage of the population. For instance, witnesses such as Muhammad Akbar Khan, District Judge, Bannu, Kazi Mir Ahmed Khan, Vice President of the Peshawar Municipality, Sadullah Khan, Muhammad Nasir Khan, District Judge, Dera Ismail Khan, and Mr R. Inayatullah of the Education Service from the N.W.F.P., were in favour of marriage at a reasonable age and most of them favoured legislation to bring this about. Their main argument was that there was no question of violating religious injunctions or constituting an interference with the tenets of Islam; on the contrary, such legislation would be in consonance with the spirit of Islam.[46] As in the N.W.F.P., Muslims from the Punjab generally favoured the raising of the age of the consent to at least fifteen years. This was the view of, among others, Justice Agha Haider of the Lahore High Court, Malik Feroz Khan Noon, Minister for Local Self Government, Nawab Muhammad Hayat Khan Noon, Deputy Commissioner, Gujranwala, Shaikh Sirajuddin, Deputy Commissioner, Jhang, Malik Zaman Mehdi Khan, Deputy Commissioner, Mianwali, and Mian Abdul Aziz, Deputy Commissioner, Hissar.[47] Similar views were expressed by the witnesses from Bengal, including

Noor Ahmed, Chairman of the Chittagong Municipality and Azizul Haq, Member of the Legislative Council. They did not consider that early marriage was due to any religious injunctions. The enforcement of the law in curbing the practice, the former suggested, could be strengthened by generating strong public opinion against the offence and offenders. This could be achieved through vigorous propaganda as well as by the formation of women's protection leagues consisting of members of all communities in every village.[48] Like in the other provinces, the Muslims of the United Provinces also seemed to be veering round to change in the matter of child marriage. Sayyed Nawab Ali, a resident of Lucknow, favoured the bill by stating that 'the Law of Islam in such matters is elastic and judged in the light of progressive teachings of the Prophet'. Justice Sayyed Wazir Hasan was of the opinion that enforcement of such a law by legislation could not be considered as an interference with the tenets of Islam but could be treated by the people as an interference with their domestic affairs.[49] Maulvi Inayatullah from Lucknow did not deny the importance of such law for Muslim women but argued that such legislation had to be implemented only by Muslim rulers.[50]

In Muslim-minority provinces such as the Central Provinces, Madras and Bombay, too, large numbers of Muslims seemed to favour change in the matter of child marriage. Abdul Kadir, Pleader, Amraoti and Fazal Husain, Honorary Secretary, District Council, Balaghat, suggested that only a girl at the age of sixteen years or above would be in a position to give her consent to cohabitation.[51]

Questions now began to be raised about the plight of orphaned minor girls who were put into the custody of their guardians and became the hapless victims of the misbehaviour of these relatives. The number of such girls less than ten years of age who had been married by these guardians themselves just for the sake of their property was 26,400, noted Mr T.A. Sherwani, M.L.A. the United Provinces.[52] This was entirely against the principles of Islam but had never as such been challenged by society. Given this, the State was the only agency which could prevent these abuses through the enforcement of law. Sherwani was also of the opinion that such sort of legislation did not interfere with the *Shariat*; on the other hand, the matter directly dealt with *fiqah*, which could be changed as it had been changed before. Now, if it was to be changed, it could only be done by the legislature.[53] The legislature, he suggested, should choose one of two courses: to enact either civil legislation or penal legislation. However, in the case of the latter there would be less amendment to be made and comparatively more people would accept it as it would not be seen as such a great interference with Islam.[54]

Abdul Qadir, M.L.A. from C.P., observed that, while the opponents of change sought to strengthen their stance by arguing that the *ulama* themselves were against it, in actual fact people were not so bound by the opinions of the *ulama*.[55] The resistance against this proposed measure was simply the outcome of the misplaced belief that it would interfere with religion. It was a fact, M.A. Jinnah, M.L.A. from Bombay noted, that to begin with, people always looked upon these semi-religious usages and practices as the very foundation of their society and any suggestion or reform to change this usage was strongly resisted. In countries like India, he suggested, where public opinion was not so developed, reforming agencies should not allow themselves to be influenced by public opinion which could resent social reform in the name of religion. On the other hand, he said, Muslims had to have the courage to say 'No we are not going to be frightened by that'.[56]

CHILD MARRIAGE: CERTAINLY AN EVIL

Much evidence was gathered from Muslims describing child marriage as an unmitigated evil, destroying the health as well as the progress of the nation. The main causes of child marriage, many of them believed, were illiteracy and lack of awareness. Given this, the only solution, suggested Khwaja Hasan Nizami, Sajjada Nashin and Mutawalli of the Dargah of Nizamuddin Auliya, was legislation, to fix the minimum age of marriage of girls in India. Without this, the law of consent could not be effective. To make it more beneficial to the interests of Muslims in India, however, he suggested giving the comprehensive powers to Muslim religious leaders and *Kazis* that they had enjoyed during Muslim rule.[57]

Mobilization of public opinion was another important suggestion made by some witnesses. They recommended the widespread use of propaganda against the evils of child marriage. For this purpose, the services of paid *mullas* and *maulvis*, in the opinion of Mazheruddin, editor of Al-Aman, Delhi, could prove to be a very effective vehicle.[58] It was also suggested that special institutions for women be set up all over the country, through which they could become self-reliant, capable of earning an honest living and would, thereby, be prevented from being forced into crime or destitution.[59]

WOMEN AND THE SARDA LEGISLATION

The restoration of women's social rights emerged as a major issue for educated women and their organizations. As soon as the Sarda Bill was introduced, women decided to support it. They arranged meetings and passed several resolutions in this regard. The written statements and oral evidence presented by these women to the Committee highlighted the fact that they themselves wanted to do away with the legal disabilities that had virtually enslaved them. In her note, Mrs Brilal Nehru cried out in anguish: 'my heart aches at the thought of the sufferings of the girl-wives. Our whole report is a plea on behalf of these victims of blind custom and usage. It is because of my deep sympathy for them that I want to try more efficacious means than those which have been tried and found wanting.'[60] An increasing number of women, it appears, were no longer willing to remain mute victims of laws that clearly and heavily discriminated against them.

Some women's organizations, too, made strenuous efforts in support of legislative change. The Begum of Bhopal, presiding over the second annual meeting of the All-India Women's

Conference in Delhi in 1928, called for mustering support for the Sarda Bill, then in the legislature, designed to raise the legal age of marriage.[61] At the 1929 Hyderabad session of the All-India Muslim Ladies Conference, Abru Begum, the Honorary Secretary, urged women to support the campaign to raise the age of consent for marriage.[62]

The common cause of an Indian sisterhood was further strengthened by the All-India Women's Association and the Women's Indian Association. Several Muslim women, including Begum Hamid Ali, Lady Abdul Qadir, Mrs Asif Ali, Begum Aziz Rasul, Mrs Akhtar Husain, Mrs Kazi Mir Ahmed, Begum Hamida Momin and Mrs I.F. Hasan actively participated in the efforts of the former association. From its very inception, it aimed at removing the evil of child marriage. Speaking at its opening session in 1927, the Maharani of Baroda said that the practice of female child marriage had cruelly deprived little girls of all the joys of childhood.[63]

Even after the passing of the Sarda Bill into law, the All-India Women's Conference continued its efforts to make the law more effective. An important resolution was passed during its twelfth session held at Nagpur in 1937 which condemned the unnatural and devitalizing custom of allowing immature girls to become wives and mothers on the grounds that it robbed them of their right to education and freedom and seriously impaired their mental, moral and physical growth.[64] In the same way, the Women's Indian Association emphasized the need for women to secure their civil rights through legislation. To remove the evil custom of child marriage, the Association passed several resolutions, including one that was passed by the first International Conference held under the auspices of the Association in 1936 at Calcutta.[65]

It should be noted that this great desire to improve the social status of women was not limited only to these nationwide associations but also became an important issue for local organizations working in different parts of the country. One such example was the Women's Conference, Madras. The Conference urged parents to recognize the rights of their daughters by giving them the opportunity of receiving higher education so that could prolong their stay in their parental home.[66] The Mysore Ladies Conference strongly urged women of the state to benefit from legislation that would raise their social status. At one of its meetings which was held under the presidentship of Lady Ismail, the wife of Sir Muhammad Ismail, the Dewan of Mysore, it demanded that the enactment of legislation on the lines of the Sarda Bill should be immediately introduced in the state by fixing the minimum age of marriage for girls at sixteen and for boys at twenty-one.[67]

After collecting the views of various social and religious bodies as well as medical and women's associations, the Committee finally submitted its report to the Legislative Assembly on 20 January 1929. It made several recommendations and suggestions relating to the proper age of consent for establishing marital relations and the registration of marriages. The Bill was enacted on 23 September 1929 and came into force on the first day of April 1930. In 1938 the Child Marriage Restraint (Second Amendment) Act added a new section to the Act, empowering the courts to issue an injunction prohibiting the proposed marriage of a child if they came to know that such a marriage was likely to take place. The abolition of child marriage was a woman's issue, but perhaps more important it was a measure which tested the desire of Indians to modernize. It was propagated as a symbol of a desire to elevate women's social status as independent persons.

THE ENFORCEMENT OF MUSLIM PERSONAL LAW (SHARIAT APPLICATION BILL)

A peculiar problem that the Muslims had come to face was what position they should adopt *vis-à-vis* legislation that seemed to interfere with their own personal laws. Although some secular laws dealing with the realm of the personal, such as the Child Marriage Act of 1929, were accepted, other measures provoked strong opposition on the grounds that the *Shariat* had already prescribed rules for these matters. For instance, this was the response to legislation such as the Married Women's Property Act of 1876, the Indian Succession Act 1885 and the Guardian and the Wards Act of 1890. It was precisely to circumvent this problem that the Kazi Act was passed in 1880 providing for the appointment of *kazi* who would advise the court on matters related to the *Shariat*.

At the beginning of the twentieth century, the attention of the *ulama* was increasingly drawn to the fact that customary law at variance with Islamic legal principles was being adhered to by several communities among the Muslims of the country. As a result of this, Muslim women were not being given any share in inheritance and this was a blatant violation of the commandments of the Quran. To remove these disabilities, the *ulama* tried to persuade Muslims to give up customary laws. Their efforts brought to the Indian statute book a number of local and central enactments abrogating the non-Islamic customs followed by many Muslims in India. The earliest of these laws was the Mapilla Succession Act of 1918 and the Cutchi Memon Act of 1920.

The efforts of the *ulama* in this direction gained momentum after the formation of the *Jamiat-ul-Ulama-i-Hind* in 1919. From its very inception the *Jamiat* made organized efforts for the 'restoration' of Muslim personal laws. Several resolutions were passed under the presidentship of leading *ulama*. In 1926 the cause was further strengthened with the publication of Maulana Ashraf Ali Thanawi's monograph, *al-Ghasab-al-Mirath* (Usurping the Heritage). Alongside these developments, a changing attitude of some of these religious reformers towards customary practices that had bound women in chains came to be reflected in many of their writings. One of the example was Maulana Mahvi Siddiqi, a local religious leader of Madras, who idealized the woman of the time as socially conscious, more independent in her thinking and committed to her cause.[68]

The practical outcome of the efforts of the *ulama* came in the form of the introduction of Muslim Personal Law. The first step forward was taken by the provincial branch of the *Jamiat-ul-*

Ulama-i-Hind of the N.W.F.P. In 1927, the *Jamiat*, at their annual meeting at Peshawar, passed a resolution demanding the enforcement of Muslim Personal Law. This was followed by the introduction of the Muslim Shariat Bill in the Council in 1934. It was moved by Khan Habibullah Khan, a non-official Member of the Council. Its objects and reasons were highlighted by Kudah Baksh, a Member of the Legislative Council,as follows:

> For several years past it has been the cherished desire of the Muslims of the N.W.F.P. that customary law should in no case take the place of the Muslim Personal Law. The matter has been repeatedly agitated in the press as well as on the platform (of the *Jamiat*). The *Jamiat-ul-Ulama-i-Hind* has supported the demand and invited the attention of all concerned to the urgent necessity of introducing a measure in the Council to this effect. Customary Law is a misnomer in as much as it has not any sound basis to stand upon and is very much liable to frequent changes and cannot be expected to attain any time in future the certainty and definiteness which must be the characteristic of all laws. The status of Muslim women under the so-called customary law is simply disgraceful. The introduction of Muslim Personal Law will automatically raise them to the position to which they are naturally entitled.[69]

During the same year the Bill was referred to a Select Committee, established under the chairmanship of G. Cunningham, the Finance Member of the Council. The Committee submitted its report to the Legislative Council of the N.W.F.P. on 20 July 1935. There were some suggestions made by the Committee, including the removal of the word 'adoption' from Clause 2 of the original Bill. In the meanwhile, an important booklet referring to the position of Muslim women according to the Quran was published by the Nawab of Hoti. It led to the widespread realization that, instead of the sacred Law of God, Indian Muslims had been apparently continuing to follow the customs of their forefathers, as a consequence of which women were treated worse than animals.[70] Under these un-Islamic customary laws, after the death of a father the whole of his property went to his son while the daughter would not get anything.[71] In this situation, the enforcement of Muslim Personal Law was considered particularly advantageous to women as it granted them inheritance rights. Ultimately, the Bill succeeded in securing favour in and outside the Legislative Council and the Act was passed in November 1935.

The effort of the N.W.F.P. Legislative Council was welcomed by Muslims of other parts of India. It was given a high profile by the Muslim press and was considered as one of the most important efforts ever made in the best interests of the Muslim women.[72]

In 1935 a similar Shariat Bill was introduced in the Central Legislative Assembly by M.H.M. Abdullah, M.L.A. from the West-Central Punjab. In explaining the importance of the Bill, he stated that it would secure uniformity of law among Muslims throughout British India in all their social and personal relations. By doing so, the claims to family inheritance rights of women, who, under customary law, were debarred from succeeding to the same, would automatically be secured.[73]

The Bill was referred to a select committee. After its preliminary meeting on 28 July 1935, the Muslim members of the Legislative Assembly held an informal meeting and, as a result of that, a revised draft of the Bill was prepared and presented at the general meeting of the Select Committee.[74] The Committee circulated the revised Bill to elicit public opinion. The main supporters of the proposed legislation were various the Muslim religious bodies, including the *Jamiat-ul-Ulama-i-Hind*, *Anjuman-e-Ittihad-e-Islam*, Madras, *Anjuman-i-Islam*, Gauhati and the *Anjuman-i-Islamia*, Jorhat, as well as women's organizations and several individuals. They spoke out vehemently against those Muslims who chose to follow the *Shariat* in the matter of marriage and divorce but conveniently ignored it at the time of the distribution of inheritance and family property.[75] Such practices were widely prevalent among Muslims belonging to the agricultural classes, particularly in the Punjab. Under the Punjab Law Act IV of 1872, Muslim women had been deprived of their share in agricultural lands on account of the fact that many Indian Muslims were originally converts to Islam and still wanted to be governed by the laws which they had followed before they had become Muslims.[76] The intensity of the sentiment generated by this issue was reflected in the writings of reformers like Rashid-ul-Khairi, the editor of *Ismat* and champion of the cause of women. He lamented:

> The Muslims of Muhammadpur, whether they are black or white in colour or Sayyed or Pathan in caste, are all dishonest in their dealings. From prostitution to polygamy they did each and every thing to fulfil their personal desires. But what a shame that when the time came to distribute their property according to Islamic law, they themselves humiliated their daughters and sisters.[77]

Under such circumstances, argued Fazl-i-Haq Pracha, M.L.A. from North West Punjab 'one could predict without any fear of contradiction that such resentment which is based on honest grounds will provoke women to undignified agitation to redress their wrongs.'[78] Under the new law, noted its supporters, the economic status of women would improve considerably, and even the non-Muslim members of the Assembly called it a major step in the right direction. Dr G.V. Deshmukh, M.L.A. from Bombay, hoped that the implementation of Muslim Personal Law would also be followed by the other communities and women would be able to achieve the same economic status as men.[79]

However, along with these favourable responses, the Bill was strongly opposed by several provincial Governments, Associations and certain individuals. Their main argument was that some customs and usages of law were so old and so well established that their replacement with the *Shariat* would seriously disrupt the whole fabric of society as most Muslims were governed by local customs which deprived women of property rights. Such opponents of the legislation demanded that the implementation of Muslim Personal Law should be left for provincial Governments to decide. They would act according to the needs of their own Muslims.

Justice Niamatullah from Lucknow opposed the proposal by calling it a 'slip-shod Bill' which did not take any account of the number of statutory provisions which were in conflict with it, and which widely differed from province to province. If an omnibus bill of this description passed into law, the result would be endless confusion for the large number of ancient *zemindar* families who had been following for generations certain rules of succession recorded in the *wajibularzes* (administration certificates) in their villages.[80] Similar concerns were expressed by the Chief Commissioner of Ajmer and Marwara who stated that, as in other areas, the people of that region would not like any change in their customary practices and that female inheritance would not be accepted at any cost.[81] In the view of K.M. Akram, D.S.P., Madras, the situation was particularly complicated in the case of inter-marriage between two families following different codes and the courts would perhaps find it difficult to remove a dispute under such circumstances.[82]

On the other hand, non-officials declared that the Bill would cause general distress among rich Muslim trading sects who would never agree to be governed by the *Shariat* in this particular matter. For example, in Bombay groups of Muslims such as the Khoja and Bohra communities were governed by Hindu law in matters of succession. A change in their personal law, observed the Bar Association of Virajpet, would necessarily affect and upset many contractual relations entered into under the existing settled law. In this situation it was not right to force any change in the personal law of the party unless there was an unmistakable demand for it. Thus, the proposed legislation would place tremendous hardship on people as the entire structure of society would be undermined and the disadvantages might far outweigh any advantage gained by the Bill.[83]

It should be noted that during the final reading of the Bill Quaid-e-Azam Muhammad Ali Jinnah also proposed a significant amendment, the purpose of which was that, instead of enforcing the law of Islam compulsorily for all Muslims, every Muslim should, for the time being, be given discretion to opt between the Islamic law and customary law. As he was a moderate politician his main motive was to save the future of the Muslim League by securing the interests of landlords and nawabs. Referring to the Cutchi Memon Act, under which the Memon community was given an option between the Muslim law and customary law of inheritance, he suggested incorporating similar provisions in the proposed Bill.[84] Jinnah's proposal was strongly opposed by the *Jamiat*, whose members argued that there was no such provision in the N.W.F.P. Shariat Bill which was the basic starting point of this Bill. In the end, the rapidly growing community consciousness among Muslims in India worked to tilt the balance in favour of the enforcement of the Muslim Personal Law Application Act in 1937. The Bill was eventually enacted on 16 September and was given the name of the Muslim Personal Law Application Act 1937. It also incorporated the provision suggested by Jinnah. Meanwhile, the *Jamiat* continued with its protest. In 1942 Muhammad Ahmed Kazmi moved in the Legislature Assembly an Amendment Bill seeking the repeal of Jinnah's proposal and the restoration of the original provisions drafted by the *ulama*. The Amendment Bill, however, could not get support in the Assembly and the Act as enacted in the Shariat Act of 1937 remained applicable. It seemed that the Government was also interested in securing the interests of landlords as, in its view, guaranteeing the security of the socio-economic interests of particular Muslim groups was indispensable in consolidating British rule. Despite all these disabilities, however, the Shariat Act provided the first ray of sunlight for groups and individuals seeking to change the social as well as political status of Muslim women in India.

THE DISSOLUTION OF MUSLIM MARRIAGES ACT 1939

The most important enactment among the legislative measures that were adopted relating to Muslim personal law was the Dissolution of Muslim Marriages Act of 1939. This was the only legislative measure which introduced a substantive reform in the Muslim law of the various schools as applied in British India.

The Quran expressly sanctions the dissolution of a woman's marriage in case of necessity by stating: 'if a woman is prejudiced by a marriage, let it be broken'.[85] While, this principle was accepted by all the schools of Islamic law, with respect to the circumstances in which it should be applied the schools of Islamic law greatly differed from one another. At one extreme was the Maliki School which allowed the *kazi* to dissolve a marriage of a Muslim woman on a wide variety of grounds. On the other extreme was the Hanafi School which restricted women's rights to seek the dissolution of marriage by a *kazi*, especially by a non-Muslim judge.

In India, Hanafi law was followed, at least in theory, by most Muslims. Upon the conversion to another religion by a Muslim woman, some Muslim jurists laid down the principle that the marriage would not be dissolved and that the woman would be imprisoned till she returned to Islam. In British India, however, it was not possible to enforce this device: various rulings of the courts were based on the notion that if a Muslim woman refused to return to her faith it would result in the dissolution of her marriage.[86]

The situation became particularly serious during the early decades of the twentieth century. Many cases were reported in British India of Muslim women desiring to put an end to their marriage by seeking refuge under the above-mentioned principle of Islamic law and, just for the purpose of getting their marriage dissolved, renouncing their faith. Muslim organizations and social reformers became aware of this situation and began thinking of ways and means to arrest the tendency among Muslim women to renounce Islam simply because religious law did not allow them to get rid of their husbands lawfully. Growing apostasy on these grounds was said to be the result of the selfishness of Muslim men who denied to their women the rights given to them by Islam. Pained by this, Rashid-ul-Khairi, stated:

As a social reformer I tried my best to convince the Indian Muslims
for the necessity of *Khulah*. But I never succeeded in my efforts.
At last, when the time of decision of the suit of divorce of Qaisar
(a daughter of one of my close friends) came, I went to the *kazi* at
the request of Qaisar's father. The *kazi* was my class fellow at
school. By giving the reference of that friendship I requested the
kazi to give Qaisar her Islamic right of *Khulah*. He (the *kazi*) said
to me that though 'you are very right in your point of view but if
I would give this right to Muslim women, the decision will destroy
the whole Muslim society in India and thousands of married women
will run away from their husband's houses. The obstinacy of the
kazi led Qaisar to change her religion. Her apostasy was declared
in the supplement of Curzon Gazette which was published from
Delhi at that time.[87]

Alongside the social reformers, this issue represented a great
challenge for religious leaders, in particular the *Jamiat-ul-
Ulama-i-Hind*, which devoted itself to this task. In 1935 several
bills were drafted by the *Jamiat*, based on a book, *al-Hilat-al
Najiza* (A Lawful device), compiled by Maulana Ashraf Ali
Thanawi with the help of Mufti Kifayatullah and Maulana
Husain Ahmed Madani. The work, which was published by in
1932, enumerated in detail the principles of Maliki law which
Muslim judges could apply to dissolve a Muslim woman's
marriage in special circumstances.[88] On the basis of the
recommendations of the book, a Bill was introduced in the
Central Legislature by Muhammad Ahmed Kazmi, M.L.A. from
Meerut, as well as a member of the Jamiat. The statement of
objects of the bill was announced by Husain Imam, M.L.A.
from Bihar and Orissa. He pointed out:

There is no provision in the Hanafi Code of Muslim Law enabling
a married Muslim woman to obtain a decree from the Court dissolving
her marriage in case the husband neglects to maintain her, makes her
life miserable by deserting or persistently maltreating her, or
absconds, leaving her unprovided for and under certain other
circumstances. The absence of such a provision has entailed
unspeakable misery to innumerable Muslim women in British India.
The Hanafi jurists, however, have clearly laid down that in cases in

which the application of Hanafi law causes hardship, it is permissible to apply the provisions of the Maliki, Shafi or Hanbali law. Acting on this principle the *ulama* have issued fatawa to the effect that in cases enumerated in clause 3, Part A of this Bill, a married Muslim woman may obtain a decree dissolving her marriage. As the courts are sure to hesitate to apply the Maliki law to the case of Muslim women, legislation recognizing and enforcing the above-mentioned principle is called for in order to relieve the suffering of countless Muslim women. The courts in British India have held in a number of cases that the apostasy of some married Muslim woman dissolves her marriage. This view has been repeatedly (expressed) at the bar, but the courts continue to stick to precedents created by rulings based on an erroneous view of the Muslim law. The *ulama* have issued *fatawa* supporting non-dissolution of marriage by reason of wife's apostasy. The Muslim community has, again and again, given expression to its supreme dissatisfaction with the view held by the courts. Thus, by this Bill the whole law relating to the dissolution of marriage is brought at one place and consolidated in the hope that it would supply a very long-felt want of the Muslim community in India.[89]

The bill was vigorously debated by the Muslim press. One argument emphasized that neither society nor the existing law had helped Muslim women secure release from tyrannical husbands. In some cases they had even been constrained to change their faith in order to rid themselves of their cruel husbands.[90] Sir Zafarullah Khan stated that the outstanding merit of this Bill was that it provided various grounds on which divorce could be obtained by a woman under the Muslim Law in very definite, clear and precise terms, and any judge, whether Muslim or non Muslim, would not have much room left for doubt with regard to them.[91]

The Dissolution of Muslim Marriage Act was enacted in March 1939 along with the changes made in the original Bill at the insistence of the Select Committee. The Act mainly dealt with (i) grounds for the dissolution of marriage and the method of dissolution, and (ii) the personnel of the court authorized to try suits relating to the dissolution.

GROUNDS FOR DISSOLUTION OF MARRIAGES

The Dissolution of Muslim Marriages Act provided specific grounds on which a Muslim wife could seek a judicial divorce. It specified eight such grounds and added that the court could also dissolve a marriage on any other grounds recognized by Islamic law.

The first ground for the dissolution of marriage was based on the principle of *Mafqud-ul-Khabar* (a person regarding whom it is not known whether he is alive or dead). According to Maliki law, the wife of a missing person is entitled to observe the *iddat* of the death on the expiry of four years from the date of his disappearance.[92]

The second set of grounds for the dissolution of marriage was the husband's neglect in or failure to provide for the maintenance of the wife for a period of two years. This provision covered the Shafi law in which dissolution would be effected between husband and wife because the husband had proved unwilling to retain her according to usage.[93]

The third ground provided that the wife was entitled to the dissolution of marriage if the husband had been sentenced to seven years' imprisonment or more, provided the sentence had become final.[94]

The fourth ground for the dissolution of marriage was based on the failure of the husband to perform his marital obligations. This clause of the Act covered the provision of Maliki Law under which the wife had the option of claiming a dissolution of marriage if the husband had failed to perform his marital obligations, without reasonable cause, for a period of three years.[95]

The fifth ground covered those cases where the husband was impotent at the time of marriage and continued to be so. It was provided that before passing a decree on this ground, the Court would, on application by the husband, make an order requiring the husband to satisfy the Court within the period of one year that he had ceased to be impotent and if the husband could satisfy the Court within such a period, no decree would be passed on this ground.

The sixth ground provided in the Act was that the wife could file a suit for the dissolution of the marriage if the husband had been insane for a period of at least two years or was suffering from leprosy or a virulent disease. In this context, Hanafi law only considered those defects which made consummation impossible, such as impotency and mutilation of the male organ. On the other hand, the Maliki, Shafi'i, Hanbali and Jafri schools considered these sufferings as entitling women to claim the dissolution of their marriages.[96]

The seventh ground covered the clause of option of puberty. It was provided in the Act that the wife who had been given in marriage by her father or other guardian before she reached the age of sixteen years could repudiate the marriage before attaining the age of eighteen years, provided that the marriage had not been consummated.[97]

The eighth ground of the dissolution of marriage covered those cases where a husband treated his wife with cruelty which included:

(a) Habitually assaulting her or making her life miserable.
(b) Associating with women of ill-repute or leading a disreputable life.
(c) Attempting to force her to lead an immoral life.
(d) Disposing of her property or preventing her from exercising her legal rights over it.
(e) If he had more wives than one, not treating her equitably in accordance with the injunctions of the Quran.[98]

INDIAN COURTS AND SUITS RELATING TO THE DISSOLUTION OF MARRIAGES

One major objection raised by *ulama* to the legislation was that the jurisdiction under the Act was not reserved for Muslim judges alone. Clause six of the Bill, which was moved by Ahmed Saeed Kazmi in the Central Legislature, provided that suits of the dissolution of marriage on the part of Muslim women should be held in proper courts under the supervision of Muslim judges and, when the presiding officer was not Muslim, the suit should be passed from one place to another until it could find a Muslim official. After the decision, the suit would then be referred back to the original court. In the case of appeals against the decision of the trial court, people would have to look to the high court and their cases should be heard and decided again by a Muslim judge.

The practical implementation of this clause was very difficult, in particular in those provinces, as pointed out by Mr J.A. Thorne, (Nominated Member of the Government of India), where the number of Muslim judges and Muslims in general was small. In the presence of such complications, the enforcement of the Act would not prove very beneficial.[99] The proposal for such communal tribunals, said Sardar Sant Singh, M.L.A. from the west-Punjab, would only show distrust of judges of communities other than one's own in the matter of administration of personal laws introduce a narrow mentality that should be avoided at all costs.[100] He further criticized those members of the Assembly who demanded removing the matter from the civil courts and handing it over to courts that were presided over by one community, on the grounds that it was akin to introducing the principle of *imperium in imperio*.[101] M.S. Aney, M.L.A. from Berar, said that since it was a matter of the administration of justice,it could be accomplished by relying upon men, irrespective of religious background, who had been recruited according to the true spirit of law and in the best interests of people.[102]

THE MUSLIM STANDPOINT

Conservative Muslims demanded the kind of religious freedom that might be exercised in every walk of life without the imposition of artificial arrangements from a foreign Government since India was no longer *dar-ul-Islam*. After the ruling of various courts in British India, the idea was further strengthened that the enforcement of Muslim Family Law could not be accomplished without the appointment of Muslim authorities in such institutions. The great mover in this campaign was the *Jamiat-ul-Ulama-i-Hind*, which demanded that the Government should take heed of this. They put the entire blame for the enactment of such 'un-Islamic' measures on Muslim League members of the Legislature who did not support the demand of the *Jamiat* on account of political rivalry. Their principal target was the leadership of Jinnah, who had a progressive outlook on the matter of legal reforms.[103] Thus, the objections of the *Jamiat* in this matter continued even after the passing of the Act. In 1940 the Central Committee of the *Jamiat* approved certain amendments in the Act under the presidentship of Maulana Husain Ahmed Madani. Beside this, many *fatawa* were issued during the period arguing that, if a non-Muslim could not perform the ceremony of Muslim *nikah*, there was simply no way in which he could be justified in dissolving a Muslim marriage.[104]

After the enforcement of the Act, several cases were registered by women and by their relatives. However, it was not an entirely smooth affair for them. In the first place, the court procedure in these suits was often too expensive to contemplate. Besides the court expenses (approximately twenty rupees), a large amount had to be paid to a lawyer as a fee and this proved impossible for poor women who were already suffering from maintenance negligence on the part of their husbands and wanted to dissolve their marriage on these grounds.[105] Secondly, social restrictions appeared as a major hindrance to getting through this procedure. For instance, arguing their case was a very difficult task for *purdah*-observing women who had to go to court from time to time over a long period.[106]

To remove these legal and social difficulties, several suggestions were made, especially by educated Muslim women. Some of them demanded that these suits should be given first priority and that in the course of ruling special arrangements should be made which would include the construction of waiting rooms for women in the compound of every court as well as fixing the maximum time of decision of such suits.[107] Secondly, they called for Talaq Fund Committees in every town with the cooperation of local Muslim *ashraf* and lawyers who would provide counselling and financial support on a voluntary basis and the arrangement of women's processions and meetings for the wider propagation of awareness about this pressing social problem. Above all, they encouraged *purdah*-observing women to step outside their seclusion to generate public awareness about the plight of women either through their writings or by telling the world about their miserable lives.[108]

* * *

Taking an overview of this whole social process, it can be said that legislation was considered as necessary to protect women from existing social practices that had enslaved them. The terrain of rights had been largely mapped according to the way that law had developed in the modern western world. We cannot say that revolutionary changes occurred as a result of the introduction of these new laws. Yet, while the process took a long time to mature, gradual changes occurred in every walk of life. For instance, the Child Marriage Restraint Act sought to increase the number of women in the field of higher education. In the same way, the proportion of mothers, less than fifteen years of age slightly decreased to 46.51 per 1,000 in 1946 as compared to 51.25 in 1929.[109]

As regards the framework of Islamic doctrine, religious symbolism was interpreted to a large extent to match existing perceptions about the status of Muslim women while legislation was used as a means to regain for women the rights that the *Shariat* had provided for them. The emphasis, therefore, was on providing Muslim women with better economic and social options which helped to improve the overall status of Muslim women.

In this way, two parallel situations came to prevail over the period in question: fihrstly, the change from the point of view of women was for the better, and one which was slowly but surely helping to break down taboos that obstructed their abilities, aptitudes and potential to contribute to national development, beyond the confined role of their household activities; and secondly, successive Governments' social policies tried to bridge the distance between individual aspirations, the prevailing social environment and the objectives of national well-being. Here was another way—through the legislative processes of the colonial state—that new public space was opened up for Muslim women.

NOTES

1. Shahida Lateef, 'Defining Women through Legislation' in Zoya Hasan (ed.), *Forging Identities: Gender Communities, and the State*, pp. 35–58.
2. *Report of the Age of Consent Committee 1928–29*, (Government of India, Central Publication Branch, 1929), p. 12.
3. Ibid., p. 110.
4. This orthodox Hindu point of view was stated by Pundit Nand Kishore, in his evidence given before the Age of Consent Committee, p. 111.
5. Ibid., p. 112.
6. Ibid., p. 24. (The actual figures were taken and calculated from the Census Report of India 1921).
7. Ibid., p. 24.
8. Ibid., p. 30.
9. Ibid.
10. Ibid., p. 50.
11. Ibid., p. 33.
12. Ibid., p. 36.
13. Ibid., p. 65.
14. Ibid. Appendix V-B, p. 308
15. Ibid.
16. Katherine Mayo, *Mother India*, (Jonathan Cape, London, 1927).
17. Mrinalini Sinha, 'Reading Mother India: Empire, Nation and the Female Voices', *Journal of Women's History*, Vol. 6, No. 2, 1994, pp. 6–40.
18. Ibid., the actual review was published in *Young India* in 1927.
19. *The Daily News*, 15 August 1927, MSS. Eur. 186, n.p., IOL.
20. *The Statesman*, 10 August 1927, ibid.
21. Cornelia Sorabji (1866–1954), was the daughter of Rev. Sorabji Kharsedji, a Parsi converted to Christianity. After getting education in law, first at Poona and then at Oxford, Cornelia took the cause of the *purdah nashin* Indian women who were suffering through legal disabilities because of their confinement in *purdah*. From 1904–1923, Cornelia worked as a Lady Assistant to the Courts of Wards in Bengal, Bihar, Orissa and

Assam. She was one of those who championed women's emancipation in particular for the restoration of their social and political rights. She was also the Honorary Secretary of the Bengal League for Women's Social Service, established for the spread of social awareness among local women.

22. Mayo to Sorabji, September 1929, Mss. Eur. 165, IOL, p. 359.
23. *Report of the Age of Consent Committee*, pp. 99–100.
24. Ibid., Appendix VI-A, pp. 325–27.
25. Ibid.
26. Abstracts are taken from the written statement, dated 23 August 1928 of Miss Khadijah Begum Ferozuddin, Professer of History, at Lahore College, *The Age of Consent Committee: Evidences 1928–29*, oral evidences and written statements from the Punjab, (Government of India Central Publication Branch, Calcutta, 1929), p. 255.
27. Abstract is taken from the Proceedings of Bengal Judicial Department, dated 26 June 1928, No. 2380-2401.J., p. 4. IOL.
28. A written statement of Dr. M.I. Balfour to *The Age of Consent Committee: Evidences 1928–29*, witnesses and statements from the Bombay Presidency, Poona and Central Provinces and Berar, (Government of India Central Publication Branch, Calcutta, 1929), p. 39.
29. Written statement of Miss Khadijah Begum Ferozuddin, *The Age of Consent Committee: Evidences 1928–29*, oral evidences and written statements from the Punjab, p. 257
30. Written statement of Haji Ismail Choudhury, to *The Age of Consent Committee: Evidences 1928–29*, oral evidences and written statements from Bengal, (Government of India Central Publication Branch, Calcutta, 1929), pp. 101–105.
31. *Report of the Age of Consent Committee*, p. 114.
32. Ibid., p. 2.
33. Ibid., p. 101.
34. Ibid., p. 113.
35. Ibid., p. 6.
36. *Legislative Assembly Debates*, Official Report, fifth session of the Third Legislative Assembly from 18–26 September 1929, Vol. IV, (Simla, Government of India Press, 1930), p. 1142.
37. Ibid.
38. Ibid., p. 1155.
39. Ibid., p. 1140.
40. *Report of the Age of Consent Committee*, pp. 276–77.
41. Quran, 4: 6. Ibid., p. 277.
42. Ibid., p. 278.
43. Ibid., p. 279.
44. Ibid.

45. Tahir Mahmood, *Muslim Personal law: Role of State in the Subcontinent*, (Vikas Publishing House, New Delhi, 1977), p. 53.
46. *Report of the Age of Consent Committee*, p. 31.
47. Ibid., p. 26.
48. *The Age of Consent Committee: Oral and Written Statement from Bengal*, Vol. 11, (Government of India, Central Publication Branch, Calcutta, 1929), p. 219.
49. *Report of the Age of Consent Committee*, p. 219.
50. Ibid.
51. Ibid., p. 88.
52. *Legislative Assembly Debates*, Official Report, 18 to 26 September, 1929, fifth session of the Third Legislative Assembly, (Government of India Press, Simla, 1930), p. 1150.
53. Ibid.
54. Ibid., p. 1154.
55. Ibid., p. 1159.
56. *Legislative Assembly Debates*, Vol. IV, fifth session of the Third Legislative Assembly, 23 August to 17 September 1929, pp. 667–68.
57. *Age of Consent Committee: Evidences 1928–29, from the provinces of Punjab, Delhi, and the N.W.F.P.*, (Government of India Central Publication Branch), p. 506.
58. Ibid., p. 505.
59. Abstract is taken from a written Statement, dated 10 August 1928 of Atiya Begum to *The Age of Consent Committee: Evidences, 1928–29, Witnesses from the Bombay Presidency, Poona and Berar*, Vol. III, (Government of India Central Publication Branch, Calcutta, 1929), p. 273.
60. Note by Mrs Brijlal Nehru, to the *Report of the Age of Consent Committee*, p. 157.
61. Gail Minault, 'Sisterhood or Separatism: The All-India Muslim Ladies Conference and the Nationalist Movement' in Gail Minault (ed.), *The Extended Family: Women and Political Participation in India and Pakistan*, pp. 83–108.
62. *Salana Report: All-India Muslim Ladies Conference*, held at Hyderabad on February, 1929, MEC. Report, n.d., pp. 1–70.
63. *The Statesman*, 20 January 1927, n.p.
64. *Proceeding of the Annual Meeting of the All India Women's Conference*, Nagpur Session, 1937. Q/I/FC/49, pp. 168–70, IOL.
65. Mona Hensman, 'Report of the First International Conference of Women in India', *Stri Dharma*, Vol. XIX, No. 4, May 1939, pp. 126–27.
66. *The Indian Ladies Magazine*, News and Notes Section, Vol. 11, No. 5, December 1928, p. 267.
67. Ibid. Vol. 111, No. 3, October 1929, p. 145.

68. Maulana Mahvi Siddiqi expressed this new social behaviour through his poems occasionally published in *Ismat*, for example see Vol. 50, No. 6 June 1933 and Vol. 62, No. 1, January 1939.

69. *The N.W.F.P. Muslim Personal Law (Shariat Application Bill 1934).* Introduced in the Legislative Council of N.W.F.P., see Notification No. 732 L.C. dated 29 March 1934, L/P&J/7/667, pp. 1–2, (IOL).

70. By giving the statement during the session of the Legislative Council of N.W.F.P., Malik Kudah Baksh, referred to this Booklet which was published to define the status of women according to Islamic teachings, see the *Proceedings of the N.W.F.P. Legislative Council, 3rd March and 6th November 1935*, Ibid., p. 16.

71. Ibid.

72. Several Muslim Newspapers such as *Haqiqat*, *Hamari Awaz*, were urging the Indian Muslims to give their whole hearted support to the Bill and get it passed. So, they might regain their lost honour, see Satyanand Joshi, Government Reporter, *The Note on the Press*, Confidential, No. 28 of 1936 for the Weekending 11 July 1936, (Superintendent Printing and Stationery, U.P., Allahabad, India).

73. Extracts from the *Official Report of the Legislative Assembly Debates*, Reference Papers, (Record Department Parliamentary Branch, 19 May 1939), L/P&J/7/943, pp. 2528–44, IOL.

74. Among the several amendments of the Committee were those of the substitution of the phrase 'Muslim' for 'Moslem', the exclusion of the word 'including British Baluchistan' from the sub clause 2 of Clause 1, according to the Government India Act 1935. Another amendment was the insert of the word 'save' as regard to agricultural land after sucession and finally the substitution for the word 'divorce' with the 'dissolution of marriage.' Ibid., n.p.

75. See in this context the Statement of the Secretary of *Anjuman-e-Islam*, Jorhat to the Select Committee, Judical Department Record, No. J 507/ 4100 GT. Government of Assam, dated 20 July 1936, ibid., n.p.

76. See the Statement of Sir Muhammad Yamin Khan, M.L.A., from Agra, *Official Report of the Legislative Assembly Debates: Opinion on the Muslim Personal Law (Shariat Application Bill*, (Reference Papers, Record Department, Parlimentary Branch, 19 May 1938), ibid., pp. 2529–44.

77. Raziq-ul-Khairi, 'Savan-e-Rashid-ul-Khairi', *Ismat*, Vol. 113, No. 1 and 2, July and August 1964, p. 704.

78. See the statement of Fazal-i-Haq Paracha, *Official Report of the Legislative Assembly Debates Opinion on the Muslim Personal Law*, 19 May 1938, pp. 2528–44.

79. Shahida Lateef, *Muslim Women in India: Political and Private Realities 1989–1990*, p. 70.

80. Letter from Secretary to the Government of the United Provinces to the Government of India, *Legal Department Record*, No. F. 129-135, 21 July 1936. L/P&J/7/943, n.p., IOL.

81. Ibid.

82. Letter from Secretary to the Government of India to the Government of Madras, *Legal Department Record*, No. 412-6, dated 9 July 1936, ibid., n.p.

83. See the Statement of Bar Association, Virajpet, ibid., n.p.

84. Tahir Mahmood, *Muslim Personal Law*, p. 31.

85. Quran, 4: 34–35.

86. Tahir Mahmood, *Muslim Personal Law*, p. 54

87. Raziq-ul-Khairi, *Savan-e-Rashid-ul-Khairi*, pp. 494–95.

88. Tahir Mahmood, *Muslim Personal Law*, p. 55.

89. *Government of India, Legislative Department Record*, 1938, L/P&J/7/ 1839, n.p., IOL.

90. See, *Hamari Awaz*, and *Qaumi Akbhar*, Satyanan Joshi, Government Reporter, *Note on the Press*, Confidential No. 9, for the Weekending, 29 February 1936, (Superintendent Printing and Stationery, Allahabad, 1936), p. 3.

91. *Legislative Assembly Debates*, seventh session of the Fifth Legislative Assembly, 31 January to 22 February 1938, Vol. 1 (Manager of Publication Delhi, Government of India Press, Simla, 1938), p. 877.

92. The four years rule is, however, not inflexible according to Maliki Law. If someone is missing after battle between the Muslims and non-Muslims, the wife of that missing person is required to wait for a year only. According to *Bidayat al Mujtahid*, of Ibn Rushid, the wife of such person can observe *iddat* soon after the battle. The period of four years can be reduced to one year when the wife has already waited for a considerable time for her husband or when it is feared that she may be led astray on account of the absence of her husband and may commit that which is not lawful, as noted by Maulana Ashraf Ali Thanawi in *Heelat al Najiza*. It would thus appear that under Maliki Law the period of four years can be reduced on the principle of necessity or the exigency of the situation. In this situation no fault can be found with the provision of the Clause 1 of the Dissolution of Muslim Marriages Act of 1939, see Aftab Husain, *Status of Women in Islam*, (Law Publishing Company, Lahore 1987), p. 671.

93. Under the Shafi Law, the inability of the husband to provide maintenance, wilful or otherwise, is a cause for dissolution of marriage by a *kazi*. The view of Imam Shafi is also shared by the Hanblis. On the other hand, Jafris and Zaidis hold the same view as the Hanafis. According to Hanafi Law, failure to maintain wife is no ground for dissolution of marriage. In this case the *kazi* shall authorise the wife to raise loans on the credit of the husband, ibid., p. 672.

94. The basis of this rule is the principle of disappearance of the husband or his remaining missing otherwise than on the principle of *Mafqud ul Khabar*, according to Shafi and Hanafi laws this is not a ground for the dissolution of marriage. But according to Hanbali law, husband's disappearance for six months without any excuse is sufficient. Malikis have two views; according to one: three years' disappearance confers such rights upon the wife of such person; the other view states: one year is sufficient, ibid., p. 676.

95. This provision also contravenes the Quranic principle of *faimsakun bil maaruf* (must be retained in honour) or *au tasrihun bi ehsan* (or released in kindness). It would not be lawful for the husband to torture his wife by keeping her in suspense by desertion and by failing to perform his marital duties, see Quran, 2:29.

96. The Hanafi Law only considers those defects as ground for dissolution of marriage which make consummation impossible. Such defects are impotency and mutilation of the male organ. On the other hand Maliki and Shafi laws consider insanity and leprosy to be defects which entitle the woman to claim dissolution of marriage. For example, leprosy, according to these laws, is included in such defect because of infection which is transmitted to children, and no woman would like to have intimate relations with a husband suffering from such disease, see Aftab Husain, *Status of Women in Islam*, p. 680.

97. The provision of matters relating to child marriage and option of puberty as well as the question of repugnancy is according to the law of the Quran and sunnah, see the first section of this chapter.

98. The right of dissolution of marriage on the ground of cruelty accrues from the contravention of the injunction of the Quran which explains that woman must be retained in honour or released in kindness. According to Islamic teachings, marriage is designed to serve as a check on immorality. If a man himself leads an immoral life or forces his wife to lead an immoral life, his actions are incompatible with the object of marriage. In the same way, assaulting or abusing the wife is also likely to make her life miserable. Islam does not allow spouses to live a life of perpetual agony. Hanafi Law does not consider the dissolution of marriage on the basis of cruelty. On the other hand Shafi law provides that if the discord between husband and wife is of a grave nature, the *Kazi* would appoint two arbitrators, one to represent each party enjoined in the verse of the Quran that 'And if you fear a breach between them (husband and wife) twain, appoint an arbiter from his folk and an arbiter from her folk. If they desire amendment Allah will make them of one mind.' The agent can separate the husband and wife, see Quran 4:35.

99. *Legislative Assembly Debates*, seventh session of the Fifth Legislative Assembly, 31st January to 22nd February 1938, p. 319.

100. Ibid., p. 626.
101. Ibid.
102. Ibid., p. 320.
103. Tahir Mahmood, *Muslim Personal Law*, p. 58.
104. By giving the reference of the *fatawa*, issued by *Taj-ul-Ulum*, Lucknow, Sayyed Ahmed Raza Jaffri argued that without the appointment of Muslim judges, the cases of the dissolution of a marriage of Muslim woman could not be conducted, see his article, 'Qanun Tansikhat-e-Nikah-e-Muslimat ka Hashar', *Ismat*, Vol. 76, No. 4, April 1946, pp. 294–95.
105. *Tehzib-e-Niswan*, Vol. 43, No. 32, 10 August 1940, pp. 777–79
106. Ibid.
107. Ibid.,Vol. 43, No. 42, August 1940, p. 511.
108. Jamila Begum, 'Tansikh-e-Nikah Act', Ibid., Vol. 43, No. 37, 15 September 1940, pp. 930–32.
109. *Report of the Health Survey and Development Committee*, Vol. 1, p. 7.

5

OPENING UP A PUBLIC SPACE FOR WOMEN: THE ROLE OF POLITICAL ENFRANCHISEMENT

The campaign for Indian women's suffrage which began after the enactment of the Montagu-Chelmsford Reforms in 1919 sought to bring about radical changes in the role of women in public life. Central to this new development was the idea of sex-equality as symbolized by the vote. This, in turn, went on to influence their own perception of themselves, encouraging them to determine their personal arena, their national role, their interests, and their activities. It also provided them with a platform from which they could influence both the Governments as well as political parties to support their cause. Moreover, it increasingly led to the realization, as the Report of Indian Statutory Commission in 1930 noted, that India could not reach the position to which it aspired in the world until its women played their due part as educated citizens.[1]

The growing awareness on the part of Indian women had a curious double-faced character of its own. Initially, feminist groups sought to mobilize all women, without consideration of community, on the basis of common issues such as education, health care and the struggle against such social evils as child marriage. One of the earliest examples of women from different communities coming together on a larger scale was the formation of women's organizations like the *Mahila Parshad* (Ladies's Congress) in 1908 and the *Bharat Stri Mahamandal* (All India Women's Organization) in 1910.[2] As they pursued their objectives, these organizations were also extending in practice the feminist agenda from social to political rights. This enabled them to bring the issue of their civil rights to the centre of the national political stage. Their cause also received publicity and support at the international level, particularly from some British women's groups.[3]

However, growing communalism between Muslims and Hindus had critical consequences for the women's movement in the country. The hardening of the communal divide did not leave women untouched. We can see this happening in the campaign against the partition of Bengal, when Hindu women were mobilized on a large scale by employing traditional Hindu motifs of goddesses of war and of the country itself as the Mother goddess.[4]

The foundation of Muslim League in 1906 represented a major political step taken towards the crystallizing of a distinct Indian Muslim community identity. The campaign for a Muslim University at Aligarh proved to be another important landmark in the same direction. This movement, as Minault and Lelyveld have noted, was 'an effort to create an all-India Muslim Constituency and to carve out for it a decisive piece of political power'.[5] Muslim women made generous donations for the establishment of the Muslim University 'National Fund Scheme'.[6]

The fact that Muslims were in a minority in India went on, over time, to mould the very character of the socio-political reforms that began to be introduced in the early twentieth century. Western educated Muslims were increasingly concerned about the implications of this status for their political future and community interests. Thay stressed on the necessity of communal safeguards to protect them from the sheer numerical predominance of the Hindus. Replying to the memorandum presented by a deputation of Muslims headed by the Aga Khan, Lord Minto, the then Viceroy of India declared that 'any electoral representation in India would be doomed to mischievous failure which aimed at granting a personal enfranchisement regardless of the beliefs and traditions of the communities composing the population of this Continent'.[7] Lord

Minto's reply to the deputation was characterized by Lady Minto
(in her diary) as 'nothing less than the pulling back of sixty-two
million people from joining the ranks of the seditious
opposition'.[8] From then onwards special safeguards and
reservations for Muslims were introduced by the Government.
These measures further strengthened communal consciousness
not just among the Muslims, but among other communities as
well. Women, too, did not remain immune from this.
Increasingly, the political mobilization of women came to
interact both with national as well as communal agendas. To
examine this process, the present chapter mainly focuses on the
following points:

(a) Constitutional developments *vis-à-vis* women's status in
    India.
(b) Muslim women and the construction of community politics.
(c) Muslim women and the general elections of 1946.

CONSTITUTIONAL DEVELOPMENTS *VIS-À-VIS* WOMEN'S STATUS IN INDIA 1919–1935

The question of women's suffrage was first raised from the
platform of the Women's Indian Association in 1917. A
delegation which was organized by an Irish suffragette, Margaret
Gillespie Cousins, and led by Sarojini Naidu, waited upon the
committee headed by Mr Montagu and Lord Chelmsford to ask
for the enfranchisement of Indian women. The idea, however,
was rejected on the grounds that orthodox opinion would oppose
it. Also that the social conditions of India made it premature to
extend the franchise to Indian women when so large a proportion
of the male electors themselves required education in the
responsible use of the vote.[9] When the Government of India Bill
of 1919 was enacted, it excluded women from the vote, but the
statute allowed provincial assemblies to drop the exclusion
clause if they so wished. The exclusion clause was then dropped
by some of the provincial assemblies: Madras was the first

province to give women the right to vote in 1921, Bombay and U.P. gave the right of a vote in 1923, while in Bengal the right was given in 1929. Among the Indian states the initiative was first taken by the State of Travancore in 1920 and its example was later followed by the states of Mysore and Cochin.

Having won the right to vote, some women were admitted to these legislatures. Dr Lakshmi Amil, for instance, was not only elected as a member of the Madras Legislature but was also nominated its Deputy President. She introduced the *Devadasi Bill* which aimed to reform the Hindu custom of offering girls for temple prostitution.[10] However, because their participation in politics was still very limited, women continued to insist on the expansion of their suffrage particularly through organizations such as the Women's Indian Association and its allies. They demanded the removal of property qualifications which disqualified most women as they had no independent share in family property.[11] The number of those women who possessed property in their own right—a franchise qualification—was exceedingly limited. Another limitation was that no woman was entitled to sit in the Council of State or to vote in elections to it. In this situation, the political reforms of 1919 were considered to be wholly inadequate and a great need was felt for further representation of Indian women. The first elections for the new legislatures took place in October 1920. The extent to which the property qualifications limited women's participation can be seen from Table 1.

Table 1
The proportion of provincial electorates according to male and female population on the basis of property qualification in 1921

Province	Electors, male and female (women electors in square brackets population	Proportion of male electors to adult male population	Proportion of female electors to adult female population
Bombay	7,59,000 [39,000]	13.4 %	.8 %
Bengal	11,73,000 [38,000]	9.7	.3
U.P.	15,89,000 [51,000]	12.4	.4
Punjab	6,97,000 [21,000]	11.9	.5
Bihar & Orissa	3,73,000 [Nil]	4.6	Nil
Assam	2,50,000 [3,000]	14.2	.2
C.P. & Berar	1,69,000 [Nil]	5.2	Nil
Madras	13,65,000 [1,16,000]	11.6	1.0

Source: See note 12.

In 1926, when the third Assembly elections were held, there was some increase in the number of women voters in different provinces. The striking disparity between the number of male and female voters, however, remained. In Madras, where the total number of voters was 2,77,582, the number of women voter was only 18,375. In Bombay, in the United Provinces and in the Punjab, the corresponding figures were 1,59,418 and 4,404 1,94,458, and 6,071 and 82,929 and 2,065 respectively.[13]

This great disparity was a major issue for the Simon Commission which was set up in 1927 to examine the working of the Montagu-Chelmsford Reforms. In its report, the Commission considered the question of women's suffrage to be a key issue on account of the remarkable progress which had been made in the country since 1919. The Commission desired to increase the existing ratio of women to men voters, but felt that it was far better to adopt the measure gradually, though steadily, by reconsidering the qualification of women's franchise. The Commission suggested further qualifications for women's franchise which included (i) being the wife (of more than twenty-five years of age) of a man who had a property qualification to vote, and (ii) being a widow over that age, whose husband at the time of his death was so qualified. In addition, it was recommended that educated women over twenty-one years of age be considered qualified in exactly the same way as men.[14]

The Commission, however, produced an immediate outcry in India on the grounds that it had no Indian members, that the fate of the country was being decided over the heads of Indian representatives and that it was, therefore, a national insult. As a result, in 1929 a boycott of the Simon Commission was organized across India which was supported by all the major political groups in the country. The All Parties Conference held in the same year demanded adult suffrage for both men and women.

WOMEN'S SUFFRAGE AS A NATIONAL PHENOMENON

The British response to Indian opposition to the Simon Report was to call for a series of Round Table Conferences to discuss constitutional reforms. These conferences played an important role in promoting women's suffrage in the country. The first Conference started in London on 12 November 1930. Indian women were represented by Begum Shah Nawaz and Mrs P. Subbarayan, both of whom believed that women needed reserved seats on the grounds that this was a necessary route for achieving parity with men.[15] A memorandum was submitted by them during the first session of the Conference. It demanded (i) that special considerations should be given to the political status of women under the new constitution by reserving seats for them in legislatures and (ii) that the property and educational qualifications for women should be removed. To fulfil these demands they proposed that a clause be inserted in the constitution, or any declaration of fundamental rights attached to it, stating that sex would not be a disqualification in any way and that men and women would have equal rights of citizenship.[16] In the same way, property and educational qualifications for the vote were considered quite inadequate because only a small number of women held property in their own right and few were educated. In addition, they sought to have the voting age reduced from 25 to 21.[17] In arguing for special reserved seats for women, they pointed out that more than a hundred and twenty million 'hapless' women in India were denied many basic rights and that it was for the sake of those women that seats should be reserved in different constituencies.[18]

Both Begum Shah Nawaz and Mrs Subbarayan also had a chance to address the first session of the Conference under the Chairmanship of Ramsay Macdonald. On behalf of the women of India, Begum Shah Nawaz made an earnest appeal to the Chairman, saying:

We have taken our problems in hand, and are trying to tackle them day by day; with the help of God we hope to achieve-and achieve very soon—that Western freedom of speech and action, combined with Eastern restraint which is the ideal of our womanhood. The social reform of a country depends mostly upon its women. With the best intention in the world, a foreign government may introduce excellent measures of social reform, but because it is a foreign government, the reforms advocated by it are always looked upon with suspicion. As soon as we have the legislation of our country in our own hands, we can better do away with some of the social evils existing today, just as Japan, Turkey, Persia, Mysore, Baroda, Bhopal and Travancore have been able to do. Almost as soon as our men got the franchise, they did not hesitate in giving us our share; and now that the women of India are coming forward and taking an active part in the political life of the country, the solution of all these problems will not be difficult to find. With women to guide in social matters, the men of a country can achieve greater success in social reform.[19]

Similar views were expressed by Mrs Subbarayan at the Eighth Plenary Meeting of the Conference. She directly related the progress of the new India to the political status of women by saying that 'if India is to take her rightful place among the modern nations of the world her women should be given full opportunity to contribute their share to her service.[20]

However, the participation of both Begum Shah Nawaz and Mrs Subbarayan and their demand for the reservation of seats for women was strongly opposed by those groups of women who were lobbying the issue on feminist as well as on nationalist grounds. For example, in one of its letters to Lord Snell, Under Secretary of State for India, the Women's Indian Association's (London Branch) demanded the extension of women's representation on a national level, arguing that as both the women (Begum Shah Nawaz and Mrs Subbarayan), due to their communal and regional backgrounds, could not become the real representatives of Indian women as a whole.[21]

The Congress boycott of the first Round Table Conference appeared in the form of Civil Disobedience Movement in India in 1931. By taking advantage of this movement, many nationalist feminists in particular belonging to Congress rejected all suggestions for the reservation of seats for women. But all of a sudden, a dramatic change occurred in their attitude after the Gandhi-Irwin Pact in 1932 and the Congress's consent to participation in the second Round Table Conference. The nationalist feminist Mrs Sarojini Naidu, the President of the All-India Women's Association and the former President of Congress, was invited to attend the second session of the Round Table Conference alongside both Begum Shah Nawaz and Mrs Subbarayan. Due to these new developments, nationalist feminists succeeded in dominating the scene. Two different memorandums on the question of the reservation of seats for Indian women were presented on the one hand by Mrs Subbarayan, and on the other by Begum Shah Nawaz and Mrs

Sarojini Naidu. Mrs Subbarayan's Memoranda was based on the belief that if ordinary channels of election were to be opened to women, it was unlikely that they would be able to secure any seats in the elections. Even in western countries, where it had been the custom for women to take part in public affairs, only a very few of them were elected to the Legislatures.[22] On the other hand, in a country like India, as she noted, where there was still strong prejudice on the part of both men and women against their coming into councils, it was not easy for women to become involved in the legislating process until public opinion reached the proper level of education when women candidates would be accepted in ordinary polls.[23] In replying to the objections raised by the three women's associations (All India Women's Conference, The Women's Indian Association and the National Council of Women in India) she argued:

> Their opposition is apparently based on the belief that, if equality of civic rights is granted to women in India, equality of opportunity in civic service will automatically follow, and that, owing to the part played by women in the recent political struggle women now realise their strength and do not require special provision. These theories seem to me to be far removed from the realities of the situation. These three women's organizations are associations of importance, but I cannot admit that they speak for the entire womanhood of India. While welcoming the fact that the political struggle has brought many thousands of women out into public life, I feel it essential to acquire a true perspective of the whole picture, and to realise that there remain more than a hundred and twenty million women and girls in India who are still in a state of civic inertia and who have not yet attained self-confidence or political consciousness. It is for the sake of this overwhelming majority of women that I believe special provision to be necessary. I am convinced that one practical step forward, which will ensure the presence of women on the Legislatures, working side by side with men as a normal feature of our political life, will do more for them than any theories of equality. [24]

On the other hand, the second Memorandum, which was presented by both Mrs Sarojini Naidu and Begum Shah Nawaz on behalf of the three women's associations of India, criticized those small groups of people either in India or in Britain who justified 'temporary' concessions to secure the adequate representation of women in the Legislatures through reservation of seats, nomination or co-option whether by statute, convention, or at the discretion of the provincial and central Government. Any form of preferential treatment, they warned, would be to violate the integrity of the universal demand of Indian women for absolute equality of political status.[25] To keep the issue at the centre of political debate they also referred another joint Memorandum which was endorsed by the three Indian women's associations in August 1931. The Memorandum demanded the rights and obligations of all citizens without any bar on account of sex, or disability, religion, caste, or creed in regard to public employment, office, power or honour and the exercise of any trade or calling.[26]

In fact, the increasing participation of nationalist feminists in the Conference was the outcome of the increasing engagement in women's issues on the part of Congress and the Muslim League. In particular, Gandhi became an important advocate of the expansion of the presence of women of all classes and cultures in public life. Mr Gandhi's understanding had grown through time from his early image of womanhood which revolved around home and family to his appeal in the civil disobedience movement of 1930 to women to come out of their houses and join the public protest.[27] In this context, Sarojini Naidu was the voice of Gandhi at the Round Table Conference. Thus, on 30 November 1930 she echoed her leader:

if we have not succeeded in solving for the moment those purely artificial questions of vulgar fractions, that arithmetic which divided a power into little fractions for this community and that community, I do not feel that it affects in any way the vital issue of liberty for my land.[28]

As regards the Muslim League, its early attitude towards the role of women and their emancipation was reflected in the form of the tribute which was paid to remarkable services of 'Bi Amman', the mother of Muhammad Ali and Shaukat Ali, and Begum Hasrat Mohani during the *Khilafat* Movement.[29] However, when the enthusiastic period of the *Khilafat* Movement ended, the League turned its whole attention to constructing community politics rather than to broadening Indian nationalism. In this situation the question of women's political enfranchisement was dealt with through the reservation of seats for them on the basis of particular qualifications suggested by the Simon Commission. Arguments emphasized that most voters had little idea of the full value and effect of their votes.[30] On such grounds the participation of Begum Shah Nawaz and her demand for the reservation of seats for woman in the first session of the Conference can be cited as an example of League's particular behaviour in this regard.

The changing tone of the League, however, could be found in the form of the joint Memorandum presented during the course of the second session of the Conference by Sarojini Naidu and Begum Shah Nawaz on behalf of nationalist feminists. The League fully supported the idea that women should be qualified to vote on the basis of their property and education and not on the basis of their husbands or other relatives.[31] It seems that the changing behaviour of the League towards women's political status was the outcome of a specific assurance of the Muslim share of power that was provided in the Communal Award. More women's votes would add to the numerical strength of Muslim community in India. Jalal describes this change as 'a product of political calculations, and not a sign of a sea-change in its attitude towards women'.[32] In general, on the part of Indian women, however, although this action surrended the feminist agenda to the preoccupations of the politics of identity, it was a bold step which helped to prise open further space for women in national life.

BRITISH FEMINISTS AND THE QUESTION OF INDIAN WOMEN'S POLITICAL RIGHTS

British feminists played an important role in keeping the issue of the political rights of Indian women at centre stage. In the past British women activists had been believers in the role of the British Raj in improving and reconstructing Indian society. In the early twentieth century, however, their concerns increasingly came to clash with the developing politics of the colonial state. In consequence, they became part of the growing discourse between the colonial state and Indian political organizations over the future role of women.

The construction of feminism under the formative influence of this democratic process was naturally specified as a logical and organic link between the women of imperialism and colonialism. Besides these new developments in the context of colonial and imperial relationships, the shared resistance of the feminists of both east and west towards the idea of women as an 'inferior sex', biologically and socially ordained, led to the realization that at least women could share with each other the sorrows and griefs of their lives.

Practical support from British women came as a stimulus to the beginning of the women's suffrage movement in India during the First World War. At the same time as they were fighting for further extension of their rights in Britain. Practical support came again in 1930 when they demanded that they as well as Indian women should be represented in the forthcoming Round Table Conference. Before the Round Table delegates arrived in London, the issue became more important after the involvement of several British women's associations.

Prominent among these were the Women's Freedom League, National Union of Societies for Equal Citizenship, St. Joan's Social and Political Alliance, Conservative Women's Reform Association, Edinburgh Equal Citizenship Society, and The Young Women's Christian Association of Great Britain. They sent several letters and memoranda to the Prime Minister Ramsay Macdonald and Mr W. Wedgewood Benn Secretary of

State for India. They demanded the participation of British women in the proceedings of the forthcoming Round Table Conference.[33] An appropriate role, in their opinion, could be played only by those women who had awareness and knowledge of India and its social problems in particular with reference to Indian womanhood.[34] Among the names recommended by these associations were Eleanor Rathbone, M.P., H.M. Hamilton, M.P. and Susan Lawrence, M.P., Mrs Pethick Lawrence, President, Women's Freedom League and Lady Irwin, the wife of the Viceroy of India Lord Irwin.[35] The Government refused to consider their representations. But two Indian women were nominated for the Conference.

The nomination of these women, however, was challenged by British organizations, although the grounds of this opposition were rather different from that of Indian feminists. For example, the Young Christian Women's Association of Great Britain called it an 'inadequate representation' which could not be engaged in framing and working for the new constitutions of India.[36] Associations like St. Joan's Social and Political Alliance, were of the opinion that this disability could be removed only if the women of India were represented by their nationwide associations. For this purpose the Association proposed the names of Mrs Annie Besant, Mrs Sarojini Naidu, Mrs Hamid Ali, Mrs Brijlal Nehru, Mrs Kamaladevi Chattopadhyaya, Rani Rajwadi, and Mrs Rama Rau.[37] It should be noted that the driving force behind this motivation was the Women's Indian Association (London branch) that had already been involved in the campaign against both Begum Shah Nawaz and Mrs Subbarayan on the grounds of their communal and regional background as well their anti-feminist behaviour during the course of the first session of the Conference.

Indeed, the Association succeeded in winning the unanimous support of British feminists in the form of joint statements and meetings occasionally held at London. One prominent example was the formation of a joint deputation including Mrs Brijlal Nehru, Miss A. Mehta and Lady Ginwade (The Indian Women's Association), Miss Clare Collison and Mrs Littlejohn (The

British Common Wealth League), Dr Knight, (The Women's Freedom League) and Miss Hynes, (St. Joan's Social and Political Alliance). The Deputation met Lord Snell, a Parliamentary Under Secretary of State of India, and presented a memorandum. It demanded that Indian women should have a voice in the selection of representatives to the Conference and nothing could be done for the formation of an Indian Constitution unless men and women of this country did it together.[38]

Similar efforts were also made by many individuals, prominent among those was Eleanor Rathbone.[39] Before the Round Table delegates arrived in London, she had given much time to a Memorandum devoted to the status and welfare of Indian women in the future constitution of India. The Memorandum appeared in print in December 1930 with the signatures of a group of men and women experienced in Indian affairs including five women Members of Parliament, Lady Astor, Lady Cynthia Mosley, Megan Lloyd George, Edith Picton-Turberville and Eleanor herself, while Sir Philip Hartog acted as a chairman of the group.[40] It criticized the existing franchise position as it affected women largely as a result of the property qualification. It demanded the extension of the right of a vote not only by accepting the recommendations of the Simon Commission but also through its further extension to the wives and widows of men with property qualifications.[41] It also emphasized the need to secure women's rights through their participation in all those committees and sub-committees designed to deal with the enfranchisement of India.[42]

Although British feminists were not able to secure their representation at the Conference, their continuous efforts provided a stimulus to female suffrage that they experienced during the British suffrage campaign in the early decades of the twentieth century. In the case of India, however, it was not a straight fight between suffragists and anti-suffragists but a simple process of democracy and the demand for political rights for women.[43]

THE FORMATION OF INDIAN FRANCHISE COMMITTEE AND THE PRESSING DEBATE OF WOMEN'S POLITICAL STATUS

To address franchise issues in India, the Franchise Sub-Committee of the Indian Round Table Conference recommended the creation of the Indian Franchise Committee under the chairmanship of the Marquess of Lothian, Parliamentary Under Secretary of State for India. In the light of the letter of instruction written by the Prime Minister Ramsay MacDonald, the Committee paid special importance to the question of securing a more adequate enfranchisement of women than the existing system, which applied to women the same qualification as to men and had produced a woman's electorate numbering less than one-twentieth of the total male electorate.[44]

WOMEN'S STAND POINT

As soon as the procedure of the formation of the Franchise Committee began in December 1931, several women's organizations and feminist groups, in Britain as well as in India, began to pressurize the Government on this issue. In particular, after the possibility of nominating a British woman to the Franchise Committee, they set out to make the best of this opportunity. The names proposed for this nomination included Mrs Pethick Lawrence and Dr Maud Royden, who it was considered had already won the confidence of Indian women during the course of the Round Table Conference. Among the other names proposed, were Mrs Eva Hubback, Parliamentary Secretary to the National Union of Societies of Equal Citizenship, and Miss Margaret Fry, the Principal of Somerville College, Oxford. However, most of the organizations and feminist groups thought that Eleanor Rathbone should be appointed to the Franchise Committee as she had by this time acquired an exhaustive knowledge of the Indian franchise problem as a whole, as well as its bearing on the political status of women. There was much disappointment among women's organizations therefore when Miss Mary Pickford, M.P. a leading woman Conservative was nominated instead of Eleanor Rathbone.[45] Among the Indian women, Mrs Subbarayan was nominated as a Member of the Committee. This was a great defeat for those feminists who believed in full adult suffrage for men and women, and desired to solve the problem on equal basis. The selection of Mrs Subbarayan, despite the demands of Indian nationalist feminists, reflected the Government view that full adult suffrage was not yet a practical proposition.

THE FRANCHISE COMMITTEE AND INDIAN WOMANHOOD

The Committee started its work in India on 1 February 1931 and visited most provinces. Everywhere, many women including some strict *purdah* observing women came forward as witnesses either through the representation of their organizations or in an individual capacity. Another important aspect of the issue was the growing interest of many Muslim women in sharing these views with their Hindu and Christian counterparts. One specific example was that of the women of Madras, where the Women's India Association and Muslim Ladies Association collaborated in mobilizing women in the Presidency to influence government policy. Both Rahmat-un-issa Begum and Nazir Husain Begum, the Vice President and Secretary of the latter Association, appeared before the Franchise Committee in *purdah*. In their joint statement, they emphasized their support for an adult franchise based on registration and payment of a small fee.

The qualifications of property and some sort of literary test, as they said, were not justified in the social context of Indian women whose position still had to be protected through laws such as the *Shariat* legislation.[46] The same concerns came from the women of Bengal, both Muslims and Hindus. The property qualification in their opinion would only enfranchise 41,000 women out of an adult female population of 11.2 million. They demanded the enfranchisement of literate women who were above twenty-one years old.[47] The women of Bihar and Orissa suggested that the qualifying amount of property held in their own right by women should be fixed at a minimum payment of Rs three as rent or tax on rented estate.[48]

The nationalist campaign on the question of women's political status was led by the All-India Women's Conference. With the collaboration of its Hindu and some Muslim members, the Conference targeted the idea of women being disqualified by their sex from voting. In one of its letter sent to J.G. Laithwaite, Secretary of the Franchise Committee, Mrs Lakshmi Rajwade, President of the All-India Women's Conference, argued that any attempt to solve the question of the proper enfranchisement of women that was based on the possession of property through a male relative must necessarily be foredoomed to failure as it would obviously tend to perpetuate the idea of dependency of woman on man.[49] She said that it was quite opposite to the very root of the principle of equality of the sexes for which the womanhood of India was actively struggling.[50] Moreover, the condition of the property qualification was very unfair to poor women who would never be able to exercise their right of a vote. She argued that in this situation mere literacy could not become the real test of qualification. It was obvious that a woman who was considered fit to manage her household duties was competent to cast the vote. Thus any conditioning, of the right of franchisement on the grounds of either property or literacy qualification was entirely at variance with the principle of equal rights and equal opportunities for all.[51] She emphasized that any man or woman on reaching the age of twenty-one should be entitled to the free exercise of the vote.[52]

The All-India Women's Conference also sought to convince other women's organizations to take the same line of argument. The efforts of the All-India Women's Conference, the Women's Indian Association and the National Council of Women in India, came in the form of a joint declaration submitted to the Franchise Committee in 1932. The pressing point was the introduction of the system of adult suffrage which was looked upon by these associations as the only way to symbolize democracy in India.[53]

THE QUESTION OF THE RESERVATION OF SEATS ON COMMUNAL BASIS

The question of the reservation of seats on a communal basis was a challenging issue for nationalist feminists who strongly repudiated it either through their associations or in their individual capacity. Their objection to being dragged into communal controversies was based on their desire not to undermine their joint struggle through which they had been opening up this important public space for themselves. In one of their letters to Lord Lothian, the Women's Indian Association, Egmore, Madras strongly opposed the proposal for the formation of separate communal electorates for either men or women. Such expedients, they warned, would not prompt unity among the communities, castes, creeds and races of India. The idea was even rejected by those women who had favoured the general reservation of women's seats in different constituencies. One example was Mrs Subbarayan, who now declared to the Committee that

> in fairness to the demand made by women, (associations) and in the best interests of the country any special constituencies that may be formed for them should comprise all voters, men and women, of all classes, castes and creeds in the area concerned. Women's representatives in the legislatures should be there not as members of particular communities but as representatives of women of all castes and creeds.[54]

However, in the presence of growing communal tension and party politics it was not easy for Indian feminists to sustain their demand for long. In particular, the minority nature of the Muslim community led to the realization that communal settlement was the very foundation of the constitution in India and, unless the foundation was soundly laid, the safety of the whole structure would be imperilled forever. The arguments of Muhammad Yakub, M.L.A. and Members of the Franchise Committee, reflected these views:

There is one more point in this connection which needs elucidation, and it is this as regards the joint and separate electorate, Muslim women will have to be bracketed with their men, and cannot be allowed to go outside the community. It was pointed out that Muslim women's witnesses were opposed to communal electorates. But, in the first place, only about a half-a-dozen Muslim women, selected by provincial committees were produced before our Committee as witnesses and they cannot be considered as representing the views of all the Muslim women in the country. In the second place what these witnesses demanded was the general adult suffrage, and nothing more and nothing less. The question of separate or a joint electorate could not arise according to their recommendations. None of them has advocated electorate for Muslim women in case where adult suffrage was not granted and separate electorates formed the basis of enfranchisement for the Muslims.[55]

THE RECOMMENDATIONS OF THE COMMITTEE

Examining all these factors, the Committee arrived at two recommendations. The first was to increase the number of women on the electoral roll in order to compel candidates to consider their interests and opinions, to awaken political interest between women and to make their vote an effective lever particularly in providing reforms of special concern to women and children.[56] The Committee was of the opinion that both the property and educational qualifications as suggested by the Indian Statutory Commission were quite inadequate and would not remove the disparity in voting strength between men and women. It was also of the opinion that this disparity would cause great dissatisfaction among women's organizations and others who gave individual evidence on the grounds that it would perpetuate the idea of dependency of women on men and would merely duplicate the husband's vote.[57] In addition the proposed educational qualification would not work because the number of women who would obtain the franchise would be quite inadequate with the ratio of men to women ranging from 8:1 in Madras to 68:1 in Assam.[58]

To overcome this disparity, the Committee proposed two extra qualifications designed to expand the number of women voters: (i) literacy and (ii) being the wife of a voter possessing a certain property qualification. As regards literacy this was defined for census purposes as the ability to read and write a letter in any language. In this way it was considered necessary for those women who could read and write to satisfy the officer in charge of the electoral roll, either by a personal application or by the production of a certificate, that they could fulfil the condition.[59] In the case of a certificate it was said that it should be provided by an authority appointed by the local government such as a magistrate or school teacher, or an inspectress of schools.[60] The provision of literacy as suggested by the Committee would provide an opportunity to vote for unmarried women particularly Muslim women who received their education privately and did not take any public examinations.[61]

The Committee recommended for enfranchisement as council voters the wives of all male voters who possessed the required property qualification except in the Central Provinces where due to the poor economic condition of the province the Committee suggested lowering the property qualification.[62]

Using these two new franchise qualifications, the Committee made a major step towards achieving female equality with men. Table 2 shows the outcome of these proposals.

Table 2
The approximate number of women receiving the vote under various franchise qualification

Province	Independent and property qualification	Literary qualification	Husband's property qualification	Total woman's electorate	The ratio of men to women
Bombay	50,000	1,63,000	5,92,000	7,50,000	4.1
Bengal	5,00,000	3,77,000	8,00,000	15,00,000	4.1
U.P	4,14,000	1,28,000	11,00,000	15,00,000	4.1
Punjab	1,01,000	85,000	3,76,000	4,50,000	5.1

Bihar & Orissa	46,000	77,000	2,80,000	3,50,000	9.1
C.P.	70,000	40,000	2,66,000	3,50,000	5.1
Assam	30,000	40,000	1,92,000	2,20,000	4.1
Madras	7,18,000	3,45,000	7,00,000	15,00,00	4.1

Source: See note 63.

The second recommendation of the Committee dealt with the question of filling the special seats for women in the provincial councils. Although the Committee agreed with the idea of open competition as suggested by the All-India Women's Conference, and other women's associations, it could see that women would be hindered by the prejudice against women taking part in public life and the difficulties in the way of women travelling about to canvass a constituency.[64] The Committee offered alternative solutions to the problem. The first was setting apart seats for women in selected urban areas. The electorate for the purpose in each such area were to belong to that particular area, both men and women; and the voters were to have two votes each, one in the general constituency, and the other for the women's seat.[65] The second was that women could stand for any constituency for which they were qualified, and those women who, if not returned at the head of the poll, obtained the highest percentage of votes as compared with the number of electors on the roll in the constituencies in which women competed, were to be declared elected, up to the number of seats specially reserved for women.[66] There were some issues over which the Franchise Committee suspended judgement: the number of seats to be given to Hindus and Muslims and the number of seats to be given to women.

WOMEN AND THE REPORT OF THE JOINT SELECT COMMITTEE

In April 1933, a Joint Committee of both Houses of Parliament was appointed, with Lord Linlithgow as Chairman, to consider the future Government of India with special reference to the recommendations of the Indian Franchise Committee and the

White Paper proposals published after the third Session of the Round Table Conference.

The suspension of a franchise for women on the communal question led women's representatives (both British and Indian) to concentrate their whole attention on the matter of the extension of the franchise. They targeted the great disparity between the number of male and female voters and the high educational standards proposed in the White Paper. They sought to convince the Committee of the necessity for strengthening the position of women under the new constitution. The development of this social consciousness among the women of India was appreciated by the Committee which declared 'nothing could be more disastrous at this juncture than to create the impression among the women of India that the proposed Constitution treated them of less equal citizenship'.[67] The Committee recommended that the proposals of the White Paper concerning women's franchise be modified. Their recommendations included: (i) that application requirements should be dispensed with altogether; (ii) that literacy qualification should be substituted for the educational qualification; (iii) that the wives, pensioned widows and mothers of Indian officers, non-commissioned officers and soldiers should be enfranchised; and (iv) that the wife of a man who was qualified as an elector under the new constitution should also be enfranchised.[68]

THE FORMATION OF THE INDIAN DELIMITATION COMMITTE

The Indian Delimitation Committee was formed on 31 July 1935 to prepare a complete scheme of delimitation of the constituencies, whether territorial constituencies or constituencies allotted to representatives of special interest, in the legislatures to be established under the provision of the Government of India. Among the important matters of women's franchise discussed by the Committee were the nature of the constituencies, methods of registration and arrangements for facilitating the polling of women.

THE NATURE OF WOMEN'S CONSTITUENCIES

In the matter of the reservation of seats for women, the Committee agreed to secure an adequate representation of women in the legislatures in touch with women's feelings. The more important matter in view of the Committee, however, was the quality of work rather than quantity: the class of candidates should be selective and committed to their aims.[69] For that purpose the Committee suggested the framing of small and selected constituencies for women which could also become helpful in minimizing difficulties and obstacles likely to be met by a candidate in maintaining contact with her constituency.[70]

The recommendations submitted to the Committee by local governments about the reservation of seats, revealed distinct differences of opinion on this subject. For instance, the Governments of Bombay, Madras, the United Provinces, and the Punjab suggested dividing the seats for the representation of women between the urban and rural areas. Bengal Presidency, Bihar and Orissa, Sindh and the Central Provinces however favoured the reservation of seats exclusively to urban areas, while the Government of Assam recommended a permanent single constituency for woman in the area of Shillong.[71]

The most important feature of this new development was the reservation of seats on a communal basis. The different local Governments recommended the reservation of seats for women in special constituencies meant for women, where the proportion of the population of a particular community was high as compared to other communities. For example, in Madras there was one Muslim seat among the eight seats reserved for women which covered the area of Madras City, Chittoor, Madura, and Malabar.[72] The Government of Bombay reserved one seat for a Muslim female representative in Bombay City.[73] In the United Provinces, two seats were reserved for Muslim candidates covering the area of Lucknow and Moradabad. The former was considered the centre of traditional strength of Muslim influence for urban constituencies while the latter district had the largest Muslim female population in the U.P. with the highest percentage of literacy (1.7) of any district.[74] In the Punjab two seats among seven were allotted to Muslim women. The urban constituency covered the areas of the Municipality and Cantonment of Lahore and the rural seat was reserved for Jullundur.[75] In the provinces of Bihar one out of four seats covered the areas of a Muslim female constituency which dealt with the Patna City Municipality administered by the Patna Administration Committee.[76] In the province of Sindh one out of two seats was allotted to Muslims which included the limits of Karachi Port Trust, Manora Cantonment and the municipalities of Hyderabad, Larkana, Sukkur and Shikarpur.[77] While the Government of the Central Provinces, Assam and Orissa suggested special constituencies for women but not on a communal basis.[78]

Indeed, the decision was the reverse of what the nationalist feminists wanted. It was greatly opposed by different women's associations in India as well as in Britain. In India, The All-India Women's Conference started a campaign against the reservation of women's seats on 'communal basis'. The matter was also criticized by the Liaison Group, a joint working committee of several British women associations and the All India Women's Conference. Mrs Ray, the Convenor of the Liaison Group appealed for propaganda work in Britain to urge the necessity of revision of the legal status of women in India.[79]

The efforts of the nationalist feminists, however, proved a cry in the wilderness. Above all, the political wrestling match between the Congress and the League divided their audiences (into the columns of the emotional adherents to which they belonged.) The first appearance of these feminists as communal feminists took place with the demand for the conversion of general seats for women into ones for Hindu female candidates. They believed that if the general seats could be contested by any non-Muslim candidates, the prospect of Hindu women securing the seats would become remote. Therefore it was suggested by them that it should be made clear that these general seats would be reserved for Hindu women.[80]

THE REGISTRATION OF FEMALE VOTERS

Another important matter discussed by the Committee was the registration of female voters. Provincial Governments had different views about this proposal. Prominent among those were the nature of social problems which varied from one place to another. For instance, it was brought to the notice of J.G. Laithwaite, the Secretary of the Indian Delimitation Committee, by the Reform Officer Calcutta, that in the case of married men they would avoid registering the names of their wives (particularly in the case of property qualification on behalf of a husband) as, it was considered a matter of great embarrassment that the names entered on the provincial rolls were indicated as the 'wife of A B C'. On the other hand the situation was quite different where the name of women under educational qualification had been entered by registration officers.[81] The same expression came from the Political and Reform Department, Bombay. In view of social customs, as the Department pointed out, the registration of women was a particularly difficult task and practical difficulties involved were too great to permit the responsibility for the preparation of this part of the roll being imposed on the offices of the Government.[82] In this case it would be more convenient as suggested by the Department that printed forms should be left at each house by village officers who should get them filled as far as possible.[83] On the other hand, in the opinion of the Reform Officer, Punjab as mentioned, in one of his letters to Mr Rhodes, the Joint Secretary of the Committee, the lack of belief in the importance of the vote was the main hindrance in the way of women registering for the vote. He suggested that the major role in this regard could be played by candidates who could prepare the voters by telling them of its importance.[84] The situation in the N.W.F.P. was particularly complicated. In the view of the Secretary to the Government, if the officials charged with the preparation of the male electoral roll were to make house to house enquiries regarding wives who might be qualified for enfranchisement, there would in some cases be a great danger of misunderstandings and possibly serious breaches of the peace.[85]

Apart from the specific difficulties which arose in connection with the application requirement, it was anticipated that, in the early stages of the new constitution, there would be difficulties more or less serious in most provinces in connection with the exercise of the franchise by women. Considering the great interest which was shown by Parliament in facilitating the registration in those provinces in which applications was required under the provision of the Act, and in facilitating polling by women in all provinces, the Committee suggested that leaflets should be issued on a very large scale well in advance of each election, containing the electoral qualifications and similar information. Official notices would in addition be published before the preparation of the electoral roll, calling for applications and explaining the position in regard to their registration.[86] In addition to this proposal, the Committee went on further to suggest that husbands should be allowed to apply on behalf of their wives for registration in all provinces except Punjab and Assam where religious and social reasons were mentioned on the part of the roll of a woman as the 'wife of A B C'. Only in the case of the U.P. a concession was given to women so that they could make their application by letter.[87]

Among the other matters which directly related to the election of women were those of the arrangements for facilitating the polling of women. Several suggestions came from different provincial Governments. After examining all the possibilities the Committee came to the conclusion that it would be desirable if the local Governments spared no effort to arrange that in the special women's constituencies a woman should be in attendance at each polling booth. She would be able, as the Committee said, to assist women who were uncertain of the procedure to be adopted or who felt diffidence in asking questions of male officers.[88]

The recommendations of the Committee were incorporated in the 1935 constitution. Under the new constitution forty-one seats were reserved for women in different provinces on general and communal bases.[89] Table 3 shows the number of seats and voters under the terms of Schedule V, paragraph 8 (B) of the Government of India Act, 1935.

Table 3
The number of women's seats and voters in different provinces on general and communal basis in 1935

Province	Nature of constituency (urban and rural)	No. of seats in different constituencies	Female population in different constituencies	No. of female voter
Bombay	General	5	8,42,135	1,99,041
	Muslim	1	8,310	4,257
Bengal	General	2	3,86,399	63,948
	Muslim	2	1,02,294	9, 380
	Anglo-Indian	1	N.A.	N.A.
U.P.	General	2	12,75,455	1.32,473
	Muslim	2	2,22,838	30,903
Punjab	General	1	1,40,080	62,612
	Muslim	2	2,61,196	38,844
	Sikh	1	3,99,951	56,987
Bihar	General	3	2,11,027	45,484
	Muslim	1	38,238	2,808
C.P.& Berar	General	3	1,65,000	71,000
Assam	General	2	10,900	21,00
Orissa	General	2	1,30,013	10,400
Sindh	General	1	N.A.	N.A.
	Muslim	1		
Madras	General	6	14,86,610	2,10,077
	Muslims	1	70,031	9,028
	Indian Christian	1	20,502	5,404

Source: See note 90

MUSLIM WOMEN AND THE CONSTRUCTION OF COMMUNITY POLITICS

The communalization of female political identity started after the Act of 1935. Before looking at this new political discourse we should keep in mind the background to these developments. The key to this was the general dissatisfaction of Muslims with the Nehru Report of 1928. Although nationalist Muslims, gave their full support to Motilal Nehru, (Chairman of the Nehru Committee), many of its recommendations embodied Congress's vision of a political arrangement for the future of India, denying the right of Muslims to separate electorates and denying their constituent status at the centre as equal to Hindus.[91] After the formal rejection of Muslim demands at the national convention in Calcutta, the majority of Muslim leaders realized that they had failed to convince Congress to arrive at some communal settlement. Mr Muhammad Husain, the Chairman of the Reception Committee of Muslim League in the course of his speech at the twenty-first session of the League, held at Allahabad in 1930 said

> if the mentality of the Hindus would change and the Muslims were assured that their traditions, their religion, their education and their language would not be annihilated and they would be treated like other sons of India, the Muslim would cease to bring up the question of the protection of their rights. But their past experience in local Boards, in every department of the administrations, and even in trade, had been to the contrary.[92]

The hollowness of Congress's claim to speak on behalf of the entire Indian people provided a space to League to show its political strength and the worth of its political claims as a 'representative organization' of Indian Muslims. The formulation of 'fourteen points' by Muhammad Ali Jinnah, after consulting several Muslim leaders became a directive principle for the political future of the majority of Indian Muslims on behalf of the League. One important part of this new strategy was the presidential address of Sir Muhammad Iqbal in the course of the twenty-first session of the League held at Allahabad in 1930. Iqbal called for a Muslim India within India, a state in the north-west consisting of the Muslim majority region of the Punjab, N.W.F.P., Sindh and Baluchistan. The creation of autonomous Muslim States in his view would be in the best interests of India and Islam.[93] For India as he pointed out,

> it means security and peace resulting from an internal balance of power; for Islam, an opportunity to rid itself of the stamp that Arabian Imperialism had given, to mobilize it laws, its original spirit and with the spirit of modern times.[94]

After getting the 'permit of' political identity in the form of the Communal Award in 1932, Indian Muslims, were determined to hold on to it and reject any diminishment of the solid gains that they had made through it. They were not prepared to surrender anything without adequate recompense. The provisions of the Communal Award were incorporated in the Government of India Act in 1935. The result of the general elections of 1937 undermined the claim of both Congress and League to represent their constituencies. Although the former secured clear majorities in six provinces, the results showed that it had very little influence on Muslim masses. The Muslim League also failed to prove itself as a 'popular representative organization' of Indian Muslims: out of a total of 485 Muslim seats, it was able to capture only 105 However, events after the 1937 elections demonstrated that if there was any party which could claim to represent the Muslims, then it was the 'League'. The undemocratic attitude of the Congress, particularly in those provinces where they obtained ministries, meant that Muslim communities had to face certain difficulties. Muslim children who were getting their education in government schools were forced to salute the congress flag and to sing the *Bande Mataram*. 'A hundred and one small pin-pricks and irritations cropped up daily', declared Begum Ikramullah, the Muslim League activist—unimportant in themselves, they were like the proverbial leaf which indicated the way the wind was blowing and the indication in this case was that it was blowing towards Hindu imperialism and Hindu domination which would attempt to exterminate eight hundred years of Muslim influence and culture.[95]

In 1937, it was possible to see Muslim women playing an active role openly in community politics. This development was made possible by the reorganization of the League, under the presidentship of Jinnah. Before this, neither Muslim women nor the League considered the matter of women's political rights and role seriously, concentrating instead on women's social uplift as mentioned before. The main reason was that the *nawabi* and the *begmati* style of leadership of these pioneer organizations could not cater for these kinds of demands. The *zenana adab* with its high 'falutin' language, expensive jewellery, and glittering dresses of the women of Muslim *ashraf* families could deflect attention easily away from the social activities of these organizations. However, by the late 1920s, the growing interest in modern education (English) among the women of *ashraf* families and their social interaction with the women of other communities changed their social outlook. In particular, the formation of All-India Women's Conference, included many Muslim women who began to discuss their social as well as the feminist agenda on national and international level. Specific examples were those of Begum Hamid Ali and Begum Shah Nawaz who worked together for the cause of women.

In the long run, however, women could not escape from the emergence of separate nationalism. The growing rift between the two communities fostered an entirely different environment. Shaista Ikramullah noted how tension was growing daily and communal feeling even poisoned social relations. Several of her Hindu friends dropped her completely and relationships with others became strained and difficult.[96] In this situation the only way of survival seemed to be the consolidation of community and its interests. For Muslim women, an important role was played by women's magazines and newspapers, whose writers began to express a growing interest in nationalist politics. For example, Shaista Ikramullah warned Muslim women in *Ismat* that their continued ignorance about the changing political situation could destroy the whole struggle which had been started for the safeguard of community interests.[97] Gohar Iqbal, a local poetess of Meerut called this struggle a 'Nagmha-e-Bedari' (A Song of Awakening) in one of her poems, published in *Ismat*. And the role of women was called by her 'a light of early morning which tears the darkness and sorrows of the night'.[98] In the same way another female writer, Fatima Jafar from Delhi, called on Muslim women to follow the examples of the women of Turkey, Egypt and Iran who were changing the course of their history. She criticized her Indian Muslim sisters who were ignoring this responsibility by saying that this game (politics) was only meant for men who could bear the burden of responsibility.[99]

On the national level, the Muslim League now began to organize and involve women in politics. Early work of this kind had been led by Begum Muhammad Ali Johar, a Member of the Central Working Committee of the League, who also presided over the women's annual meetings held under the auspices of the League in different parts of India. In 1938 the League established an All-India Muslim Women's Sub-Committee, which aimed to coopt Muslim women to organize them for its cause. The objects of the Sub-Committee, discussed in the twenty-sixth session of the League, held at Patna in 1938 were as follows:

(a) To organize Provincial and District Women's Sub-Committees under the Provincial and District Muslim League.

(b) To enlist a large number of women to the membership of the League.

(c) To carry on an intensive propaganda among Muslim women throughout India, in order to create in them a sense of the great political consciousness.

(d) To advise and guide them in all such matters as mainly rest on them for the uplift of the Muslim society.[100]

Most of the pioneer women, nominated for All India Muslim Women Sub-Committee were the sisters and wives of the League's politicians of the various provinces.[101] These pioneering women political workers did much to awaken political consciousness among women and to carry the message of the Muslim League into the homes and to the ladies who until then were completely unconcerned about politics. In 1940 when the League passed the Pakistan Resolution at Lahore, one remarkable feature of the session was the unprecedented number of women who attended it. Another significant event of the same year was the demonstration of militant behaviour by Muslim women. The procession of a small number of women against the arrest of Muslim leaders and the banning of the Khaksar Party, which had joined the Pakistan movement, was the beginning of this new attitude which continued during the course of the whole struggle. On 18 June another demonstration was carried out both by men and women at Lahore. The police tried to stop it and when they refused, arrested the men and asked the women to return home. The women refused to do so and hence for the first time women were arrested for their political activism.[102]

In 1941 another step to extend the activities of Muslim women was taken through the formation of the Muslim Girl Students Federations. Before that the Muslim Federation for Boys was already working under the presidentship of the Raja of Mahmoodabad. However, in the presence of *purdah* and other social restrictions it was found necessary to form a separate federation for female Muslim students. The Girls' Federation was launched by Lady Abdul Qadir, Shaista Ikramullah, Fatima Begum, and Miss M. Qureshi These women went from college to college to spread awareness and to seek support for the idea of Pakistan.[103] In February 1942 a Conference of the Federation was organized in Delhi at the Anglo-Arabic College. The great significance of the Conference was the participation of a large number of unmarried girls, coming unchaperoned from other cities, staying in a place with people unknown to their families, which was a revolutionary development.[104] The Girls' Federation also proved to be the vanguard of the Women's Sub-Committee touring the countryside holding public meetings and establishing the League's message for Muslim women there.[105]

In 1942 Jinnah took a direct interest in women's committees and in his tours addressed large gatherings of women. By this time the participation of women in the Pakistan Movement were in full swing. They composed songs usually along the lines of 'Pakistan' is our birth right; we will pass through many storms; we will live or die for 'Pakistan'.[106] Begum Salma Tasadduque Husain[107] acknowledged the role of Jinnah by saying:

> it was Jinnah who took women out of the seclusion of their homes and brought them to the forefront to tackle the hard realities of life. He invariably urged in his speeches that women should be made active participants in the struggle because they are the second arms of the nation. Life without them would be incomplete.[108]

In this way the movement that freed the country also freed women from the bondage of the four walls of the house and they were accepted as members of a society which so far had exclusively belonged to men.

The presence of the newly-formed Women's National Guard in 1943 further signified the acceptance of an entirely new role for women. They were no longer bound to remain at home in isolation and under heavy protection. In wearing the uniform of white *pajama*, white *kurta* and green *dupatta*, the women of the National Guard collected funds, sold badges and propagated the idea of Pakistan. Their appearance in public and interaction with strangers was a 'violation' the unwritten but centuries old rule of *purdah* and confinement for Muslim women.[109]

MUSLIM WOMEN AND THE GENERAL ELECTIONS
OF 1946

The elections of 1946 were very important because they were the test of Muslim League's claim of being the sole representative of the Muslims of British India. The challenge was also taken up by the women members of the League who toured the countryside relentlessly canvassing for the League. Due, in part, to these efforts the League won a tremendous victory in the elections. In particular in the Punjab from where two Muslim women Begum Shah Nawaz and Begum Salma Tasadduque were contesting the women's seats, 75 per cent of the Muslim voters had turned up to cast their vote, and the opponents had their deposits forfeited.[110] During the course of the election, the women of the Punjab even ignored the interests of their brothers or husbands, who, being Government servants supported the ruling Unionists Party. Their new confidence can be seen by the examples of Miss Mumtaz Shah Nawaz (daughter of Begum Shah Nawaz) and other younger members of the League who picked up the women's voters in the presence of agents of the Unionist Government at every polling station. Miss Mumtaz was a 'terror' for her opponents and delivered fiery speeches.[111]

In the same way in Bengal, the Muslim League was able to secure an absolute majority in the legislature. During the election much of the work was done by students and women. It was the first time that Muslim women took part in political activity. In getting her exhilarating experiences during the election campaign of her cousin (Husain Shaheed Suhrawardy) in Kharagpur (Bengal), Begum Shaista Ikramullah stated that it brought women into the forefront of public life. The political struggle had somehow generated enough enthusiasm to sweep away all prejudices and taboos. Women worked in towns and villages among every stratum of society and tried to get votes for the Muslim League.[112]

MUSLIM WOMEN AFTER THE ELECTIONS

Soon after the elections the League Ministry was formed in Bengal under Husain Shaheed Suhrawardy. On the other hand, in the Punjab, the League had still not done enough to form a government. When the League was not able to form the ministry there, League supporters continued their campaign on the streets. As a result various League leaders including Begum Shah Nawaz were arrested. On hearing of their arrest, a large number of Muslim women came out into the streets where they faced *lathi* charges and tear gas.[113] On 27 January 1946, sixteen Muslim women were arrested and Section 144 was imposed, forbidding public demonstrations. They were taken into custody by the police, but they were not put in jail. Instead they were taken miles away from Lahore and were left in deserted places, from where they had to come back on their own.[114] The increasing and persistent protests of women resulted in the arrest of many of their leaders who were put behind the bars. These included Begum Shah Nawaz and Miss Mumtaz Shah Nawaz, Begum Salma Tasadduque Husain, Begum Kaka Khel, Miss Iqbal Rathore, Miss Husan Ara Hafizullah and Miss Nusrat Jahan. They were not even allowed to see their relatives. In particular, the daring act of Miss Shah Nawaz of hoisting a green flag made out of her own *dupatta* on the top of the jail in Lahore annoyed the Sikh lady jailer, Mrs Saudagar Singh. She ordered the women's guard to beat all these women. This action further increased the number and size of demonstrations in front of the jail and the Secretariat.[115] At the end of February, the achievement of one thirteen-year-old girl student Miss Fatima Sughra fixed itself in the annals of Indian Muslim women's as well as Pakistan's history: she hoisted the Muslim League flag on top of the Secretariat after pulling down the Union Jack.[116] All these women were released on 28 February and their protests spread to other parts of British India.

The women of the N.W.F.P. in particular, became involved in street politics. Many of them were injured in a railway accident while they were protesting on a railway bridge. The driver of the train who appeared to be a Hindu drove the train at accelerated speed under the bridge. Some of the women lost their balance, fell from the bridge, and were injured.[117] In the same way, the Congress Ministry of the N.W.F.P. put hurdles in the way of those Muslim women who were going to attend the historic Muslim rally at Peshawar. However, the women of the N.W.F.P. carried on the tempo of the movement. One of their great achievements was the emergence of a women's War Council in early 1947. The Council set up an underground radio station called the Pakistan Broadcasting Station. The station operated without being traced right up to 14 August 1947 when they gained their destination in the form of 'Pakistan'.[118]

* * *

In the light of this new political discourse, it seems, as Kumar has stated, that the women's movement was absorbed into the struggle for independence with the result that the issue of women's emancipation was felt by many to have been resolved if not pushed to one side.[119] On the other hand, in the opposite view of Khawar and Shaheed, the independence struggle actually sought to change the discourse of age-old traditions and social restrictions by requiring women to cast off their veils and allowing them to enter into the public arena.[120] Their abilities in this way were not only acknowledged by their men-folk but also utilized in the construction of community interests. Thus, they proved themselves as a 'powerful potential source of political activity'.[121] Such potential, in their opinion, however, has usually appeared as a temporary enthusiasm and when the moment of crisis is over women are asked to take a back seat, to return to their kitchens and children.[122] Likewise, in the opinion of Jalal, the action of these women (participants in the Pakistan movement) was largely as appendages of their men. She has categorized many of these women either as mothers, wives, daughters and sisters of influential Muslim politicians. But she has also acknowledged that many women participated with neither the advantage of a privileged background nor political connections.[123] Their participation, however, in her view, may have been something of a liberating experience which was too brief to bring qualitative change in their lives. In other words, simply taking part was more attractive than the cause itself.[124] According to Jalal, the mobilization of women in a political movement such as the campaign for Pakistan, instead of undermining conventional attitudes, caused them to be reasserted with a fresh vengeance.[125]

Despite these reservations, one cannot dismiss the achievements of women's struggle. The splendid role of Muslim women during the course of the Pakistan Movement was the outcome of the confidence which many of them had already come to experience either through their education, their growing awareness of their socio-political rights or through their growing participation in public life. When the struggle for Pakistan was over, they utilized these experiences to try to define their role in the newly emerged state and society. They did not automatically surrender their preoccupation with a feminist agenda and continued to apply it to their lives. One specific example of this was the All-Pakistan Women's Association which became a symbol of women's feminist behaviour in the history of the struggle for women's social rights in Pakistan.

In the same way, while we cannot deny the importance of the leading role of Miss Fatima Jinnah, Begum Shah Nawaz and other prominent women who were the wives, mothers, and daughters of Muslim politicians; we cannot ignore the historical fact that such kinds of mass movements as the Pakistan Movement cannot succeed without the vital presence of common people. Despite this, emotional exploitation in the name of religion often dominates the scene. Particularly in South Asian politics the religious phenomenon has sometimes appeared as a dynamic force, but local social norms especially concerning women's lives have sometimes been just as influential. The question of *izzat* or honour has created 'risks' for women seeking to cross these limitations. But the developments of the decades leading up to independence had produced important shifts in society's outlook and temperament. The construction of women's character as an individual person as well as an important part of society led to the realization by many that the presence of women could consolidate the cause and not damage the honour of their male relatives. One specific example was of the women of the Punjab and N.W.F.P. who became part and parcel of the Pakistan struggle on the basis of their own social experiences which they had already acquired. So, taking a view of all these facts, the role of these women can be seen as a part of a continuous struggle which had started after the First World War with them seeking a greater role in the public arena. While their involvement may have been 'fun', it was not 'frivolous' but represented a serious commitment to change.

NOTES

1. *Report of the Indian Statutory Commission*, Vol. 1, (His Majesty's Stationary Office, 1930), p. 53.
2. Radha Kumar, *The History of Doing*, p. 54.
3. Barbara N. Ramusak, 'Catalysts or Helpers: British Feminist, Indian Women Rights and Indian Independence' in Gail Minault (ed.), *The Extended Family: Women Political Participation in India and Pakistan*, pp. 109–50.
4. Radha Kumar, *The History of Doing*, p. 85.
5. Gail Minault and David Lelyveld, 'The Campaign for a Muslim University 1898–1920', *Modern Asian Studies*, Vol. 8, No. 2, 1974, pp. 145–189.
6. *Khatun*, Vol. 8, No. 1, January 1912, p. 29.
7. V.P. Menon, *The Transfer of Power in India*, (University Press, Princeton, 1957), p. 10.
8. Ibid. p. 10.
9. *Report of the Indian Statutory Commission*, Vol. 1, p. 49.
10. Ibid.
11. Ibid.
12. Ibid., p. 191.
13. Ibid., p. 223.
14. Ibid.
15. Radha Kumar, *The History of Doing*, p. 86.

16. *Printed Memorandum*, (presented by Begum Shah Nawaz and Mrs Subbarayan, during the course of the first session of the Round Table Conference, held at London in 1930), Sri Ram Sita Press, Madras, 1930, pp. 1–18.
17. Ibid.
18. Ibid.
19. *Proceedings of the Indian Round Table Conference*, first session, 12 November 1930–January 1931, (His Majesty's Stationery Office, London, 1931), p. 115.
20. Ibid., p. 446.
21. Letter to Lord Snell, Under Secretary of State for India, from the London Committee of the Women's Indian Association, dated 18 May 1931, (Q/I FC/92, n.p., IOL.
22. 'Representation of Women in the Indian Legislature', 'memorandum submitted by Mrs Subbarayan to the Indian Round Table Conference, see the proceedings of the Conference, second session, 7 September 1931–1 December 1932, Appendix 13, (His Majesty's Stationery Office, London, 1932), pp. 97–99.
23. Ibid.
24. Ibid.
25. Memorandum Representing the 'Views of a Number of Indian Women's Organizations', presented by Mrs Sarojini Naidu and Begum Shah Nawaz, ibid., pp. 99–100.
26. Memorandum on the 'Status of Indian Women in the Proposed New Constitution of India', ibid., pp. 100–102.
27. Radha Kumar, *The History of Doing*, p. 83.
28. The Indian Round Table Conference, second session, p. 261.
29. See, 'Proceedings of the Sixteenth Session of the All-India Muslim League', held at Bombay in December 1924, in Sharifuddin Pirzada (ed.), *Foundation of Pakistan: All-India Muslim League Documents 1906–47*, Vol. 2, (National Publishing House Karachi, 1970), p. 70.
30. Ibid. *Seventeenth Session held at Aligrah*, in December 1925, p. 55.
31. Ibid. *Twenty-third Session held at Howrah*, in October 1933, p. 199.
32. Ayesha Jalal, 'The Convenience of Subservience: Women and the State of Pakistan', in Deniz Kandiyoti (ed.), *Women Islam and the State*, (Macmillan, London, 1991), pp. 77–114.
33. For example, in one of her letters to Ramsay MacDonald, dated 17 April 1930, Mrs Pethick Lawrence, President of Women's Freedom League requested that the possibility of a British woman participant in the forthcoming Indian Round Table Conference be considered. Also, Mrs Corbett Ashby, President, National Union of Societies for Equal Citizenship, in her letter dated 13 October 1930 and Miss Barry, Honorary Secretary, St. Joan Social and Political Alliance in her letter dated 13 October 1930 requested Mr Wedgwood Benn to arrange for the

participation of a British woman representative, see Q/1FC/92, n.p., IOL.

34. See letter of Mrs Corbett Ashby, dated 13 October 1930 which she wrote to Mr Wedgwood Benn in this regard, ibid., n.p.

35. Mrs Milne Robertson, Secretary Edinburgh Equal Citizenship Society, proposed the names of these British women in her letter dated 13 October 1930 to Mr Wedgwood Benn. The same reprsentatives were also proposed by St. Joan's Social and Political Alliances and British Common Wealth League in their letters to Ramsay MacDonald, see, ibid., n.p.

36. Ibid.

37. Ibid.

38. Ibid.

39. Eleanor Rathbone belonged to a Lancashire family that had long associated with business and legislative politics in Liverpool. She was born in London on May 1872. Her early education was private. In 1893 she went to Oxford and got her degree from Somerville College. During this period she formed close friendship with feminist activists such as Margery Fry and Barbara Bradley Hammond. In 1894 Eleanor Rathbone returned to Liverpool and became involved in public roles, first as an assistant to her father now retired from Parliament, and then in her own social spheres. She entered into legislative politics in 1909 and was elected as a first woman member of the Liverpool City Council. She also showed great concern for Indian feminist activists and their efforts for the right of political franchisment for Indian women, see Mary D. Stocks, *Eleanor Rathbone: A Biography*, (Victor Gollancz, London, 1949)

40. Ibid., p. 150.

41. Ibid.

42. Ibid.

43. Ibid., p. 152.

44. *Indian Franchise Committee*, 1932, (His Majesty's Stationery Office, 1932), p. 81.

45. Ibid., pp. 152–53.

46. *Indian Franchise Committee*, Selection from Memorandum submitted by Individuals and Oral Evidences, Vol. 4, (His Majesty's Stationery Office, London, 1932), p. 453.

47. 'Memorandum on the Franchise of Women by the Women of Bengal', presented to the Indian Franchise Committee, (N. Mukherjee Art Press, Calcutta, 1932), pp. 1–12.

48. *Indian Franchise Committee, Selection from Memorandum Submitted by Individuals and Oral Evidences*, p. 170.

49. Letter from Mrs Lakshmi Rajwade to Mr G.J. Laitthwaite, dated 26 February 1932, E-Ind/85, Q/IFC/49, pp. 1–4, IOL.

50. Ibid.

51. Ibid.

52. Ibid.

53. *Indian Franchise Committee: Selection from Memorandam Submitted by Individuals and Oral Evidence*, p. 86.

54. Indian Franchise Committee, pp. 206–209.

55. Ibid., pp. 197–99.

56. Ibid., p. 85.

57. Ibid.

58. Ibid.

59. Ibid., p. 86.

60. Ibid.

61. Ibid.

62. Ibid., p. 87.

63. Ibid., p. 88.

64. Ibid., p. 85.

65. Ibid., p. 89.

66. Ibid.

67. *Proceedings of the Joint Committee on the Indian Constitutional Reforms*, Session 1933–34, Vol. 11, (His Majesty's Stationery Office, London, 1934), p. 271.

68. Ibid.

69. *Government of India Act 1935: Report of the Committee appointed in connection with the Delimitation of Constituencies and Connected Matters*, Vol. 1, (His Majesty's Stationery Office, London, 1936), p. 123.

70. Ibid.

71. Ibid., p. 125.

72. Ibid., p. 127.

73. Ibid., pp. 127–28.

74. Ibid., p. 130.

75. Ibid., pp. 131–32.

76. Ibid., p. 132.

77. Ibid., p. 134.

78. Ibid.

79. *Bulletin of Indian Women's Movement*, issued in connection with the Liaison Group of British Women's Societies (British Common Wealth League, Six Point Group, Women's Freedom League and the Women's International League) that worked in cooperation with the All-India Women's Conference. Dated October 1937, Q/IFC/37, n.p., IOL.

80. See the joint letter of various women's associations (The All-India Women's Conference, the All-India Muslim Ladies Conferenc, Bharat Stri Mandal, The Congress Committee and the National Council of Women in India) to the Secretary of Indian Delimitation Committee, dated 2 October 1935, ibid., n.p., IOl.

81. Letter of Mr R.N. Cilehrist, Reform Officer, Calcutta, to Mr Laithwaite, dated 23 December 1935, D.O.N. 4914, A.R., Bengal Secretariat, ibid., n.p. IOL.

82. Letter from Mr C.W.A. Turner, Chief Secretary to the Government of Bombay, to Mr C.K. Rhodes, Joint Secretary to the Government of India, dated 4 January 1936, N.R. 266, Political and Reform Department Bombay, ibid., n.p., IOL.

83. Ibid.

84. Letter from R.J.S. Dodd, Reform Officer, Punjab, to Mr Rhodes, dated 26 December 1935, F.14/2/35 F., ibid., n.p., IOL.

85. Letter from Mr M. Macann, Secretary to Government of N.W.F.P. to Mr Rhodes, dated 26 December 1935, No. 947/38/48 R.O., ibid., n.p., IOL.

86. Indian Delimitation Committee, p. 35.

87. Ibid.

88. Ibid., p. 138.

89. The following extent of Constituencies meant for women in different provinces were: Madras Presidency: the city of Madras, Ellore Municipality, the Municipalities of Tellicherry, Calicut, Cuddalore, Bellary, Dindigul and Tinnevelly; Bombay Presidency: Bombay city (Girgaum and Bhuleshwar) Ahmedabad city, Poona city, Dharwar district; Bengal Presidency: Calcutta, Dacca; The United Provinces: Benaras, Meerut, Cawnpore district north and east, Lucknow city, and Moradbad district; The Province of Punjab: Lahore city, Lahore Municipality and Cantonment, and Amritsar; The Province of Bihar: Patna city, Muzaffarpur town, and Bhagalpur town; The Central Province and Berar: Nagpur city, Jubbulpore city and Amraoti; Assam: Shillong town and Cantonment; Orissa: Cuttack town and Berhampur; Sindh: Hyderabad city-cum-Karachi city and Karachi city, see Government of India Act: Report of the Committee appointed in connection with the Delimitation of Constituencies and Connected Matters, Vol. II, (His Majesty's Stationery Office, London, 1936).

90. Figures are derived and calculated from the Government of India Act 1935: *Report of the Committee appointed in connection with the Delimitation of Constituencies and Connected Matters*, Vol. 11, Appendix-IV, p. 10, Appendix-V, p. 35, Appendix-VI, p. 71, Appendix-VII, p. 99, Appendix-VIII, p. 126, Appendix-IX, p. 151, and Appendix-XIV, p. 223.

91. Uma Kaura, *Muslim and Indian Nationalism: the Emergence of the Demand for India's Partition 1928–40*, (Manohar Book Services, New Delhi, 1977), p. 165.

92. 'Proceedings of the Twenty-first Session of the All-India Muslim League' held at Allahabad, December 1930, in Sharifuddin Pirzada (ed.), *Foundation of Pakistan: All-India Muslim League Document 1906–47*, Vol. 11, p. 153.

93. Ibid.

94. Ibid., p. 160.

95. Begum Shaista Ikramullah, *From Purdah To Parliament*, (Cresset Press, London, 1963), p. 87.

96. Ibid.

97. Begum Shaista Ikramullah, 'Musalman Auryatan aur Sayasit', *Ismat*, Vol. 55, No. 3, September 1935, pp. 243–44.

98. Gohar Iqbal, 'Nagma-e-Bedari', *Ismat*, Vol. 61, No. 4, October 1938, p. 298.

99. Fatima Jafar, 'Sayasit main Auryoton ka Hisa', *Ismat*, Vol. 57, No. 3, 4, September and October 1936, pp. 313–14.

100. Proceedings of the All-India Muslim League Twenty-sixth session Patna, in Sharifuddin Pirzada, (ed.), *Foundation of Pakistan*, Vol. 11, p. 318.

101. The following women were nominated to the Central Sub-Committee of the All-India Muslim League: Punjab: Begum Shah Nawaz, Lady Abdul Qadir, Mrs Rashida Lateef and Lady Jamal Khan; Bengal: Begum Shahbuddin, and Mrs Ispahani; Bombay: Miss Fatima Jinnah, Mrs Faiz Tyabji, Begum Hafizuddin; U.P.: Begum Habibullah, Begum Aziz Rasul, Begum Wasim, Begum Muhammad Ali, Begum Nawab Ismail Khan, and Miss Rahilla Khatun; C.P.: Miss Nadir Jahan, Begum Nawab Siddique Ali Khan; Bihar: Lady Imam and Begum Akhtar; Assam: Miss Ataur Rahman and Miss J. Khan; Sindh: Lady Haroon, Lady Hidayatullah, Begum Shahban and Mrs Hatim Tyabji; Delhi: Mrs Husain Malik, Mrs Najmul Hasan, and Begum Rehman; N.W.F.P.: Begum Haji Sadullah, Mrs Khwaja Allah Buksh; Madras: Mrs Ayisha, Kulhamoro and Mrs Qureshi, ibid.

102. Begum Shaista Ikramullah, 'Women in Politics', *Quaid-i-Azam and Muslim Women*, Ministry, of Education, Government of Pakistan, (National Foundation, Karachi, 1976), pp. 43–35.

103. Ibid.

104. Ibid.

105. Khawar Mumtaz and Farida Shaheed, *Women of Pakistan: Two Steps Forward and One Step Back* (Zed Books, London, 1987), p. 45.

106. Begum Salma Tasadduque Husain, 'Saviour of Muslim Women', *Quaid-i-Azam and Muslim Women*, pp. 20–33.

107. Begum Salma Tasadduque Husain, (born in 1908) joined the Muslim League in 1937 and worked under the guidance of Jinnah. She won a seat of the Provincial Assembly of the Punjab in 1946 and worked as a member till 1958, ibid.

108. Ibid.

109. Khawar Mumtaz and Farida Shaheed, *Women of Pakistan*, p. 45.

110. Begum Salma Tasadduque Husain, 'Saviour of Muslim Women' pp. 20–33.

111. Ibid.

112. Begum Shaista Ikramullah, *From Purdah to Parliament*, p. 125.

113. Khawar Mumtaz and Farida Shaheed, *Women of Pakistan*, p. 46.

114. Begum Salma Tasadduque Husain, 'Saviour of Muslim Women' pp. 20–33.
115. Ibid.
116. Ibid.
117. Khawar Mumtaz and Farida Shaheed, *Women of Pakistan*, p. 47.
118. Ibid.
119. Radha Kumar, *The History of Doing*, pp. 93–94.
120. Khawar Mumtaz and Farida Shaheed, *Women of Pakistan*, p. 47.
121. Ibid.
122. Ibid., p. 48.
123. Ayesha Jalal, 'The Convenience of Subservience: Women and the State of Pakistan', pp. 77–114.
124. Ibid.
125. Ibid.

6

OPENING UP A PUBLIC SPACE FOR WOMEN: THE ROLE OF LITERARY CULTURE

The debate on the status of women during the first half of the twentieth century was significantly different from that of the nineteenth century reformist movement in British India. These new concerns were further developed in the later years (1929–47) by the enactment of social legislation, women's modern education and their new political role. It led women to understand their problems from their own standpoint rather than that of men. The response which came from women sought to explore the connections between women and social transformation as well as their appropriate role in the new public life. To meet these new challenges many women shared their views through different channels and expressed their social problems and their solutions. One expression of these new experiences was the emergence of a women's literary culture which came to express women's views on their changing role in society. Note should be taken that, up to this time, the world of letters had been only confined to the women of aristocratic families, who, for instance, played an important role in creating literature for women during the second half of nineteenth and early twentieth century. One example was the Begums of Bhopal, whose reformist work helped to set an example for the generation that followed.

However, the expansion of literary activity to include middle class women led to a change in the content of women's literature. Arguments emphasizing the changing role of middle class women emerged as an important part of the colonial debate in British rule. As most of the issues directly related to women, their voices proved to be a narrative terrain of bitter social realities as well as the creation of dreams and desires. These voices began to explore the new market providing a forum within which they could consider issues such as womanhood and gender complexity, marriage and divorce, *purdah*, female education and the idea of greater freedom and greater opportunity.

Under this new dispensation the emergence of women's journalism provided an opportunity to understand women's lives from their own point of view. The multi-dimensional approach of women's magazines offered a new and broad space for writers to air their views on a range of topics, particularly those which could not be resolved by legislation, such as the disadvantaged positions of daughters and daughters-in-law in particular and the inferior position of women in general. However, the need to find a solution to these social problems was increasingly pressing in the context of the changing social role of women. Thus writings about the social status of women and their new role became helpful not only to establish the agenda of reform, but also to debate the definition of feminism and its historical application in the cultural context of Indian society. Taking a general overview of these writings about the shaping of Indian Muslim womanhood, the present chapter focuses on the following points:

(a) The recovering of female voices through women's journals in Urdu.
(b) The nature of women's writings.
(c) The production of new kind of domestic literature.
(d) Women and social transformation.
(e) The reassessment of Indian Muslim womanhood.
(f) Awareness, criticism and deviation from traditional patriarchy.

THE RECOVERING OF FEMALE VOICES THROUGH WOMEN'S JOURNALS IN URDU

Between 1920–47 many Urdu journals by, for and about women were published in British India for circulation throughout the country. Although the purpose of all these journals and newspapers was to transmit new ideas among women, *Tehzib-e-Niswan* and *Ismat* had the particular purpose of campaigning to improve women's status. These were not just any ordinary women's journals. Their volumes relate the long history of the struggle of Muslim women to improve their status in the eyes of society and to reinterpret Islamic teachings, while at the same time expressing feminist beliefs within the existing system.

TEHZIB-E-NISWAN AND *ISMAT*: CHAMPIONS OF THE WOMEN'S CAUSE

The weekly *Tehzib-e-Niswan* (Reform and Womanhood) was founded by Sayyed Mumtaz Ali in Lahore in 1898 in partnership with his second wife Muhammadi Begum. After the death of Muhammadi Begum in 1908, the co-editorship of this newspaper passed into the hands of Waheeda Begum, the daughter of Sayyed Mumtaz from his first wife. When Waheeda Begum died in 1917, the newspaper was edited by Sayyed Imtiaz Ali (the son of Mumtaz Ali and Muhammadi Begum) who was the last editor until the end of the publication of *Tehzib-e-Niswan* in 1948.

The driving force behind Mumtaz Ali's publishing of *Tehzib-e-Niswan* lay in his own experiences and concerns. From his childhood he had a chance to observe many women from his own family who were leading their lives in a state of misery and social discrimination. This inspired him to do something for these suppressed creatures which he finally succeeded in doing in 1898 through the inspiration of Muhammadi Begum (an educated daughter of distant relatives) whom he married after the death of his first wife. Within hours of their marriage, so it is said, the happy couple had decided to launch a newspaper for the promotion of general awareness among women.[1] The

Tehzib-e-Niswan appeared at a time when education for Muslim women was not very popular among the *ashraf*. Women's knowledge was usually confined to the reading of the Quran and a few *hadith* without understanding their meanings. To express their thoughts in writing was considered more than a sin for them.[2] In this situation, the publication of *Tehzib-e-Niswan* caused resentment amongst many *ashraf* families. They accused Mumtaz Ali of inciting women to revolt, but he was not deterred from his work of reform. He inspired Muslim women to write down their feelings and to share their social experiences with one another.[3] The early issues of *Tehzib-e-Niswan* contained pieces on female education and useful information about household management. A constant theme of *Tehzib-e-Niswan*, as Minault has noted, was the 'reform and simplification of custom, the need to eliminate wasteful expenditure on rituals, dowry and ornaments'.[4] As the years went by, the growth of education and socio-political awareness among women led to a widening of the range and variety of topics. In addition to their traditional experiences about home and family, they were now exploring the root causes of women's suppression, and reassessing their social status and defining their public role. Thus, by the 1930, the readers of *Tehzib-e-Niswan* had come a long way in the scope of their interests, their ability to organize as women, and their ability to champion their own interests in education, in legal rights and in lowering the barriers of *purdah*.[5] It should be noted that during the course of the Pakistan Movement, the national and political activities of Muslim women were highlighted in the pages of *Tehzib-e-Niswan*. The forum of *Tehzib-e-Niswan* provided a 'laboratory' through which women became able to analyse the impact of their socio-political experiments on their personal lives. A specific example was the serialized debate, *Aurat Ghulam Nahin* (Woman, not a Slave), which became the most popular topic of the years 1944–45. Almost all the well-known female writers of *Tehzib-e-Niswan* participated in this debate and shared their views about the changing role of women. Prominent among them were Khawar Durrani, Riffat Husain, Salima Begum, Sultana Kazia, and Jamila Begum.

The second popular journal *Ismat* (Chastity) was founded by Rashid-ul-Khairi in Delhi in 1908. The driving force behind this cause was the person of Sheikh Abdul Qadir, the editor of the well-known Urdu journal *Makhzan*, published from Lahore. In 1908 when Sheikh Abdul Qadir temporarily moved the office of *Makhzan* from Lahore to Delhi, he persuaded his friend Rashid-ul Khairi to bring out a journal to raise a voice for the social rights and duties of women.[6]

From 1908 to 1922, the publication of *Ismat* continued under the editorship of Rashid-ul-Khairi. Unlike Mumtaz Ali, although Rashid-ul-Khairi could not get the services of an educated wife for the co-editorship of his journal, his wife, Mubarak Zamani, provided assistance in his early writings for *Ismat*. For instance, she made major contributions to the chapters on tailoring, sewing and embroidery of women's clothes in his novels serialized in *Ismat*, *Subh-e-Zindagi*, (The Dawn of Life) and *Salehat*, (Chaste Women).[7] In the same way, she contributed the *begumati* language of Delhi, the correction of idioms, the narration of old *zenana* customs and folk songs which appeared in these novels.[8] In 1923 Raziq-ul-Khairi, the eldest son of Rashid-ul-Khairi, assumed the editorship of *Ismat*. With the assistance of his wife Khatun Akram, a well-known writer, he was able to raise the standard and to increase the circulation of the journal. The reformist writings and works of fiction on social issues written by Khatun Akram became especially popular among the readers of *Ismat*.[9] However, this association between the two did not last long: the young Khatun Akram died in 1924. Raziq ul-Khairi married a second time in 1929. Amina Begum was not as educated as Khatun Akram, but learned good lessons from her father-in-law and husband. In later years she helped her husband in editing *Ismat*.[10]

Like the *Tehzib-e-Niswan*, the early period of *Ismat* seemed to be devoid of writings by women. Lack of education and social restrictions made it difficult for women to write. Thus, in the early period *Ismat* contained mostly the writings of Rashid-ul-Khairi himself. To inspire women to write, he usually wrote his articles under various female pseudonyms.[11] In this way, he gradually encouraged real women to become the pioneers of women's journalism in Urdu. Prominent among them were Sayyeda Jahreia, Nazar-ul-Baqar, Attiya Faizi, and Khujista Akhtar Banu Suhrawardy. These were the women whose writings became a bridge between house and house, a way to combat domestic isolation and loneliness. They presented an image of Indian Muslim womanhood, creating a literary text to suggest that writing itself was a natural and noble act that could have a broad and salutary impact on society. The front page of *Ismat* also gave visual expression of this aspiration. It showed a woman sitting on a chair reading a book. Her bright and shining eyes seemed to reflect the inner satisfaction attained from personal discovery. She seemed to believe in the power of the word that opened a completely new world and new possibilities for herself and enhanced her sense of awakening.

Note should be taken of the fact that Khairi's writings under his own name included social and moral articles, short stories and novels which played an important role in spreading the idea of emancipation among the Muslim women of India. This will be investigated below.

It is difficult to determine the precise circulation figures for both these journals during this particular period. Unlike male readers, female readers were not necessarily found in the streets but rather at schools and in homes. Reading aloud was frequently carried out in the context of the family. Usually an educated woman or girl offered to read a journal to her uneducated female kin. In the same way, the readership of journals was also extended by passing the printed text around. Estimates of the number of female readers of *Tehzib-e-Niswan* and *Ismat* should thus be blended with a profile of real readers.

The early circulation of these journals was limited as most of the women were not educated and the reading of journals was generally considered morally harmful for them. In the case of *Tehzib-e-Niswan*, for instance, Mumtaz Ali stated that for the first six months he used to publish one thousand copies and post them to the addresses of 'respectable families'. This response continued until 1900 when the circulation of *Tehzib-e-Niswan* was not exceeding 200.[12] With the gradual expansion of female education however, the habit of reading of female journals developed among the women of the middle class as well. As a result the circulation of *Tehzib-e-Niswan* also increased, reaching, 1,750 copies in 1924.[13] The average circulation during the period 1930–1947 was between one to two thousand.

Like the *Tehzib-e-Niswan*, the early years of *Ismat* revolved around similar difficulties; the continuous returning of copies not only discouraged Rashid-ul-Khairi but also pushed him into financial crisis. However, at the later stage when the editorship of *Ismat* came into the hands of Raziq-ul-Khairi, the circulation increased along with its standard. In 1926, 2,500 copies were circulated which increased up to 5,000 in 1929.[14] During the period of 1930–1947, the circulation of *Ismat* was between 3,000 and 5,000.[15]

Taking account of these journals, it becomes obvious that both had the same objectives behind their foundation. Both, were run by husband and wife teams. They encouraged educated women of different classes and social groups to express their feelings and social experiences by submitting their writings for publication. In the same way both had the same reforming social agenda: to improve the status of women by helping them with better education and awareness of socio-political rights.

THE NATURE OF WOMEN'S WRITINGS

Before looking at different kinds of women's writings it seems necessary to point out the particular social imperatives and impulses that sought to transform society in the late nineteenth and early twentieth century British India. The great mobilization of urban society through the wider expansion of modern education and through jobs in the colonial administration led to the crystallization of a new middle class culture. The women of this middle class culture began to see new possibilities for changing their social position. The model of ideal womanhood which they presented entailed the modernizing of traditional norms and regulating gender relations both in and outside the home. In this way their approach towards the new structure of society became a basic characteristic of their reforming venture. This pushed forward their writings to express their desire for self-identification and self-expression. Women sought to break into literary space, first veiled by pseudonyms and then later lifting their veils and revealing their identities. Through this act they acknowledged their individual existence and gained public recognition.

THE CLASSIFICATION OF WOMEN'S WRITINGS

Women's writings published in *Tehzib-e-Niswan* and *Ismat* can be categorized as:

(a) Producing a new kind of domestic literature.
(b) Commenting on social, economic and political changes taking place in the world around them.
(c) Rethinking the pattern of a woman's life.

Besides confronting these issues, both the journals also included poetry, short stories, serialized novels, women's letters to the editor, and matrimonial and other advertisements.

THE EMERGENCE OF A NEW KIND OF DOMESTIC LITERATURE

Foreign influence and indigenous concerns reshaped Urdu language and literature during this period. As more and more new subjects became topics of public discussion, language underwent a considerable evolution. New words were invented to convey new political concepts, a new vocabulary was created for the domestic realm. Phrases emerged for defining terms such as 'a housewife', the concept of new 'womanhood' and the knowledge of domesticity.

It should be noted that essay-writing, more than any other genre, aided in this transformation. Its revitalized language and new forms helped literature to expand its variety and range. Part of this process involved the creation of a new kind of domestic literature. It dealt with the reshaped ideology of family life and concepts of domesticity. As the greater part of domestic life revolved around women—their maternal role in particular—became the key issue of the modern demands.

THE RELATIONSHIP BETWEEN MOTHER AND CHILD: THE FIRST KEYPOINT OF DOMESTIC LITERATURE

The relationship between mother and child was believed to begin immediately after the onset of the pregnancy of a woman. The basic necessity during this period, as suggested by Saeeda Zamiruddin in *Maan ki Sehat* (The Health of the Mother) was the maintenance of the health of the expectant mother which could be achieved through proper diet, fresh air, proper ventilation and positive thinking.[16] In the context of social restrictions like *purdah* and confinement, which led to women being forbidden to go outside, the proper way to get fresh air, she suggested, was to go to a nearby opened window and do the exercise of long and fresh breathing.[17] In the same way maintaining the cleanliness of the house could save women from the danger of diseases like tuberculosis and anaemia.[18]

The second stage of child care was looking after the new born babies. To keep them healthy and cheerful it was the duty of their mothers to take care of their diet, sleep and cleanliness. For example, in the matter of diet, as Miss S.R. Karminia explained in *Maon ko Hidayat* (Instruction for Mothers), when babies began to cry women assumed that this was because they were hungry, without thinking about the other possibilities of the cause of their restlessness which could be colic pain, a sore throat, or uncomfortable clothing. To overcome these minor problems mothers should know, she suggested, the basic methods of child care and the proper use of medicines.[19]

The third stage of this procedure lay in the training of growing children. Indeed, a mother was considered the most important and effective source of training and knowledge for her children. To fulfil such a great responsibility the appropriate type of mother who could play this role was debated by many women writers. For instance, in the opinion of Sayyeda Kishwar Ara, as she stated in *Aurat aur Tarbiyat-e-Kirdar* (Woman and the Training of Character), an educated, well-trained and well-behaved mother could perform her duty appropriately.[20] However, a higher educational qualification should not be comsidered as the only criterion of good motherhood. Much depended on the awareness and concern of a mother who sought to train her children in a proper way. The person of Hazrat Fatima, the daughter of Prophet Muhammad (PBUH), for instance, could become the best example for mothers. Hazrat Fatima, brought up and trained her sons, Hazrat Imam Hasan and Hazrat Imam Husain, in such a way that they became the symbol of bravery and modesty in the history of Islam.[21]

However, in addition to this concept of ideal motherhood, the recognition of historical changes in the institution of Muslim motherhood was another challenging issue discussed by many female writers. They debated how they should paint the features of an ideal motherhood which would be acceptable both for social and religious institutions of the time (in context of the transformation from tradition to modernity). One of the prominent features noted by them was the need to maintain a 'balanced behaviour' between child and his parents. Why the use of 'parents' instead of 'mother'? In arguing for this change, Mrs A. Shaheed, for instance, said, in one of her essays, *Tarbiyat ke Chand Usool* (Some Principles of Training), that it was a more suitable term, given the changing structure of middle class family life, in which women were also shouldering a public role alongside men. Hence both the parents were considered equally responsible for the upbringing of their children.[22] Under these circumstances, she suggested, parents should agree upon a plan for the training of their children. Otherwise, for example, a child would get confused if he was given two different explanations for one and the same action.[23] Another point she stressed was the need for a positive approach towards the training of growing children. For instance, if a child was doing some thing different, it did not mean that he was wrong and should be rebuked by his parents. On the other hand, parents should keep in mind that children were their future and that the future would naturally differ from that of the past or even the present.[24] In general, however, as she advised, it was the duty of parents to make sure that their children were obedient, modest and faithful.[25]

WOMEN AND DOMESTICITY: THE SECOND KEY ISSUE OF DOMESTIC LITERATURE

In discussing the subject of women and domesticity many female writers dealt with those refined manners and principles that could make women's lives more useful not only for their families but also for themselves. This was thought to be particularly important in cases where the housewife was educated, because of which she would be expected to be more competent in managing her household than an uneducated woman. For example, it was a great challenge for an educated wife to achieve a balance between her domestic and social life. In one of her writings, *Larkiyon ki Talim aur Dastkari* (Girls' Education and Handicraft), Ghadir Fatima emphasized the need for this balance in the married life of an educated woman. For example, after becoming a father, usually, the love and attention of the husband which was previously reserved for his wife converted into the love of a peaceful domestic life. He expected that when he came back home after a long day of hard work, he should be warmly welcomed by his wife, gat his children should be neat and clean and the house should be tidy. On the other hand, one could imagine his reaction if he found that exactly at the time of his coming home, his wife was going out to play tennis or to see some friends, leaving children and home under the care of servants. That would make him think that marrying an educated woman was the biggest mistake of his life. Such kinds of thoughts sometimes became the major reason for domestic problems.[26] In fact it was not the fault of modern education, as Ghadir Fatima argued; but the lack of domestic subjects in the educational curricula and the ignorance of mothers as regards the domestic training of their educated daughters which was the main reason for this kind of irresponsible behaviour. In these circumstances a proper allocation of time to both domestic and social activities was the only solution to avoid all these problems.[27]

WOMEN AND THEIR SOCIAL LIFE: THE THIRD KEY ISSUE OF DOMESTIC LITERATURE

Social life was seen by many writers as a new experience for middle-class women in the context of their broadening role in society. One of the ways through which women could adjust themselves to the transformed society was by reflecting on their personalities and behaviour. It seems that the incorporation of such writings in Urdu female journalism, or, in a broader sense, in Indian female journalism, was the impact of western female journalism that was directly or indirectly approaching these writers.

In the context of personality analysis, for instance, Jamila Begum, in one of her essays, *Hamari Shakhsiyyat* (Our Personality), discussed the social and psychological stresses which caused many Indian women to look much older than their actual age. One of the basic reasons lay in their married lives. After getting married early and becoming the mother of several children at a very young age, it was generally assumed that the period of a woman's youth had passed and that now she had just to wait for her grandchildren.[28] This belief led her to become serious and act as an old woman. Usually after the age of thirty many women stopped thinking about themselves. Their ignorance and carelessness about their health, indeed their lives, caused them to wallow in a state of misery and sorrow. The only solution to this problem, Jamila Begum proposed, lay in total condemnation of such sort of thinking, to keep physically

fit and to engage in healthy social activities. A balanced diet
and proper grooming would go a long way in improving their
personality.[29] For instance, obesity which usually distorted the
personality, could be reduced in many ways. Imtiaz Begum in
her work *Barhthe hue Wazan par Qaboo Pana* (Watching
Weight Gain) suggested that excess weight could be shed by
developing self-control and by using the least quantity of greasy
food in one's daily diet. The frequent use of fresh vegetables
and fruit was recommended.[30]

The selection of proper clothing was the second major issue
raised in this context by many female writers. In Shaista
Ikramullah's *Kaproh say Mutaaliq Chand Bathen* (Some Matters
Relating to Dress) the proper dress was that which could be
worn in accordance with the needs of season, place, and
function.[31] For example, it would look odd to go to a lunch
party in the month of June in a red satin dress covered with gold
and silver embroidery. On the other hand, a light coloured dress
would prove more comfortable and attractive in the summer
season. However, such glittering clothes could be worn at dinner
parties even in summer.[32] In the same way, a bulky woman with
a dark or a sallow complexion should avoid wearing light
colours such as sky blue and light purple.[33] Another important
point in Shaista's view was a consideration of the age factor. In
particular, the selection of the colour of clothing, its designing
and the matching of purse and shoes should be made in
accordance with the age of the user.[34]

As regards occasion and place, it was necessary to keep in
mind the nature of the visit. For example while visiting a patient,
as Miss A.J. advised in her *Iyaddat* (Visiting the Sick), women
should wear simple and plain clothes. It was improper to visit
a seriously ill patient wearing a glittering dress and heavy
jewellery.[35]

Women's manners and social behaviour were other important
issues discussed in these journalistic contributions. Both were
considered central features of women's public sphere. Attending
different kinds of social gatherings was a crucial aspect of
women's movement into the public sphere and women needed

to learn how to behave in this new environment. Badar Mansoori's critical writing, *Dawaten aur Hum* (We and our Parties), discussed appropriate manners for a middle-class woman. Mansoori stated that sometimes the invited woman wrongly assumed that she had not been treated properly by her host. She should remember that her host had to attend to several guests at the same time and that it was not possible for her to give her whole attention to one person. Moreover, she had to look after the other arrangements of the party.[36] In the same way any kind of whispering or winking might hurt the feelings of other persons. Another bad habit of women, as pointed out by Mansoori, was their criticism of a party after they returned home. They would often begin to criticize the food, the way it was served—in short each and every thing which they had found at their host's house.[37]

Thus, the domestic and social role of an ideal middle-class woman as summed up by these female writers was to be (i) a competent wife and mother who was able to fulfil her domestic duties properly, (ii) an appropriately educated person who was able to shoulder her social and national responsibilities and, (iii) an ideal life partner who could capture the heart of her husband through her refined manners, and her physical attraction. This she could achieve through proper exercise, adornment and stylish dress, and her ability to behave graciously as her husband's consort in social gatherings.

WOMEN AND SOCIAL TRANSFORMATION

The second category of women's literary culture was based on those writings that sought to deal with the transformation of Indian Muslim society. Among the ranges of positions from which female writers chose to approach the issue, two options stood out.

The first option was to work within a religious framework, slowly assimilating acceptable modern influences and reforming Islamic law through *ijtihad*, particularly in those local social practices which were not recognized in Islam but were given an Islamic colouring to legitimize them. For example, it was assumed by many female writers that enhancing women's religious awareness would help them sift Islamic injunctions from local customs that sought in the name of Islam to justify gender oppression. In this situation the religious awareness of educated women, as Sugrah Humayun Asghar argued in one of her writings, *Auraton ke Faraiz* (The Duties of Women), would save their lives from being sacrificed in the name of so-called religious practices.[38] By obtaining direct knowledge of Islam, on the one hand, women would be able to educate their children, and, on the other hand, would become aware of their own rights, consequently would be in a stronger position to obtain these rights.[39] The best way to acquire religious knowledge, as Salehah Abid Husain pointed out in *Auratayn aur Mutalia-i-Koran* (Women and the study of the Quran), was through understanding the meaning of the Quran. The lack of knowledge of the Arabic language, in her opinion, led *mullahs* to explain the meaning of the words of the Quran according to their own interests and biases. By understanding the Quran women could at least learn how to look sceptically at their so-called *fatawa*.[40]

As far as the social activities of women were concerned, many female writers agreed that they should not be confined to successful domesticity, bringing up children and maintaining a good relationship with relatives or friends, but that they should be expanded beyond these traditional limits. For example, in the field of female education, the central point raised by Jamila Begum's article, *Hamari Talim ka Maqsad* (The Purpose of Our Education), was the proper use of modern education: the entry of educated women into different professions it is argued would not only make them independent, but would also improve the economic condition of Muslim society as a whole.[41] On the other hand, she warned that it would be a great setback for Indian Muslims if, after receiving higher education, their girls were kept within the four walls of their houses only to wait for marriage.[42]

Opposed to Jamila's strong views, however were certain female writers who firmly believed in the socio-moral impact of modern education, rather in its economic utility. Understanding the meaning of 'modern education' and its proper application in social life was termed by them the 'necessity of the time'. In their general approach towards the terms 'western education and culture' Indian Muslims saw their society as divided into two broad groups. In their opinion the first group consisted of those people who assumed that the meaning of modernity lay in speaking English fluently, in joining clubs, in going to the cinema or in wearing western-style dresses. The second group saw this 'modern' approach as a 'destruction of character.' particulaly regarding girls the it was argued that after acquiring a modern education they became conceited, wayward, selfish and stubborn.

Such extreme views discouraged people from pondering over the real objectives of modern education. The main reason for these extreme views, as Mahmoona Qadir explained in her *Talim ke Mukhalifon se* (To the Opponents of Education), was a superficial approach towards modern education. In fact, modern education was a capacity that could be achieved through scientific knowledge and which could be used for the welfare of society. The replacement of old norms and outmoded practices by a modern approach would be worth while only if society used these means to understand the real implication of progress.[43] By giving the example of the 'sense of responsibility' of English people as individual citizens, Begum Amiruddin, a well-known social activist of Madras, raised the question of how many modern educated Indian Muslims followed this example. Unfortunately, she noted, this particular example was never followed by them. They clumsily tried to simply imitate English society without knowing its real spirit.[44] The situation was even more distressing as far as the feminist movement in India was concerned, Rafia Khatoon noted in her *Hindustan main Niswani Taraqqi ka Mafhoom* (The Meaning of Women's Emancipation in India). Generally, freedom and liberation were seen by many educated women merely in the form of 'modern' dress-designing, a bob-cut hairstyle and thick layers of make-up.[45] When these women were asked to use their skills for the social and economic progress of the country, they shed crocodile tears and used lame excuses of *purdah* and other such gender restrictions for their unwillingness to engage in such work.[46]

The second option, which challenged the former, was based on religious conservatism. The only solution, as suggested by Islamist writers, was the revival of Islam. They argued that westernization eroded women's position by encouraging materialism and undermining morality. In spite of these views, however, they did not appease the religious conservatives. The meaning of revivalism according to these Islamist writers was a better understanding of Islam or a return to 'true Islam' through religious instruction. They emphasized the early days of Islam, glorifying the characters of Khadija, Ayeshah, Fatima and Rabia Basri.[47] Issues discussed in this context included the necessity of Islamic education and the reformation of Muslim society in India.

In the field of education, Christian missionary schools were bitterly opposed by this group of female writers. One well-known name in this regard was that of Fatima Begum, who had been writing for *Ismat* since 1930. In most of her writings she emphasized the necessity of pure Islamic education as it was the only way Muslims could save themselves from further moral degradation. For example, in one of her writings, *Mission Askool ki Talim Zaroor Rang Layegi* (The Consequences of the Education of Mission Schools), she called missionary schools a 'sugar-coated pill' which would ultimately destroy Muslim society as a whole.[48] Those Muslim girls who were being educated in mission schools hardly had a chance to receive Islamic education at home, and if some of them did, they did not have firm belief in their faith.[49] In analysing this situation, Jamila Begum observed in her *Mazhabi Talim* (Religious Education) that it was not the fault of these innocent girls. The whole blunder was committed by their parents who sent their young daughters to missionary schools and never realized that what they lost by way of religious education was much more than what they gained.[50] Without acquiring religious knowledge, she warned, the material progress of Muslim society was little more than a mere mirage.[51]

As regards the reformation of Islamic society, woman's stereotyped role became the central theme for these female writers. The consolidation of woman's character as a wife and mother meant the consolidation of socio-religious norms and the well-being of society. They interpreted women's changing role and the idea of their liberation as a better understanding of these stereotyped responsibilities. The new kind of domestic knowledge could become helpful in the upbringing of children, in maintaining a good relationship with their husbands as well as other relatives. On the other hand, those women who ignored their children and homes and spent most of their time in frivolous activities in the name of social freedom or economic liberation, not only lost their femininity but also destroyed the future of society.[52]

Thus, they concluded that, since woman's primary role was as a wife and a mother, the best way to improve her situation was to educate her for a domestic vocation. The rights of women usually implied social reforms that would enhance women's position in the family. The debate on women's question, in this way, basically centred on issues such as education (mostly religious), domesticity and marital relations.

THE REASSESSMENT OF MUSLIM WOMANHOOD

Female writers of this period not only responded to socio-economic changes in British India but also tried to redefine patriarchy in different classes of society. It led them to explore the dialectical relationship between feminism and gender in the light of the changing status and role of women in society. In such a context, the reformulation of the cultural environment was considered as a central factor in changing the traditional images of Indian Muslim womanhood as well as their development in a transformed society. Thus, most of the reformist work of this period revolved around the quest for improving the social images of women and regulating gender relations. Although the passing of social legislation apparently safeguarded women's rights, but attitudes and the prevailing social norms in male-dominated society were the main obstacle in the path of their fulfilment and implementation. The only way to mitigate the intensity of these problems was to expose and resolve them not only through law but also on humanitarian grounds. This was indeed an issue of immense importance raised by these 'new' women. The quest to know what they were and what were the objectives of their lives became became a central concern. For female writers it was the most serious social issue ever to be addressed by newspapers and journals. The picture of Indian womanhood painted by these writers reflected the history of men's tyranny over women down the centuries. These oppressed women became the cruel victims of their circumstances: continuous suppression and humiliation made them an emblem of misery and wretchedness.

In identifying the root cause of women's low status and its remedy, female writers dwelt upon the following matters:

(i) The misery of women's lives and contemporary gender behaviour.
(ii) Women's awareness, criticism and deviation from Traditional patriarchy.
(iii) Possible solutions or alternative social agendas.

THE MISERY OF WOMEN'S LIFE AND CONTEMPORARY GENDER BEHAVIOUR

In India the position of women was worse than that of an animal. How was a woman's life defined? Was it as a damaged or ill-fitting shoe that could be changed, or was it better summed up in the custom of *sati* in which a woman had to be burnt with her dead husband to avoid the greater humiliation of becoming a miserable widow? In the case of widowhood she had to cut her hair and to wear only coarse cloth. Above all she was prohibited from taking any proper diet. In the same way the status of daughters-in-law was very low in Indian Muslim society, as in Indian society in general, the cruel mothers-in-law made their lives miserable. When the whole family of in-laws used to rest during the long afternoons in the burning heat of the months of June and July, she was not allowed to do so. She had to wash dishes after lunch or to make dresses for her younger sisters- and brothers-in-law.[53]

The picture of women's sorrows painted by these writers, mostly women, described the different stages of their lives.

THE BIRTH OF A GIRL

The tragedy of a woman's life started from her very birth itself. She was treated as an unwelcome guest. Members of her family felt immense sorrow and grief to hear the news of her birth. Rashid-ul-Khairi, the great champion of women's rights, in his *Sharia ka Khoon*, (The Murder of Islamic Law), cited the instance of a husband who, in a letter to his wife after hearing the news of the birth of their daughter, wrote that in his opinion the birth of a girl was worse than 'a hundred punishments'.[54] The birth of Shabana (his new born daughter) had, he maintained, destroyed his peaceful life, and at the end of his letter he prayed to God for her death.[55] Another writing of Khairi, *Alam-e-Arvah se Auraton ki Sada* (The Cry of Women from the Heavens Above) gives an account of an imaginary conversation between the souls of Indian Muslim women after their death. Their souls protested against the discriminatory attitude of society by saying:

> Before our arrival in the world people were making a lot of preparations for our welcome. Their loving arms were eagerly waiting to sway us while singing lullabies and their ears were longing to listen to our twittering. But when we arrived in this world, we came to know that we were the wrong persons. These selfish people were waiting only for sons—those sons who would spread the dishes of selfishness on the table of cruelty and would snatch away our rights and would make our lives worse than that of animals. The value of the life of a daughter in the eyes of her

parents is no more than that of a mere stone as compared to their son who is considered as a precious, brilliantly shining diamond.[56]

MUSLIM WOMANHOOD IN THE MIRROR OF CHILDHOOD

The picture of Muslim girls painted in the writings of many writers was an unhappy one, especially when they looked back to the missed chances of their childhood years. As these girls grew older the indifferent attitude of their parents and relatives became more visible. If parents had spent five rupees on the clothing of their sons, only two rupees were spent on their daughters' dress. What a shame, lamented Khairi, that these pitiful creatures and helpless prisoners were the daughters of Indian Muslims.[57] From sunrise to sunset they were forced to do domestic chores. Despite all their hard work, they had to face the anger of their parents and elder brothers. In their innocent childhood they were never able to experience the joys of life. They were never allowed to go outside and meet other people.[58] On the other hand, from the beginning of their childhood they were required to involve themselves in domestic affairs. They never forgot the days of their childhood when they used to make food for their fathers and brothers during the hottest days of June and July but were never allowed even to taste the food before their male-kin had eaten.[59] Another example presented of such kind of inhumanity was that of several families of Delhi and Lucknow who required their unmarried young girls to make embroidered caps. After working hard at this for several days, when these caps were completed, the girls were asked to throw these caps into the river.[60] Sometimes rice and red lentils would be mixed together and these poor creatures were told to separate them. The purpose of these inhuman exercises was to prepare these young girls to bear the tyranny and oppression during their prospective married lives.[61]

Even mothers had an indifferent attitude towards their daughters as compared to their sons. The best part of the food was kept for their sons, and if young daughters sometimes demanded that food their mothers used to make a lot of excuses.[62] The discrimination that was practised against girls is well exemplified in an old lullaby in Hindko in which a girl was shown as envious of her brother's diet, whereas a boy was portrayed worthy of special attention in this matter:

Come son drink
From the cup filled with milk
And let not your sisters
know about it.[63]

These girls were not allowed even to complain or cry out against this inhuman behaviour in the presence of other people. They used to lighten the burden of their misfortune and grief in some hidden corner of the house.[64] Even families who were rather well-educated and claimed that they respected the rights of women, often treated their own women badly.[65]

The Maidenhood of a Muslim Girl

The same kind of picture continued to be painted in these writings about the lives of girls as they grew older. The youth of an Indian Muslim girl or the period of her maidenhood proved to be an equal nuisance for her parents. The only solution in their view was to get her married off as soon as possible. Khairi dwelt on this in one of his stories, *Sauda-e-Naqad* (A Cash Transaction). Farzana, the heroine of the story, was among those girls whose youth became a burden for their parents.[66] She was brought up to believe that, if a young girl's parents did not pay adequate attention to her early marriage, it was a big 'sin' which could not be easily remedied. To her parents, the period of her maidenhood was just like 'a hissing snake' that could at any time mortally strike at her parents.[67] This encumbrance of the youth of a girl could be dealt with only by marriage be it with an old or sick man.[68]

The Life of a Married Muslim Woman

The description of the next phase in the life of most Indian Muslim girls was similarly bleak. Marriages were usually conducted without the consent of the related parties. Sometimes the result of these marriages was an ill-matched couple; girls of a tender age married to old men of sixty years or over. Parents, became relaxed once they had got rid of the burden of their daughters and they did not seem to mind the huge difference between the age of the bride and the groom. Usually such marriages ended with nothing for them except the early widowhood of these girls and two or three young orphans. The situation becomes more clear in the form of Rabia, the main female character of Rashid-ul-Khairi's story, *Aisi Biyahi se Kunwari Bhali* (Better a Spinster than a Woman forced into a bad marriage). Rabia was married at the age of fifteen to a sick, old, but rich man of sixty years. Five years later the death of that man causes Rabia to become a widow with three young daughters who spend the rest of their lives in a state of utter poverty.[69]

What was the definition of a wife in the opinion of Indian Muslims? asked Khairi. Nothing more than a purchased slave that was created for the service of her husband, to look after his children, and to do other domestic duties, he answered. The whole life of a married woman revolved around the anger of her husband, the taunting remarks of her in-laws, the threat of divorce and sycophancy. The misery of married life can be well visualized through one of the poems of Shafiq Siddiqui, *Mujhe Bhool Jana Meri Pyari Amman* (Forget About Me My Dear Mother), in which a married girl complains to her mother about the tyranny of her in-laws. In despair she asks how she can relate her tragic tale of suffering and misery to her mother, with her ruined youth having become a symbol of utter helplessness and despair.[70] The cavilling and incessant complaining of her in-laws, their rage and resentment and, above all, the apathetic attitude of her husband made her life worse than death.[71]

Looking around at Indian society it seemed clear that man played god with his wife—she worshipped him and even tried to sacrifice her life for him. Her actual position at home was worse than that of a maid servant. Muslim families who hired the service of maid servants usually had to pay from thirty to forty rupees per annum. The expenditure on a wife, on the other hand, was much less and she proved more submissive and punctual than the former. To stay up late at night waiting for the husband who was returning from his job or even from visiting a prostitute, was the moral duty of the wife.[72]

Muslim men often gave lame excuses for a second marriage in the presence of the first wife. *Nikah* actually meant that a Muslim husband made a solemn promise to his wife that he would look after her and make her happy. However, after a few years of marriage when this woman became the mother of several children and frequent pregnancies and breast feeding destroyed her health and figure, she often became the victim of the cruelty of her husband. He now used her pitiable state as a good excuse for his second marriage.

Another excuse often employed by men for a second marriage was the barrenness of the first wife. Soon after marriage the birth of a child became the greatest desire in the world of her in-laws. Even in the case of temporary defects that could be removed after a medical treatment, she was criticized and rejected.[73] It was never thought that the woman alone might not be responsible for this problem; and that the physical defects of the husband could also be a reason for the problem. However, the lack of such an approach or awareness on the part of male dominated society in India meant that such 'defects' were usually entered in the women's account.[74] These 'inauspicious' women were so humiliated that even to look at their faces in the morning was considered a sign of misfortune.[75]

MUSLIM WOMEN AND THE PROVISION OF *MEHER* (DOWRY)

Under Muslim law, *meher* is a settlement in favour of the wife made prior to the completion of the marriage-contract. Muslim law requires that there should always be a consideration (*meher*) moving from the husband in favour of the wife, for her sole and exclusive benefit. Another object of *meher* is the protection for the wife against the arbitrary exercise of the power of divorce by the husband. In this way, the enforcement of *meher* at the time of *nikah* has two objectives in itself. In the first place it protects the esteem and respect of the woman not only through social protocol (*nikah*) but also by providing economic security (*meher*). Secondly, it can be used as a check upon the capricious exercise by the husband of his power to terminate the marriage at will. In a general sense, *meher* is a sum of money, or other property, payable by a husband to a woman on or after her marriage with him.

Like the usurping of other socio-religious rights of Muslim women, the right of *meher* was frequently ignored by Indian Muslims. Muslim husbands had a lot of excuses to avoid making the payment of *meher*. Most husbands pressurized their wives to give up their right to *meher*, For that purpose they also tried to seek religious support from *ulama* and *maulvis*, who pronounced that those women who would give up their right to *meher* for the sake of their husbands would be rewarded in the next world. To minimize the amount of *meher* without any genuine reason was another ploy employed in the name of religion.[76] Usually the example of the *meher* of Hazrat Fatima was given in this regard and was considered as a matter of *Sunnah*. By asserting this, these *ulama* forgot that the *meher* of Hazrat Fatima was settled according to the economic status of Hazrat Ali who was, of course, very poor at the time of his marriage. However, to make this example a standard for the rest of the Muslim community was certainly not correct.

AWARENESS, CRITICISM AND DEVIATION FROM TRADITIONAL PATRIARCHY

The state of women's misery and their social degradation led these female intellectuals to criticize and pin-point the wrongs dealt out to Indian Muslim women. Their arguments emphasized the traditional patriarchy and gender complexity of Indian society which were affecting the lives of women as a whole. One of the basic reasons for women's suppression as mentioned by many female writers was the double moral standard of a male-dominated society. The picture painted by different female writers reflected a range of angles of this social hypocrisy.

WOMEN AND SOCIAL EXPLOITATION

In general, a woman was expected to show patience and loyalty, in her social behaviour. These were good qualities but it did not mean that each and every thing should be accepted without proper consideration. Such matters became acute when a large number of non-Islamic social practices were propagated in the name of religion but were never criticized by *mullahs* or their followers. One example cited by Sultana Kazia in *Zehniyyat* (Mentality), was the inferior position and the low status of Indian Muslim women. As compared to the women of other Muslim countries, they did not even know about social rights which were given to them by Islam.[77] Another example of this social exploitation cited by Riffat Husain in her *Aurat Ghulam Nahin* (Woman, is not a Slave), was the denial to women of their right to inheritance and the right of divorce from cruel husbands. The demand for divorce by women was seen by society, as if it were the murder of a father or a brother.[78] But then there were those Muslim men she criticized, who knew Islam only with reference to the privilege of four marriages. In particular, she referred to those old men who wanted to remarry, specially young girls as their previous wives were no longer able to fulfil their sexual desires.[79] Another example of this social exploitation was the double standards regarding vice and virtue for men and for women, noted by these female writers. For instance, when a man was guilty of some crime, as Mahmooda Rizvia noted in her *Aurat ki Zindaghi par ek Nazar* (A Glance at a Woman's Life), society conveniently ignored it. On the other hand, when a woman did the same, she was put to shame by the whole society. In spite of the fact that the nature of the action was the same and its punishment according to the teachings of Islam was also the same, she was never excused by society till the end of her life.[80] But if the man committed a shameful act, she was forced to spend the rest of her life with a scoundrel husband, locked up within the four walls of her house.[81]

In the context of prevailing social norms, the double standard of middle-class Indian Muslims was also highlighted by many female writers. For instance, Amat-ul-Wahy's arguments in *Rasmi Purdah* (The Customary Purdah) criticized those so-called Muslim gentlemen who, after donning Western-styled dress and joining clubs, tried to pass off as *Sahib Bahadurs* (Englishmen). But, if someone had a chance to visit their homes, their hypocrisy was easily revealed in the ragged clothes of their wives who were supposed to do their domestic work from dawn to dusk.[82] The pale complexions and emaciated bodies of these women showed that they were never allowed to go out. The houses in which these women spent their whole lives were usually suffocating, dingy and dark and even the courtyards were encircled with high walls. In this situation it was impossible for them to breathe fresh air.[83]

The Muslims of the United Provinces, in particular, were considered to be extreme in the matter of *purdah*. If their women ever got a chance to go outside, they had first to wear a heavy *burqa*, and, then, they were moved into a *tanga* (a small two-wheeled carriage pulled by a horse) which was covered with a heavy, thick cloth.[84] The situation became more ridiculous in the case of a train journey. Both sides of the pathway on the platform through which a woman had to go to reach the train were covered with bed-sheets held by her male-kin. In such a criminal way, the queen of the house had to be moved from one place to another.[85] Throughout her whole life, an Indian Muslim woman seemed to be the hapless victim of the double social and moral standards of society. For instance, it was generally assumed that she was supposed to be the owner of the house of her husband. But what sort of ownership was it? as Begum Ghulam Rasul asked in her *Hum Bechari Auraten* (We Helpless Women), that she could not spend even a single penny on her own. She did not have the right to buy anything independently for herself or for her home. In fact, she was not the owner of the house but a prisoner within the four walls of the house. She was not permitted to go outside even for some fresh air.[86]

FEMALE FANTASY OR MALE HYPOCRISY

Another prominent example of this double moral standard was the definition of 'woman' as a 'body' and as a 'behaviour'. The characteristic understanding of a woman as a body was as a mere object for 'male voluptuousness'. These fantasies were reserved by men for unknown and unseen social relations with women who were beyond their grasp and never filled a place in their real lives. The fantasy of these women as a 'body', Sultana Kazia observed in her article *Saz-e-Dilbari* (The Lovelorn Tune), was a central and key theme in male writings and discussions. Their fiction, novels and social stories were filled with such women. A woman as the most beautiful creature of the world captivated their hearts and minds: the knit of her brow was interpreted in male poetry as a star of fortune, the curls of her hair resembled a chain around the leg of a lover. Above all, a slight wrinkle on her beautiful forehead was enough to confound the whole system of the world.[87]

On the contrary, the definition of a woman as a 'behaviour' was to be found in men's relations with their daughters, sisters, and wives. Snatching off the veil of male hypocrisy, Sultana Kazia declared that, for most men, a 'woman was nothing'. She had no real status in society; her social status was judged by that of her father or husband. In the same way, she did not have any rights in her husband's house. Capturing his heart, as she was portrayed in his fantasies or thoughts, was, thus, actually a distant dream.[88]

WOMEN AND ISLAM

The misinterpretation of Islamic teachings, particularly in relation to women's status, was another issue raised in the context of the double standards of Muslim society. For example, accusing the *mullahs*, Begum Naseeruddin graphically portrayed the miserable condition of the Muslims of Nagpur in one of her writings, *Musalman Auraton main Qaumi Bedari* (National Awakening among Muslim Women). Owing to the social and cultural influence of the Hindu majority, local Muslims then knew little about the basic teachings of Islam. The *ulama* of this area, however, were not properly concerned about their religious responsibility. Their main concerns during Friday sermons seemed to be the interpretation of the beauty of *houris* (black-eyed heavenly nymphs) or the heart-rending torments of hell.[89] With regard to the Quranic verse in which God says that 'You (men) are their (women) protector', *mullahs* interpreted it to legitimize male control over women. However, the *mullah* was not the only one who could be accused of this kind of despicable behaviour. The whole male-dominated society was involved in these intrigues.[90] Begum Azam-un-Nisa's article, *Aurat aur Uski Ghulami* (Women and her Slavery), provided its readers with a graphic account of those houses in which baby girls were treated by their fathers as unwanted children and when they grew older they were driven into their husbands' homes without their consent. In doing so, why did Muslim men forget the example of Egypt, Turkey and Iran where Muslim women were enjoying complete rights of liberation and freedom? she asked.

WHAT CAN WE DO FOR OURSELVES?

The analysis of social problems led female critics to discuss the various possibilities as solutions to these issues.

Women and the Removal of Inferiority Complexes

Women's inferiority was the first and main question which they raised in their writings. The domestic environment in which a girl was brought up was often regarded as the root cause of this complex. Much of the blame it was felt rested with the mother; after all being a woman she could influence the ideas of her husband or train her son in such a way that, after marriage, he would at least be able to recognize the rights of his wife and daughter. Unfortunately, most mothers did not do that, and the sons brought up under their influence continued to treat their wives badly.[91] This was sometimes seen as an 'influence of Hindu culture' because, as Begum Aziz-ul-Hasan observed in her *Khushgawar Shadi* (A Happy Marriage), a Hindu woman, according to her religious and social roles, could not demand maintenance allowance from her son. The only way she could preserve her authority and divert the attention of her son was by degrading her daughter-in-law. She tried to teach her son that the status of a wife was no more than that of a 'shoe' or a 'maid'.[92]

Writers were keen to point out that when this kind of domestic environment generally prevailed in the society, people began to think that women were in fact inferior by nature. By doing so, however, society ignored the fact that women, too, had two ears, two eyes, the same nose and the same tongue. Indeed this was one of the best examples of gender equality given by nature.[93] In the same way, there was no difference between men and women in their intellectual qualities. Arguing this in her *Aurat ki Ghulami* (The Slavery of Woman), Riffat Husain declared that if men were proud of Jinnah and Gandhi then women were also proud of Sarojini Naidu and 'Bi Amman' (the mother of Ali brothers).[94] Similarly, in the field of literature, if men produced scholars like Nazir Ahmed and Rashid-ul-Khairi, women also produced Sultan Jahan Begum and Muhammadi Begum.

As regards poetry, if a person like Iqbal could become the best example in the field, why, she asked, were women lagging so far behind? The fact, she said, was that women were never given any encouragement in their domestic environment. Their male-kin never let them express their feelings and they remained secluded within the four walls of the house. In this situation how could women produce an Iqbal? They never got the chance to see the remains of Cordoba or the destruction of Muslim civilization which inspired Iqbal to pen his passion-filled poems.[95] Another 'reason' for woman's inferiority was, it was argued, that she could never be awarded the honour of prophethood. But Riffat argued that critics forgot who the mothers of these sacred men were. Indeed, women had received this honour and, in this way, they became the fountainhead of the luminosity which was spread in the world by these prophets.[96] She further noted that while women were often called the disciples of the Devil men conveniently chose to forget that the Devil was of a masculine gender.[97]

The second cause of woman's inferiority was her own ignorance of her rights and social status. In the first place she surrendered herself before the man, not because she was physically weak but because she did not know the difference between right and wrong. She did not realize that the purpose of her creation was not to become a slave or subordinate of a man but to become a full human being with equal rights and opportunities. Women were not animals who could be handed over from one person to another.[98] They must remember, as Salima Begum suggested in her *Aurat Ghulam Nahin* (Woman, not a Slave), that their first and foremost duty was to be a respectable person, which was more important than to be mothers of those men who were usurping women's rights by confining them to their homes and letting them die of tuberculosis or anaemia. These 'selfish' men never let women raise their voice against injustice and cruelty. However, now the time had come for women to protest against their oppression.[99]

WOMEN AND THE SELECTION OF LIFE PARTNERS

Another suggestion which came from some female writers was some sort of concrete change in the general behaviour and attitude of society towards women. They focused on marriage as indication of the urgent need for reform. Parents it seemed hardly considered the opinion of their children when the subject of marriage was raised. The only criterion for the selection of a son- or daughter-in-law was close kinship, close family terms or the sound financial position of the party, without considering the personal likes or dislikes of the grown-up children involved. Such marriages usually resulted in permanent misunderstanding between husband and wife. This often led to a second marriage for the husband, or forced the husband to spend most of his time outside the home, either with prostitutes or with 'dissolute' friends. In this way, although the husband and wife were both affected by this sort of marriage, the consequences for the latter proved to be far worse. Denied contact with the world outside life became intolerably suffocating for her.[100]

The situation was worse in families where the girl was not allowed to appear even before her would-be mother-in-law before marriage. Sometimes, the desire to find out some thing about the girl led her in-laws to use certain strange tactics and often, the services of maids were hired for this purpose. However, such illiterate women were not able to relate much to them except about the complexion or height of the girl, while her habits and interests remained a big mystery until the day of her marriage.[101] Thus the general habits, interests and inclinations of the engaged couple were hardly discussed by their elder kin which often proved disastrous for the marriage. If for example in the case of marriage where the groom was fond of going to the cinema or to the club and the bride was hemmed in with age-old traditions and restrictions, how could the match prove to be an ideal one?

The only way to get rid of such impediments was to ensure that, before marriage a man and a woman were able to get to know each other. By doing so, both parties would avoid the problems which could later weaken the marriage tie and badly affect their lives. Modern education for women could play a crucial role in this regard. Modern education and economic independence changed the lifestyle of many Indian women who were now in a position to choose their life partners. The basic motive behind this desire to choose one's own partner, according to Siddiqa Bano, as she noted in her *Razamandi ki Shadi* (Marriage by Consent), was the idea of a happy married life. The fulfilment of this desire sometimes appeared in the form of love marriage, rather than accepting the selection of a spouse by one's parents. In this case, modern women sometimes did not hesitate to cross the boundaries of caste and *biradari* (fraternity). Religion, however, remained an important consideration in choosing a husband.[102]

Before accusing these women of wanting to select their own partners, parents should realize, Siddiqa suggested, that it did not represent a deliberate revolt against the traditional system but stemmed from a desire to spend a better life with a better partner.[103] In the same context, Jamila Begum, in her *Muhhabat ki Shadi* (Love Marriage), bitterly criticized parents who were liberal in the matters of education and training of their children but became narrow minded when the time came for their marriage.[104] They would do well to realize, she advised, that the changing educational curricula now included love stories and romantic poetry and that the cinema, too, sought to stimulate love scenes and romanticism among younger generation. It was, therefore, necessary for parents to consider these changes and make arrangements so that, before marriage men and women are able to see and learn to understand each other within religious limitations.[105] But this rarely happened: parents and other close elderly kin were reluctant to show any flexibility. One of the main reasons, as pointed out by some writers, was the age of these relatives. When their children reached a marriageable age, most parents had long passed the age of love and emotions which would enable them to understand and appreciate the feelings of their children. The only standard for the selection of suitable life partners for their children were the sound financial position of the party or close familial relationship.[106] They must understand and accept as Safia Naqvi suggested in her *Kaghaz ki Nao* (A Paper Boat), the dramatic social changes occurring around them from which it was impossible to remain unaffected for long. It was an undeniable fact that traditional culture was dying out and age-old customs were becoming weaker day by day. The only way to meet the present challenges, in her opinion, was the reconsideration of all socio-cultural values.[107]

WOMEN AND THE CONSCIOUSNESS OF SOCIAL RIGHTS

To know how to exercise particular social rights was another solution presented by many female writers. In particular, after marriage the awareness of a woman about her social rights could save her life from many problems. In explaining Islamic marriage as a social contract, the status of the wife was presented as equal to that of the husband. The purpose of marriage for a man was now seen as acquiring a companion in the form of a wife, instead of getting a mere 'maid' or 'slave' for domestic service.[108] Mushir Fatima, in her *Shadi aur uske Lawazmat*, (Marriage and its Requirements), suggested that in this way the mutual esteem and respect of both parties for each other would be further strengthened. She stated that the fixation of the amount of *meher* at the time of *nikah* could save married women from undue threats of divorce by their husbands. Even in the case of divorce, when a woman had to pass through great economic stresses, a reasonable amount by way of *meher* could lessen her problems.[109] The exercise of the right of *khulah* was not a sin as it was thought of by most Indian Muslims. If the basic objective of marriage—love and mutual understanding—could not be attained, said Safia Khanum in her *Insaf ya Zulm* (Justice or Injustice), and it became impossible for a wife to live with her husband under the same roof, then there was absolutely no need to tolerate such misery. *Khulah* was the only solution in such a case.[110]

While supporting these individual solutions, some female writers felt that the general improvement in the image of a woman in society would be to tackle the problem in a more

holistic way. An important role could be played by leading
political organizations. This would also consolidate their national
agenda. However, as Begum Z.D. Hasan, ruefully noted in her
Badalte hue Mashriq par ek Nazar (A Glance at the changing
East), the two main political outfits in India at that time—the
Congress and the Muslim League—were completely blind to
the feminine question. When they were asked why they had
turned a blind eye to the matter they would reply that women's
issue was not on their agenda.[111]

In the same way, the utility of education as a campaigning
tool against these social problems would always be helpful in
raising awareness in Indian society about the status of women.
Finally, female education was seen as the most powerful catalyst
and tool in reshaping societal images of Indian Muslim
womanhood. Education was advocated not just for its own sake
or, as Sultana Asif suggested in *Aurat ka Nasbulayn* (The
Purpose of Womanhood), to increase the value of the would-be
bride in the marriage market or to improve her economic
condition. But what was far more important was the role that
education could play in helping society in general, and women
in particular. This could radically transform attitudes in matters
relating to women.[112]

* * *

Taking a general overview of the growth and development of
Indian Muslim women's literary culture during the period under
discussion, we can visualize the contribution that it made in the
development of a feminist discourse among Muslim women in
colonial India.[113] The recovering of hidden female voices through
a study of the texts which they produced helps us to understand
both the particular conditions of these women's lives as well as
the genesis and growth of a distinct feminist consciousness among
them. Women took up the pen and began to reinterpret society
from a radically and refreshingly new perspective. This new
perspective was not dominated by traditional patriarchal notions
of power in society. On the contrary, it challenged the dominant

socio-religious ideology and the rigid traditional boundaries that circumscribed gender relations in society at large. These female intellectuals believed that education and social awareness were crucial forces which could be employed in bringing about a new synthesis in society in general. Their endorsement of a new domestic ideology and their campaign for an ideal marital life was an attempt to refashion women's roles in accordance with the changing social context.

As regards the ideological thrust of this new approach it was neither a call to return to traditional socio-religious gender relations nor an appeal for the blind adoption of western culture. In fact it was seen as a part of the process of transforming society from tradition to modernity and a coping with the new challenges of social transformation.

It was, however, too much to expect a dramatic change in the lives of the women of the middle classes. It was less a 'revolution' than a slow process of 'evolution' in which intrinsic and gradual changes became more important than extraneous events. On the part of women these sorts of intrinsic changes helped to redefine conceptions of themselves and their place in the wider social system. Social change and the transformation of society was considered by these female writers as a serious responsibility not only as a vehicle to enable them to express themselves but also to improve the image of the Muslim community in the eyes of society at large. In this way, these middle-class female intellectuals saw themselves as a force in bringing about a new synthesis and harmony in society.

Indian Muslim society at this time was in a flux, caught up as it was in the vortex of dramatic changes taking place all around. It must be remembered that these middle-class women intellectuals were by no means fully representative of the concerns and aspirations of all Muslim women in general. The concerns of working-class women or women belonging to the agriculturalist classes, for instance, were very different, in many important respects. These were hardly reflected in the writings of middle-class women writers. Furthermore, some of the demands of these writers can possibly be seen, with the benefit of hindsight, as reflecting an excessively undiscriminating attitude in the matter of adopting feminist models from the West.

NOTES

1. Mumtaz Gohar, *Muntakhabat-e-Tehzib-e-Niswan*, (Maghrabi Pakistan Urdu Academy, Lahore, 1988), p. 8.

2. Jamila Begum, 'Salgirah Tehzib-e-Niswan', *Tehzib-e-Niswan*, Vol. 43, No. 27, July 1940, pp. 632–33.

3. Zuhra Begum Faizi, 'Tehzib-e-Niswan ke Bani', *Tehzib-e-Niswan*, Vol. 143, No. 27, July 1940, pp. 633–35.

4. Gail Minault, 'Making Invisible Women Visible: Studying The History of Muslim Women in South Asia', *Journal of South Asian Studies*, Vol. 9, No. 1, June 1986, pp. 1–14.

5. Ibid.

6. Raziq-ul-Khairi, 'Savan-e-Umri Rashid-ul-Khairi', *Ismat*, Vol. 113, No. 1 and 2, July and August 1964, p. 127.

7. Ibid., p. 411.

8. Ibid.

9. Ibid., p. 196.

10. Ibid., p. 261.

11. Ibid., p. 160.

12. Mumtaz Gohar, *Muntakhabat-e-Tehzib-e-Niswan*, p. 8.

13. *Punjab Native Newspapers Report, 1900–1925*, L/R/5/200-205, n.p., IOL.

14. Raziq-ul-Khairi, 'Savan-e-Umri Rashid-ul-Khairi', pp. 332–33.

15. *Quarterly Statement of Newspapers in Delhi Province, 1925–47*, V/25/960/48, n.p., IOL.

16. Saeeda Zamiruddin, 'Ma ki Sehat', *Ismat*, Vol. 58, No. 1, January 1937, pp. 25–26.

17. Ibid.

18. Ibid.

19. S.R. Karmania, 'Maon ko Hidayat', *Ismat*, Vol. 50, No. 4, April 1933, pp. 265–66.

20. Sayyeda Kishwar Ara, 'Aurat aur Tarbiyat-e-Kirdar', *Ismat*, Vol. 76, No. 4 April 1946, p. 245.

21. Ibid.

22. Mrs A. Shaheed, 'Tarbiyat ki Chand Usool,' *Ismat*, Vol. 72, No.1, January 1944, pp. 21–22.

23. Ibid.

24. Ibid.

25. Ibid.

26. Gahdir Fatima, 'Larkiyon ki Talim', *Ismat*, Vol. 26, No. 1, January 1939, pp. 55–56.

27. Ibid.

28. Jamila Begum, 'Hamari Shakhsiyyat', *Ismat*, Vol. 64, No. 1, June 1940, pp. 413–15.

29. Ibid.

30. Imtiaz Begum, 'Barhthe hue Wazan par Qaboo Pana,' *Ismat*, Vol. 73, No. 5, November 1944, p. 283.

31. Shaista Ikramullah, 'Kaproh say Mutaaliq chand Bathen', *Ismat*, Vol. 56, No. 2, June 1936, pp. 441–42.

32. Ibid.

33. Ibid.

34. Ibid.

35. Miss A.J., 'Ayaddat', *Tehzib-e-Niswan*, Vol. 43, No. 37, September 1940, pp. 908–909.

36. Badar Mansoori, 'Dawaten aur Hum', *Ismat*, Vol. 76, No. 5, May 1946, p. 342.

37. Ibid.

38. Sughra Humayun Asghar, 'Auraton ky Faraiz', *Ismat* Vol. 56, No. 1, January 1936, pp. 46–48.

39. Ibid.

40. Salehah Abid Husain, 'Aurathen aur Mutalia-e-Koran', *Ismat*, Vol. 73, No. 4, October 1944, pp. 209–12.

41. Jamila Begum, 'Hamari Talim ka Maqsad', *Ismat*, Vol. 57, No. 3, September 1936, pp. 303–304.

42. Ibid.

43. Mahmoona Qadir, 'Talim ke Mukhalifon se,' *Ismat*, Vol. 68, No. 5, May 1942, pp. 273–75.

44. Begum Amiruddin, 'Inglistan se Hame kya Sikhna Chahiye,' *Ismat*, Vol. 55, No. 3, March 1935, pp. 184–85. The actual interview was published in a local English language newspaper of Madras and was translated for *Ismat* by Miss Ibrahim, a local writer from Madras.

45. Rafia Khatun, 'Hindustan main Niswani Taraqqi ka Mafhoom,' *Tehzib-e-Niswan*, Vol. 43, No. 35, 31 August 1940, pp. 852–54.

46. Ibid.

47. For further detail see, Salima Begum, 'Aurat Ghulam Nahin,' *Tehzib-e-Niswan*, Vol. 48, No. 2, 10 February 1945, pp. 84–86.

48. Fatima Begum, 'Mission Askool ki Talim Zaroor Rang Layegi', *Ismat*, Vol. 51, No. 6, December 1933, pp. 452–55.

49. Ibid.

50. Jamila Begum, 'Mazhibi Talim', *Ismat*, Vol. 60, No. 2, February 1937, pp. 111–12.

51. Ibid.

52. Ibid.

53. Raziq-ul-Khairi, 'Savan-e-Umri Rashid-ul-Khairi', *Ismat*, p. 665.

54. The abstract is taken from Rashid-ul-Khairi's 'Shara ka Khoon' published in *Ismat* in 1911. Ibid.

55. Ibid.

56. Ibid.

57. Extract from one of the social writings of Rashid-ul-Khairi, 'Larki Maike Mein', published in *Ismat*, in 1919, ibid., p. 668.

58. Ibid.

59. Ibid.

60. Sultana Kazia, 'Zehniyyat', *Tehzib-e-Niswan*, Vol. 48, No. 25, 14 Janauary 1945, p. 385.

61. Ibid.

62. Ibid., p. 668.

63. Sabiha Hafeez, *The Girl Child in Pakistan: Priority Concerns*. This paper was presented at the UNICEF Strategy Conference on the SAARC Year of the Girl Child in Pakistan, held at Islamabad on 28–30 January 1990, (Pictorial Printers, Islamabad, 1990), p.18.

64. The abstract is taken from one of the social writings of Rashid-ul-Khairi, 'Jahez wa Tajhiz', published in *Ismat*, in 1908. Raziq-ul-Khairi, 'Savan-e-Umri Rashid-ul-Khairi', p. 669.

65. Ibid.

66. Abstract is taken from one of the social writings of Rashid-ul-Khairi, published in *Ismat*, in 1918, see ibid., p. 667.

67. Ibid.

68. Ibid.

69. Rashid-ul-Khairi, 'Aisi Biyahi se Kunvari Bhali', *Ismat*, Vol. 62, No. 4, April 1939, pp. 250–52.

70. Shafiq Siddique, 'Mujhe Bhool Jana Meri Piyari Amman,' *Ismat*, Vol. 78, No. 1, January 1947, p. 32.

71. Ibid.

72. Extract from Rashid-ul-Khairi's 'Muslaman Aurat ki Halat-e-Zar', published in *Ismat* in 1918, see Raziq-ul-Khairi, 'Savan-e-Umri Rashid-ul-Khairi', p. 686

73. Extract from Rashid-ul-Khairi, 'Bahnwar ki Dulhan', published in *Ismat*, in 1926, see Ibid., p. 689.

74. Ibid.

75. Ibid.

76. Extract from Rashid-ul-Khairi's 'Musalman Mard ki Khudhgarzi', published in *Ismat*, in 1934, see Ibid., p. 698.

77. Sultana Kazia, 'Zehniyyat', *Tehzib-e-Niswan*, Vol. 48, No. 24, 16 June 1945, p. 385.

78. Riffat Husain, 'Aurat Ghulam Nahin,' *Tehzib-e-Niswan*, Vol. 48, No. 9, 2 March 1939, pp. 129–31.

79. Ibid.
80. Mahmooda Rizvia, 'Aurat ki Zindagi par ek Nazar', *Ismat*, Vol. 76, No. 2, February 1939, pp. 115–16.
81. Ibid.
82. Amut-ul-Wahi, 'Rasmi Purdah', *Ismat*, Vol. 61, No. 6, December 1938, pp. 451–52.
83. Ibid.
84. Ibid.
85. Ibid.
86. Begum Ghulam Rasul, 'Hum Bechari Auraten', *Ismat*, Vol. 59, No. 4, October 1937, p. 313.
87. Sultana Kazia, 'Saz-e-Dilbari', *Tehzib-e-Niswan*, Vol. 48, No. 2, 13 January 1945, pp. 20–22.
88. Ibid.
89. Begum Naseeruddin, 'Musalman Auraton main Qaumi Bedari', *Tehzib-e-Niswan*, Vol. 49, No. 25, 22 June 1946, pp. 385–86.
90. Ibid.
91. Sakina Chirgahuddin, 'Aurat aur Mard ki Jungh', *Ismat*, Vol. 59, No. 5, November 1939, pp. 409–10.
92. Begum Aziz-ul-Hasan, 'Kushgawar Zindgi', *Ismat*, Vol. 60, No. 3, March 1938, p. 189.
93. Riffat Husain, 'Aurat Ghulan Nahin', *Tehzib-e-Niswan*, Vol. 48, No. 8, 24 February 1945, pp. 114–17.
94. Ibid.
95. Ibid.
96. Ibid.
97. Ibid.
98. See for detail Sultana Kazia, 'Saz-e-Dilbari', *Tehzib-e-Niswan*, Vol. 48, No. 2, January 1945, pp. 20–22.
99. Salima Begum, 'Aurat Ghulam Nahin', *Tehzib-e-Niswan*, Vol. 48, No. 5, February, 1945, pp. 65–69.,
100. Miss A.S., 'Byzubanohn ki Shadiyan', *Ismat*, Vol. 65, No. 6, June 1935, pp. 412–16.
101. Miss A.J., 'Intikhab-e-Ristah', *Ismat*, Vol. 65, No. 1, August 1940, pp. 156–57.
102. Siddiqa Bano, 'Razamandi ki Shadi,' *Ismat*, Vol. 74, No. 2, February 1945, pp. 88–89.
103. Ibid.
104. Jamila Begum, 'Muhabath ki Shadi', *Ismat*, Vol. 74, No. 6, June 1945, pp. 349–50.
105. Ibid.
106. Raza Jafri, 'Jinsi Rishtay aur unka Intikhab', *Ismat*, Vol. 77, No. 1, July 1946, pp. 33–37.

107. Safia Naqvi, 'Kaghaz ki Nao', *Ismat*, Vol. 75, No. 6, December 1945, pp. 408–10.

108. Amina Nazli, 'Dulhan', *Ismat*, Vol. 67, No. 4, October 1941, pp. 325–38.

109. Mushir Fatima, 'Shadi aur usky lawazmat', *Ismat*, Vol. 74, No. 4, April 1945, pp. 239–42.

110. Safia Khanum, 'Insaf ya Zulam', *Ismat*, Vol. 47, No. 4, October 1937, pp. 300–302.

111. Begum Z.D. Hasan, 'Badalte hue Mashriq par ek Nazar', *Ismat*, Vol, 48, No. 4, April 1932, pp. 292–97.

112. Sultana Asif, 'Aurat ka Nasbulayn', *Tehzib-e-Niswan*, Vol. 48, No. 15, April 1945, pp. 325–27.

113. See Appendix No. I.

Conclusion

The birth of the contemporary feminist movement among Muslim women in India can be seen as a direct response to, as well as consequence of, the growing influence of liberal and rational ideas from the West. Given the conservatism and general backwardness of the Muslim community, it was but natural that the achievements of this movement were modest rather than revolutionary. Without entering into the controversy of the debate, we can say that the question of the position of Muslim women was largely accommodated in the context of those reforms that were started to improve the social condition of Indian society as a whole. Over time, women's issues began to acquire a salience of their own and they began to receive growing attention. The first priority of these social reforms concerned various acute social problems of South Asian society. Among them, the problems of *sati* or widow burning, female infanticide, the remarriage of a widow, *purdah* or seclusion and child marriage were directly discussed as part of this new ideological discourse. The second set of concerns involved matters which were directly discussed under the label of women's social rights, their economic status and their political and national role in the colonial state. Thus, the formulation and consolidation of feminism was accommodated by Muslim women and became bound up in their cultural revivalism, their national identity, their political independence and above all in their efforts to improve the image of womanhood.

Before looking at the issues of women's emancipation which directly or indirectly were discussed under the label of feminist movement in India, it is necessary to understand the meaning of 'feminism' in the context of Indian society in general and that of Indian Muslims in particular. At first glance it seemed to be only a foreign ideology, something imported from the West and seeking to involve many local women, mostly from the newly emerged middle class, into the redefined realms of private and public spheres. Indeed, feminism itself is a western ideology, first introduced in western countries to remove the social disabilities of western women. After that the same ideology was propagated among the women of the east, in particular those belonging to colonial states. In fact, the idea of feminism was not imposed on colonial women but rather its arrival was the product of historical circumstances that created important material and ideological changes in these societies. The example of British India highlights the process by which feminism emerged as the outcome of those social reforms that were started by different agencies during the nineteenth and twentieth centuries. The social agendas of these agencies evolved into a 'hotly contested ideological terrain' in which women were used to symbolize the progressive aspirations of Indians in the colonial context.

However, the nature of changes relating to colonial women was quite different from that which affected their western sisters. In the West, the feminist agenda did not automatically involve suggestions that there should be changes made to the whole social ideology and local traditions. Most attention was paid to raising the status of women without destroying the basic social system. On the other hand, in a place such as India, the existing laws, social customs and local traditions were targeted by imperial as well as indigenous critics. In this way, the practical implementation of changes relating to Indian women became a major challenge for those working for reform. They found that if they wanted the benefits of feminism it would bring fundamental changes to their socio-religious traditions.

The way in which the feminist discourse was introduced in India can be better understood in the context of the feminist movement in Egypt which developed as a result of a historical encounter between Egypt and the West. This opened up the possibility of choice for an increasing number of women mostly from middle-class backgrounds and led to the conviction that they could become an important force for changing oppressive and unjust conditions within their own society. But this kind of feminism did not follow western models but deliberately set out to operate on Egyptian terms in the context of Egyptian society.[1]

In British India a similar process took place as the impact of colonial rule was increasingly felt and the changes which it stimulated were accommodated by local communities according to their needs and desires. Like other communities in India, Indian Muslims responded to the Western social agenda and its package of values without bringing about any fundamental changes in their social and religious systems. The three spheres in which their response was more visible were the realms of religion, social issues, and politics.

On religious grounds the early response of *ulama* distinctly differed from those of mostly social and political reformers. The considerable amount of reformist literature produced by *ulama* for Muslim women in particular during the latter half of the nineteenth and early years of the twentieth centuries was directed, by and large, towards reinforcing and consolidating further their traditional roles. The maximum change, which they were willing to allow, was rudimentary education at home for Muslim women. By idealizing the character of Muslim women as one of loyalty, moral sensitivity, and strict domesticity—her religious obligations were considered, for some, as more important for the moral purity of society than those of men.

The response, which came from Muslim political élites during this period, was rather different from those of the *ulama*. Some of them considered the uplift of Muslim women as crucial in the overall regeneration of Muslim society. They sought to persuade their community to realize the importance of women's education in the vastly changed social context of their times. One specific example was that of Badruddin Tyabji, who went so far as to send his daughters abroad for higher education.

A number of social reformers emerged at this time and proved to an important bridge between urban-dwellers—newly arrived from *qasbahs*—and the modern structures within which they now found themselves living. These reformers sought to bring about a creative harmonization between the demands of 'tradition' on the one hand, and of 'modernity' on the other. They focused, for instance, on the curricula taught in girls' schools and addressed issues of female education in both Islamic as well as western-styled institutions. Their approach towards Muslim women's emancipation sought the combination of social with religious agendas. They attempted to communicate their views to a wider circle through their writings, which included novels as well as poetry.

It should be noted that, as in the case of the *ulama*, most of the literature for the emancipation of Muslim women produced by social reformers was in Urdu. The development of this new genre of literature pointed to the emergence of Urdu as the common language linking middle-class Muslims in the various regions of India. It would not be wrong to say that these writings proved to be as popular among Indian Muslims as those of the *ulama*, and, in certain respects, more socially relevant. The popularity of this body of literature lay in the way that it directly approached issues and problems relating to Muslim women. The plots of their novels, for instance, revolved around women's lives, with their central characters speaking their own language, employing their own idioms, sharing their own feelings, and finally offering what they saw as the appropriate solutions to their own problems. Thus these works not only provided a space for the creative refashioning of indigenous culture but also an important source of guidance for women. Hence, the characters of Asghari, in Nazir Ahmed's *Mirat-ul-Arus*, Saeeda in Wazir Ali's *Nasihat ka Kiran Phool*, and Liaqat-un-nisa in Muhammad Muslihuddin's *Kuhl-ul-Jawahir*, symbolized those women who were trying to explore their identities both within, as well as increasingly outside, the *zenana*.

During the same period another initiative was taken through the formation of various associations and organizations. Among the prime concerns of several of these bodies was pursuing practical measures for social improvement. These early efforts touched upon issues directly related to women such as their attacks on social evils including women's seclusion and child marriage. The cause of women was further strengthened by the foundation of several specifically women's associations alongside those of their men-folk. This new kind of social discourse not only became a channel to discuss different issues relating to Muslim women but also it gradually offered a space to them to express their cultural experiences in the light of the transformation of Indian society. Later these concerns proved helpful for many Muslim élites in defining new dimensions in their political and constitutional struggle.

The period from 1920 to 1947 proved a real turning point in terms of opportunities and challenges for the Muslims of India. British participation in the First World War, the abolition of the Muslim *Khilafat* in Turkey and the enactment of the Montagu-Chelmsford reforms led them to revise their social and political manifestos. Many came to realize that their continued ignorance would shut them off from becoming a part of that political and social force, preventing them from being able to effect changes in the prevailing systems, laws, and legislation and above all in the political future of the country. Their favourable but cautious response had important repercussions for the changing position of Muslim women in India as well as the creation of more space for them in their private and public lives.

Hence, support for girls' education which grew during this period was based increasingly on the appreciation of its importance in the process of educating society as a whole. Despite the particular difficulties arising from local Muslim customs, the colonial government and Muslim social reformers went ahead with their efforts to promote education among Muslim girls. The former introduced special measures for Muslim girls' education in different parts of India, while the latter became major campaigners for the promotion of modern education for Muslim girls both in Urdu as well as in English. Pioneering efforts in this regard were made by Shaikh Abdullah of Aligarh and Justice Karamat Husain of Lucknow.

The achievement of these and other pioneers were communicated to a wider circle through the Urdu journals which had already been targeted specifically at women through discussing the agenda of their social reform. The most prominent of these, Sayyed Mumtaz Ali's *Tehzib-e-Niswan* and Rashid-ul-Khairi's *Ismat*, adopted a relatively radical position on the question of what a proper education for Muslim girls should be. While doing so, however, these pioneers sought to strike a comfortable balance between the demands of 'tradition' and 'modernity' within an overarching Islamic context. They were of the opinion that an ideal curriculum should be based on firm religious foundations, provide a sound elementary education, and also teach the lessons of hygiene, child bearing, and household economics. While the nature of these demands was not new or at all revolutionary, it brought about radical changes in local Muslim values. For Muslim women this kind of opportunity also enhanced their personal freedom as well as their educational qualifications. Through higher education, for instance, some Muslim women gained access to jobs which had previously been reserved solely for men, such as medicine, law, banking and even, as in the course of the Second World War, military service. Thus, the response of Muslim women, the quality of their work, and their active participation, can all be compared quite favourably with the achievements of other Indian women during the same period.

Women's space in the field of health was the outcome of the advancement of the maternity and child welfare movement in India. Social problems such as women's seclusion and child marriage developed widespread interest throughout society and produced support for the urgent need to provide medical facilities as it was considered more fit to mitigate the consequences of these social evils. Women's response towards this emerging 'scientific culture' can be seen in their frequent visit to *zenana* hospitals and maternity homes. It also encouraged many Indian women to enter into the medical profession. New public spaces, as a result, were created for women as trained nurses, and midwives gradually replaced the traditional *dai*. Alongside these developments, significant progress was made through the beginning of preventive campaigns for the adequate health protection of mother and child, passing of various pieces of legislation and the general spread of awareness. It helped

Indian women to improve their health status in general, not only as mothers or wives, but also as individuals. Early efforts can be seen through those forms of literature and books which were written to redefine women's health and their social role in the transformation of Indian society. Among Muslims this sort of work was mostly done by social reformers as well as religious authorities, who were looking at these changes according to their own points of view. Reformist *ulama*, in particular those from the Dar-ul-Ulum at Deoband, responded by attempting to increase the popularity of the Graeco-Arabic medicine system or *unani tibb*. This subject was taught as an ancillary topic at Deoband, covered a vast range of ailments, and was considered equal or even superior to the Western medical system.

In the field of social legislation, the status of women was another challenging issue raised in the context of developing more space for women in their private and public lives. Before that, the legislative reforms, such as the banning of *sati*, provided the initial stimulus for a broader attempt to improve the status of women through the agency of the law. Three main pieces of legislation which were enacted during this period—the Child Marriage Restraint Act of 1929, the Muslim Shariat Application Act of 1937, and the Dissolution of Muslim Marriage Act of 1939—were used by Indian Muslims not only to challenge existing social practices concerning women but also to draw government support to secure their communal identity and religious and political interests. For the *Jamiat-ul-Ulema-e-Hind,* for instance, it provided one more base from which to spearhead its campaign for the complete enforcement of Muslim personal law. For the Muslim League, the issue of women's rights was increasingly seen as inextricably linked with the prospects of the entire Muslim community in India. Significant sections of the League now began veering round to the view that the question of Muslim women's empowerment was inseparable from that of the community as a whole. Yet, the stand it adopted was, at best, ambiguous. While, for instance, Jinnah was reluctant to concede to Muslim women the full property rights which the *shariat* had given them, for fear of alienating powerful landlord bodies, for many Muslim women legislation of this kind represented a welcome shift from traditional patriarchy to more 'modern' gender relationships which would provide them with greater social and political space. The feminist agenda, which came from modern educated women, was summed up in the slogan that the sphere of their activities could be extended from the home to the world in keeping with the changing times. Thus, legislation was considered as both escape and protection from existing social practices. The terrain of rights had been largely mapped according to the way that law had developed in the modern world. The legal enforcement of their inheritance and divorce rights by the state led to the realization that further ignorance meant the surrender of socio-economic independence.

Another major consequence of this growing social awareness was the spawning of the movement for women's political enfranchisement, a radical development which further widened their role in the public sphere. The vote was seen as not just important in itself but as symbolizing sex-equality. It also provided women with a platform from which they could influence both the government and political parties. Over time the latter came to view the women's issue in purely communal rather than specifically gender-related terms, as markers of separate communal identities. As regards Muslim women, this was reflected in the very active part that they played in the political struggle which led to the creation of Pakistan, particularly the efforts of the Muslim League's Women's Sub-committee. Although, in many cases, the number of politically-active women was not that large, their presence in processions and rallies was sufficient to show their determination to support their cause or simply to shoulder more responsibility so others could work for freedom. Thus, the construction of women's feminist behaviour as an individual character as well as an important and integral part of society led to the realization by many Indian Muslims that the presence of women could consolidate the cause and not damage the honour of their male relatives.

The emergence of women's literary culture sought to project the women's issue according to their own views. The recovery of hidden female voices through the study of the texts which they produced during the colonial transformation of India has become a major source for understanding both the existing position of women in and outside the home as well as the development of different attitudes which led to the creation of a distinct feminist consciousness among them. In this way, the place, which they found for themselves through literary culture, was as different as that of the world created for them by men. Surely, it was not dominated by traditional patriarchal notions of power or rigid gender boundaries and roles, but represented an endorsement to refashion women's roles in accordance with the changing times. These texts, taken collectively, could in fact be regarded as a 'manifesto' of Indian Muslim feminism.

Overall, then, the period from 1920–47 proved crucial in the development of new spaces for Muslim women and the emergence of a nascent feminist consciousness among them. Yet it is important to note that this consciousness was distinctly Muslim and Indian in character. It was by no means a blind imitation of a western model of feminism. Radha Kumar, for instance, observes that, while in the west the feminist movement seems to have been directed against men themselves, in South Asia, by and large, it entailed co-operative efforts by both women as well as men for the betterment of society.[2] The fledgling Indian Muslim feminist movement reflected this by seeking a harmonious balance between 'modern' approaches and 'traditional' norms.

It must also be noted that the feminist consciousness, which emerged among sections of Muslim women in India, differed in several respects from that of Hindu women. While the Hindu reform movement and its efforts to improve the status of women was not opposed by Indian Muslims, they did not see them as applying in any way to their communities. Their arguments emphasized the ideological differences between the two communities, and, as regards women, took great comfort from the fact that Islam provided far more comprehensive rights to

women than orthodox Hinduism. Hence, most of the secular
measures and social measures concerning women which were
introduced by the Government in British India, were usually
resisted by Muslims, who saw Islam as providing woman with
her rightful share. However, Muslim and Hindu women did
actively combine to work together on some occasions, such as
during the campaign against child marriage and the struggle to
obtain the right to vote for women. But just as the same
enthusiasm which occurred in 1916 in the form of 'Lucknow
Pact' between the Congress and Muslim League later
evaporated, so most of this co-operation between different
communities of Indian women subsequently melted into thin air
as the communal temperature rose.

At the same time, the Muslim feminist movement in India
had to contend with the challenge of how their struggle fitted in
with the wider processes of change that were taking place more
or less simultaneously in other Muslim societies, particularly in
the Middle East where the 'women' question had become an
important issue for social and political reformers. It cannot be
doubted that that Islam has provided a powerful unifying force
which centred on the idea of the *umma* binding Muslims
together, and the greatest example of this universality can be
seen in the *hajj*. Yet alongside this, individual Muslim local
cultures have existed with their own characteristics and values.
The minority status of Muslims in India, for instance, combined
with their existing cultures and their past histories, endowed
them with a particular character which was specific to the
subcontinent. This influenced the way in which feminism
developed among Indian Muslim women and distinguished them
to some extent from the movements which involved their
Muslim sisters from other countries.

Drawing inspiration from western, Hindu, and non-Indian
Muslim feminist movements, Indian Muslim women, with the
help of sympathetic male members of their community, wove
these strands into a rich tapestry which depicted their visions of
what the position of women within society should be. The
framework for this endeavour, however, was provided and

contextualized in the long run by the communalization of Indian life, which fixed a kind of template for reforms among Muslims. In general, from the Muslim point of view, this communalization was linked very closely to the spirit of Islam but it also involved coming to terms with secular ideas absorbed largely from the West and put to use in support of the welfare of Indian Muslim society. One of the best example of this 'strategy' was the emergence of Pakistan itself, propagated in the name of Islam but achieved on the grounds of western democracy.

However, another debate centres on what the overall gains and losses were for Muslim women in India as a result of the decades of efforts for social changes upon which this study has focused. Immediately after the creation of Pakistan, women's participation in nation-building efforts saw a remarkable expansion in different spheres of life. A number of volunteer women's organizations sprang up in Pakistan to assist the government with massive rehabilitation schemes. On the national level, women worked as first-aid helpers and accompanied medical teams to refugee camps to help in preventive health measures. They also played a part in initiating educational programmes in these camps. But the fervour with which women's equal status in national life and their great participatory roles received high level support did not last very long. Pakistan's early years saw a corresponding rise in feudal politics, in which attitudes and norms regarding women's role and status had a low cultural grading. In the same way, the traditional religious lobbies began to adopt an increasingly hard-line position, especially after the active participation of women's associations such as the All-Pakistan Women's Association (APWA) in the movement for the enforcement of Muslim family laws.

The enactment of the Muslim Family Laws Ordinance of 1961 and the West Pakistan Family Courts Law of 1964 affected Pakistani women greatly. It was a bold attempt to accord women a legal status in their personal roles, as defined in the Quranic injunctions. The crucial question of what Islam ordains for Muslim women, however, continues to be a highly contentious issue which women themselves, and society more generally, cannot ignore. To understand why it is so a clear distinction must be made between Islam in general and its local interpretations in particular. For many Muslims, Islam provides Muslim women with all the rights that they require, but, at the same time, it is also necessary to recognize that Islam has been often moulded and re-cast in the context of individual societies. As the case of Muslim women in South Asia demonstrates, the framework of their religion together with the constraints of their immediate circumstances combined to produce the context within which they struggled to prise open and make space available to them should they want to move into it.

NOTES

1. Cynthia Nelson, 'Biography and Women's History: Interpreting Doria Shafik', in Nikki Keddie and Beth Baron, (eds.), *Women in Middle Eastern Societies: Shifting Boundaries in Sex and Gender*, (Yale Press, New Haven, 1991), pp. 312–33.
2. Radha Kumar, *The History of Doing: An Illustrated Account of Movements for Women's Rights and Feminism in India, 1800–1990*, (Kali for Women, New Delhi, 1993), p. 165.

Appendix

NAMES OF FEMALE WRITERS

The popular female writers whose names have been included here cover most of the publishing material collected during the period from 1930 to 1947. The summary of the work of these female writers has been drawn mainly from the different issues of the *Tehzib-e-Niswan* and the *Ismat* of that period. Many of these writers led anonymous lives, hence the information about them focuses on their published work and excludes detailed data concerning their own individual experiences.

AKHTAR JAMAL (NAGPUR)

Area of Interest: Short stories and general articles on women's concerns

She was one of those writers who served *Ismat* for a long time. Her simple but impressive writings not only provided entertainment to her readers but also proved a source of information. Among her prominent writings were those of *Zindigi* (Life) (*Ismat*, April 1935); *Qurbani* (Sacrifice) (*Ismat*, March 1936); *Munajat* (A Supplication) *Ismat*, May 1936; *Dehat aur Qudrati Nazare* (Countryside and Natural Scenery) (*Ismat*, January 1946); and *Ansu* (Tears) (*Ismat*, June 1946).

AMINA NAZLI (DELHI)

Area of Interest: Short stories and drama writing

Amina Nazli was a daughter-in-law of Rashid-ul-Khairi. She started to write for *Ismat* soon after her marriage in 1929. She also helped her husband Raziq-ul-Khairi in the editing of *Ismat*. Among her better-known writings were *Sufaid Zeera* (White

Cummin-seeds) (*Ismat*, February 1943); *Dawat* (Invitation) (*Ismat*, August 1943); *Hamari Naslon ki Gumrahi* (Our Misled Generation) (*Ismat*, June 1944), *Afshan* (Afshan) (*Ismat*, February 1945); *Ustani ji* (Female Teacher) (*Ismat*, March 1945); *Iftari* (Breaking the Fast) (*Ismat*, February 1946) and *Shauhar ki Shadi* (The Marriage of a Husband) (*Ismat*, May 1947).

Amtual Hafeez (Jullundar)

Area of Interest: Domesticity and health arrangments

Amtual Hafeez's writings were usually based on her personal experiences as an Indian Muslim woman. For example, her book, *Sanat wa Hirfat* (Skills) published in 1933, tells women how to improve their domestic economy. In the same way, her other articles including, *Buhtan* (An Accusation) (*Ismat*, May 1934), and *Balohn ki Hafazat* (Hair Care) (*Ismat*, June 1938) also provide useful information to readers about domestic and household affairs.

Anwar Jahan (Aurangabad)

Area of Interest: Poetry

Usually her poems deal with contemporary social issues, such as the inferior social status of women, and urged them to improve their status. For instance her poems, *Barsat* (The Rainy Season) (*Ismat*, August 1937); *Zindigi* (Life) (*Ismat* January 1938), and *Itiraf-e-Haqiqat* (The Acknowledgement of Reality) (*Ismat*, March 1940), exhort women to accept new changes in Indian Muslim society.

Asif Jahan Bilgrami (Hyderabad)

Area of Interest: Fiction and essay writing

Asif Jahan often discussed different kinds of social and domestic subjects in her essays. Her famous works of fiction *Ansu* (Tears) (*Ismat*, November 1938); *Shikayat* (A Complaint)

(*Ismat*, September 1940) and *Hum Safar* (A Fellow Traveller) (*Ismat*, November 1941), tell of the causes of the social degradation of Indian Muslim women.

ASMA SAEED (WHEREABOUTS UNKNOWN)

Area of Interest: Fiction writing

As a modern educated woman, she developed her interests both in English and Urdu literarture. Among her prominent Urdu writings were *Fazool Bahas* (A Senseless Argument) (*Ismat*, December 1935); *Shopping* (*Ismat*, October 1937); *Musalman Aurat aur Beruni Dil-Chaspian* (Muslim Women and Out-door Activities) (*Ismat*, March 1938), and *Muqaffal Kamra* (The Locked Room) (*Ismat*, January 1938).

BILQEES BEGUM (AGRA)

Area of Interest: Domestic issues

Most of her literary work was published in *Ismat* and *Tehzib-e-Niswan* while her two books, *Khana Dari* (Domesticity) (1933) and *Mushir-e-Niswan* (A Guide for Women) (1940) helped to promote the idea of domesticity and women's maternal responsibilities. She also responded to socio-economic changes and urged her readers to consider them, as pointed out in her article, *Kishti main* (In the Boat) (*Ismat*, April 1933) and *Mahol se Mutabaqat* (According to the Situation) (*Ismat*, May 1835).

BILQEES JAMAL (BAREILLY)

Area of Interest: Poetry

Her poetic work which was occasionally published in *Ismat*, later appeared in the form of a book, *Aina-e-Jamal* (The Mirror of Beauty). Her work, such as *Awaz-e-Dil* (The Voice of the Heart) (*Ismat*, July 1936) and *Subh-e-Arzu* (The Dawn of Desire) (*Ismat*, September 1936), mainly discussed moral, religious and social problems.

B.N. Ansa (Madras)

Area of Interest: Domesticity as well as general social writing
She responded to the demand for new 'scientific' domestic literature and wrote many articles on this particular subject, prominent among which were *Maon ke waste Lamha-e-Fikr* (The Moment of Worry for Mothers) (*Ismat*, April 1937); *Zindigi* (Life) (*Ismat*, March 1938) and *Mamta* (motherly love) (*Ismat*, March 1939).

Hafeeza Jamal (Hyderabad)

Area of Interest: General
Hafeeza's work mainly focused on the importance of female education, social and moral matters. In the same way she also developed her interest in domestic literature. Among her prominent writings were those of *Susti aur Jald Bazi* (Indolence and Hastiness) (*Ismat*, March 1932), and *Timardari* (Nursing).

Humira Saqib (Kanpur)

Area of Interest: Poetry and Prose writing
By naming socio-political changes of Indian society as a 'national awakening', she urged Muslim women in her poems- such as *Jagmagate Tare* (Glittering Stars) (*Ismat* May 1936); *Arz-dasht* (A Petition) (*Ismat*, December 1938), and *Sal-e-Rafta ki Lash Par* (On the Dead-body of the Past Year), (*Ismat*, December 1940)-to play their active role in the changing times.

Iqbal Jahan Begum (Bahawalpur)

Area of Interest: Fiction and general writing
In her simple style she tried to entertain her readers through her literary writings. Examples of this style include *Karamad Baythen* (Useful Hints) (*Ismat*, March 1932), and *Kaimmandar ki Dulhan* (The Bride of the Commander) (*Ismat*, February 1940).

JAHAN BANO (HYDERABAD DECCAN)

Area of Interest: General

She mostly wrote short stories and expressed her opinion on contemporary social problems, in particular those relating to women. Her fiction *Nujumi* (The Fortune-teller) is a lesson for those women who believed in superstitions.

JAMILA BEGUM (CALCUTTA)

Area of Interest: Prose writing

She was among those writers who contributed to *Tehzib-e-Niswan* and *Ismat* at the same time. She mainly focused on writing as well as the translation of novels. Her novel *Feroza* (1944) became popular among educated women. She also translated an English novel, *Who was the Murderer?* into Urdu, in 1945. She had deep insight into those social issues which were very important in women's lives.

JAMILA PERVEEN (AMRITSAR)

Area of Interest: Social and religious writing

She emphasized women's religious education through her different essays and articles, such as *Communalism aur uske Naqais* (Communalism and its Flaws) *(Ismat*, March 1942); *Aulad ka Rohani Qatal* (The Spiritual Murder of Children) *(Tehzib-e-Niswan*, December 1940), and *Aql* (Wisdom) *(Ismat*, May 1946).

KANIZ FATIMA (KANPUR)

Area of Interest: Short stories and essay writing

Like other female writers, she pursued her literary activities in the form of examination of women's contemporary social problems and their solutions. One specific example was her *Muslim Ladies Conference* (*Ismat*, February 1933), and *Paap* (Sin) *(Ismat*, November 1941).

Gohar Iqbal (Meerut)

Area of Interest: Poetry

A prominent Muslim poetess who urged her Muslim sisters to meet the new challenges of the times. Her poems such as *Zindigi* (Life) (*Ismat*, November 1937); *Sakoot-e-Shab* (The Stillness of the Night) (*Ismat*, June 1938), and *Kanwal* (The Lotus), dealt with the socio-political changes that were challenging Indian Muslims and which, she felt, would help to change their destiny.

Mahmooda Rizvia (Karachi)

Area of Interest: Short stories and general writing

She tried to cope with new challenges of the times with her simple-styled short stories and fiction. Among her writings were *Maqsad-e-Hayat* (The Purpose of Life) (*Ismat*, April 1943) and *Lumha* (A Moment) (*Ismat*, August, 1943).

Najma Ramitullah (Lahore)

Area of Interest: Poetry and General

She shared her feelings with other women writers in the form of poems, such as *Maa* (Mother) (*Ismat*, August 1943); *Shab-e-Mah* (Night in a Month) (*Ismat*, March 1944).

Nazar Sajad Hyder (Lucknow)

Area of Interest: Novel and general writing

She was one of the earliest Urdu female writers. In 1908 her first article was published in *Ismat*. Through her writings she tried to persuade women to maintain a balanced behaviour in their daily lives. For instance, her serialized novel, *Najma*, and other pieces of fiction, *Malan ki Beti* (The Gardner's Daughter) and *Hasina*, published in *Ismat* from time to time, proved a big lesson for those women who had been drawn to western culture without fully considering its advantages or disadvantages.

Naseera Sultana (Lahore)

Area of Interest: Domestic issues and food recipes

In her writings she provided different kind of recipes including some for squashes and juices. In addition she discussed household managment and child-care in various articles. Among her most popular recipes published in *Ismat* were those for *Timater ki Chatni* (Tomato Sauce) (*Ismat*, July 1939); *Amrud ki Mithai* (Guava Sweet) (*Ismat*, November 1941); *Shaljam ka Achar* (Turnip Pickle) (*Ismat*, May 1942), and *Am ka Murabba* (Mango Jam) (*Ismat*, Agust, 1945).

Nusrat Nisat (Simla)

Area of Interest: Fiction and essay writing

Her main literary achievements were *Qatil Kaun* (Who is the Murderer) and *Khawateen aur Hindustan* (Women and India) (*Ismat*, November 1940).

Safia Naqvi (Bombay)

Area of Interest: Fiction and essay writing

Muslim women's social issues were discussed at length in her different pieces of fiction and articles. Instead of accusing men, she believed that women should be responsible for removing their own failings as argued in *Kagaz ki Nao* (A Paper Boat) (*Ismat*, September 1934); *Sharafat* (Nobility) (*Ismat*, July 1937), and *Khandan ki Nak* (The Honour of the Family) (*Ismat*, 1941).

Sakina Ubadullah (Lahore)

Area of Interest: Fiction and essay writing

Alongside writing her own fiction she was also interested in translating writings of other Indian local languages into Urdu, for instance *Yaad* (Memory) (*Tehzib-e-Niswan,* March 1945), and *Shikasta Taswir ke Tukre* (The Broken Pieces of the Picture) (*Ismat*, April 1946).

SARDAR MUHAMMADI BEGUM (BOMBAY)

Area of Interest: Social, moral, historical and religious topics

Her vast observations and scholarly interests are visible in several issues of *Ismat* and *Tehzib-e-Niswan* which carried articles such as *Insan ki Qadar* (Respect for Human Beings) (*Tehzib-e-Niswan*, January 1940); *Aam Tawahhumat* (General Superstitions) (*Tehzib-e-Niswan*, March 1945), and *Dunya* (The World) (*Ismat*, April 1945). The main subject of these articles revolve around the concept of life and happiness.

SHAISTA IKRAMULLAH (DELHI)

Area of Interest: General

Shaista was one of the foremost writers to contribute to *Ismat*. She wrote for the journal as a young woman and continued to do so after her marriage. While she belonged to a very privileged class and received higher education both in India and abroad (London), her writings reflected the feelings of an ordinary Indian Muslim woman who wanted to get rid of the social restrictions without losing her socio-religious identity. Her main writings were *Khandan* (The Family) (*Ismat*, March 1933); *Ala Talim ka ek Rukh* (One Aspect of Higher Education) (*Ismat*, November 1935); *Jahil aur Talim Yafta Bibian* (Illiterate and Educated Women) (*Ismat*, August 1936); *Rail ka Safar* (A train Journey) (*Ismat*, March 1938).

SUGHRA HUMAYUN ASGHAR (HYDERABAD)

Area of Interest: Political and general

Sughra devoted much of her life to national-building activities. As an active social and political worker, she acquired vast experience of public dealings and utilized these experiences in writings such as *Mushir-e-Niswan* (A Guide for Women) (1943); *Sar guzasht-e-Hajra* (The Story of Hajra), and *Mohni* (1944). Besides these novels, her general writing also became popular among the readers of both *Ismat* and *Tehzib-e-Niswan*.

SYEEDA ASHAR (NAGPUR)

Area of Interest: Translation and general

She translated many pieces of Hindi fiction and other work into Urdu. In addition, her own stories, such as *Cinema ka Shauq* (Love for Movies) (*Ismat*, February 1935); *Farishta* (An Angel) (*Ismat*, April 1938); *Ithefaq* (Unity) (*Tehzib-b-Niswan*, November 1940), and *Muzhabi Gadagar* (Religious Mendicants) (*Ismat*, August 1945) were published both in *Tehzib-e-Niswan* and *Ismat*.

ZUHRA BEGUM FAIZI (BOMBAY)

Area of Interest: General

Zuhra's name was quite familiar to the readers of *Ismat* and *Tehzib-e-Niswan*. Among her literary work was a book, *Tundarusti Hazar Namat* (Health is Wealth) (1933) as well as several articles about women's health, household management and social problems.

ZUHRA HASHMI (BAUDAUN)

Area of Interest: Poetry

Among her poetic works, the best-known were those of *Nagma-e-Bahar* (The Song of the Spring) (*Ismat*, November 1940); *Bimar Shuhar ke Sirhane* (At the Bedside of a Sick Husband) (*Ismat*, March 1941), and *Khawateen Salaf ka Ramazan* (The Fasting month (Ramzan) of our ancestral Women) (*Ismat* December 1942).

GLOSSARY

adaab	manners.
ashraf	plural of the Arabic *sharif* meaning honourable, the term was usually used to describe Muslims descendents of immigrants to India.
aulad-e-Saleha	virtuous children.
atuji	a female teacher.
burqa	a kind of veil covering the whole body from head to foot.
dai	a midwife.
dargah	tomb, shrine.
dawa khana	a dispensary; an apothecary's shop.
fatwa	a formal opinion, given by a *mufti* or an *alim* on a point of Islamic law.
fiqa	'understanding, knowledge, intelligence' the technical term for the science of Islamic jurisprudence.
hadith	the traditions, the record of the sayings and doings of the Prophet Muhammad (PBUH).
hajj	the annual pilgrimage to Mecca.
hakim	a doctor practising one of the orthodox systems of Graeco-Arabic medicine.
haram	forbidden by the *sharia*.
iddat	waiting period of a widow or a divorced woman according to Islamic law
ijma	a consensus of religious opinion.
ikhtank-ul-rahim	a sort of swooning due to severe pain in the womb.
ijttihad	'exerting oneself to the utmost degree to attain an object' the utmost effort to understand points of Islamic law.

Imam	a religious leader, one who leads prayers in the mosque.
izzat	honour.
kazi	a judge trained in Islamic law, though often the title was inherited as a name by men with no such training.
khulah	divorce obtained by a wife for a ransom by her or some other person on her behalf.
madrasa	a secondary school; academy; seminary.
maktab	a school for teaching children the elements of reading, writing and Quranic recitation.
maulvi	a title equal to maulana.
mulla	a term often used in British India for a schoolmaster.
mehar	a dower approved by the Muslim law.
nikah	matrimony; marriage according to Muslim law.
pundit	a learned Brahman.
purdah	seclusion—the veil.
qiyas	judgement; opinion.
raj	a kingdom, rule or sovereignty.
sailan-e-rahim	Leucorrhea.
sajjada nashin	'one who sits on the carpet' head of the *pir* family.
sati	'a virtuous wife'; the faithful wife who immolates herself on her husband's funeral pyre.
sawab	the reward of virtue in life after death.
shariat	the divinely revealed law of Islam.
sura	a chapter or division of the Quran.
tafsir	commentary on the holy Quran and *hadith*.
tanga	a small two wheeled carriage pulled by a horse.
ulama	pl. of *alim*.
umma	followers of Islam.
unani tibb	Graeco-Arabic system of medicines.
wajibulares	a written representation or petition; an

agreement; an administration paper.

zamindar   Under the British, the holder of a right of property in land, who was individually or jointly engaged to pay rent to government and had the right to collect rent and to regulate the occupancy of all other tenures on his estate.

zenana   Women's apartments in a Muslim household.

BIBLIOGRAPHY

MANUSCRIPT SOURCES

India Office Library and Records, London, (IOL).
Friends of Vellore Papers, MSS.Eur. F.219.
Hartog Papers, MSS.Eur. E.221.
Shrabji Papers, MSS.Eur. F.165.
Women's Christian College, Madras Papers, MSS.Eur. F.220.

UNPUBLISHED GOVERNMENT RECORDS

India Office Library and Records, London, (IOL).
1900–47 Department Files: General, Judicial, Political. 1895–47 Records: Commission, Committee and Conference.
Arrangements for Facilitating Registration and Voting of Women, 1935–36, Q/FC/37.
Government of India, Legislative Department Record, 1938, L/P&J/1939.
Miscellaneous Papers Belonging to Lord Lothian, 1931–32, Q/IFC/92.
Muslim Personal Law (Shariat) Application Bill of 1934, (introduced in the N.W.F.P., Legislative Council in 1934), L/P&J/7/667.
Muslim Personal Law (Shariat) Application Act of 1937, and Amending Acts, 1937–43, L/P&J/7/943.
Polling of Women in Various Provinces: Papers Corresponding to Women's Vote, 1935–36, Q/IDC/37.
Proceedings: Bengal Government, Judicial Department, June 1928.
Proceedings: Madras Government Education, including Confidential, August 1920.
Punjab Native Newspapers Report: 1900–25, L/R/5/200–205.
Quarterly Statements of Newspapers in Delhi Provinces, 1925–47, V/25/960/48.
Secretariat Notes, Summarizing Proposals of Provincial Government and Committees on the Question of Women's Franchise, 1935–36, Q/IFC/49.
Women's War Efforts, 1939–45, L/1/1/1020.

OFFICIAL PUBLICATIONS

Abolition of Fees in Primary Schools (Calcutta, 1910).

Age of Consent Committees 1928–29: Oral Evidences and Written Statements from Bengal, Bombay, Delhi, N.W.F.P. and Punjab, (Calcutta 1929).

Annual Reports on Public Instruction in Different Provinces: Bombay, 1946; Central Provinces and Berar (Nagpur), 1942; Madras, 1941; N.W.F.P. (Peshawar), 1939; Punjab (Lahore), 1943; Sindh (Karachi) 1943.

Annual Reports of the Public Health Commissioner with the Government of India: Calcutta, 1924; Calcutta, 1925; Calcutta, 1931; Delhi, 1944; Delhi, 1946; Delhi, 1948.

Annual Report of the Public Health Department of Central Provinces and Berar (Nagpur, 1941).

Annual Report on the Public Health Administration of Punjab (Lahore, 1942).

Annual Report of the Sanitary Commission with the Government of India for 1917 (Bombay, 1931).

Annual Reports of the United Provinces (Allahabad, 1917, 1931, and 1951).

Bengal Public Health Report (Alipore, 1941).

Education in India in 1938–39, Bureau of Education, (Delhi, 1941).

Educational Manual of the Central Provinces and Berar (Nagpur, 1911).

General Report on Public Instruction in the United Provinces of Agra and Oudh (Allahabad, 1914, 1949).

Indian Delimitation Committee, Report of the Committee Appointed in connection with the Delimitation of Constituencies and Concerned Matters (London, 1936).

Indian Franchise Committee 1932 (London, 1932).

Indian Franchise Committees: Selection from Memorandums, Submitted by Individuals and Oral Evidences, (London, 1923).

Indian Medical Review (Delhi, 1938).

Indian Statutory Commission (London, 1930).

Legislative Assembly Debates of 1929, Fifth Session of the Third Legislative Assembly, (Simla, 1930).

Legislative Assembly Debates of 1938, Eight Session of the Fifth Legislative Assembly, 1938, (Simla, 1939).

A Memorandum on the Progress of Education in India (Calcutta, 1928).

Moral and Material Progress and Condition of India During the Year 1930–31 (London, 1932).

Problems of Urdu Training in the Bombay Presidency (Bombay, 1914).

Note on the Press, United Provinces of Agra and Oudh: No. 9, 29 February 1936; No. 28, 11 July 1936; No. 81, 22, February 1938, Allahabad.

Progress of Education in India, Seventh Quinquennial Review of Education, 1912–17, Vol. 1, (Calcutta, 1918); Eighth Quinquennial Review of Education, 1917–1922, (Calcutta, 1923); Ninth Quinquennial Review of Education, 1922–27, (Calcutta, 1929); Tenth Quinquennial Review of

Education, 1927–32, (Calcutta, 1934); Eleventh Quinquennial Review of Education, (Simla, 1939).

Proceedings of the Indian Round Table Conference, 1st and 2nd Sessions 1930–31, (London, 1932).

Proceedings of the Joint Committee on the Indian Constitutional Reforms, Session, 1933–34, Vol. 11 (London, 1934).

Public Health and Vaccination Reports of the N.W.F.P., 1940 (Peshawar, 1946).

Punjab Public Health Department: Report on the Public Health Administration of Punjab, 1940 (Lahore, 1942).

Report of the Age of Consent Committee, 1928–29 (Calcutta, 1929).

Report by the Central Advisory Board of Education on the Post-War Educational Development (Sargent Report) (Delhi, 1945).

Report on the state and Progress of Education in the Central Provinces and Berar, (Nagpur, 1942).

Report of an Enquiry into the Causes of Maternal Mortality in Calcutta (Delhi, 1940).

Report of the Health Survey and Development Committee Vol. 1, (Calcutta, 1946).

Reports of the Indian Students Department 1922–23; 1925–26; 1929–1930, (London).

Report on an Investigation into the Causes of Maternal Mortality in the City of Bombay (Delhi, 1941).

Reports of the Progress of Education in the Punjab of 1941–46 (Lahore, 1943, 1947).

Report on the Maternity and Child Welfare Work in India, 1938 (Simla, 1939).

Report on the Medical Inspection of School Children and the Teaching of Hygiene in Schools (Delhi, 1942).

Report of the Muhammadan Educational Recent Development in the Bombay Presidency (Bombay, 1914).

Report of the Second Wardah Education Committee Central Advisory Board of Education (Delhi, 1941).

Royal commission on the Public Service in India, Volume 1, (London, 1917).

Statistical Appendices to Annual Report of the Public Health Commission with the Government of India, 1945 (Simla, 1948).

The Bombay Maternity Benefit Act of 1929, No. VII, as Modified to 1935 (Bombay, 1935).

The Mines Maternity Benefit Act of 1941, No. XIX as modified to 1946, (Delhi, 1946).

NEWSPAPERS AND PERIODICALS

(Urdu)

Ismat (Delhi), April 1933; December 1933; January 1934; June 1934; March 1935; June 1935; September 1935; December 1935; January 1936; May 1936; September 1936; January 1937; February 1937; October 1937; November 1938; December 1938; January 1939; February 1939; April 1939; August 1939; November 1939; June 1940; August 1940; January 1941; May 1941; October 1941; May 1942; July 1943; January 1944; October 1944; November 1944; February 1945; April 1945; June 1945; March 1946; April 1946; May 1946; July 1946; January 1947.

Ismat (Karachi), July and August 1964.

Khatun (Aligarh), February 1909; June 1909; August 1909; October 1909; June 1910; January 1912; March 1912; May 1912.

Rafiq-e-Niswan, (Lucknow), April 1885; September 1887.

Tehzib-e-Niswan (Lahore), July 1940; August 1940; September 1940; November 1940; January 1945; February 1945; March 1945; April 1945; January 1946; July 1947.

(English)

Asiatic Review (London), January 1937.

Stri Dahrma (Madras), December 1920; January and February 1921; July 1922; May 1936.

The Modern Review (Calcutta), March 1909; August 1910; May 1911; August 1920; November 1920.

The Daily News (London), August 1927.

The Statesman (Bombay), August 1927.

The Islamic Review (Woking), June 1929; September 1929.

The Indian Ladies Magazine (Madras), December 1928; March 1929; April 1929; October 1929; April 1930.

The Indian Magazine (London), February 1886; June 1886; October 1886; February 1887; March 1888; January 1888; March 1889; October 1889.

The Ninteenth Century Review (London), March 1891.

Published Works and Unpublished Theses

(Urdu)

A.J., 'Ayaddat', *Tehzib-e-Niswan*, Vol. 43, No. 37, September 1940, pp. 908–909.

A.J., 'Intikhab-e-Rishtah', *Ismat*, Vol. 65, No. 6, June 1935, pp. 412–16.

A.S., 'Byzubanohn ki Shadi', *Ismat*, Vol. 65, No. 6, June 1935, pp. 412–16.

Abdul Rashid, Begum, 'Nazakat aur Chusti ki Jung', *Ismat*, Vol. 51, No. 6, December 1933, pp. 471–72.

Abid Husain Saleh, 'Aurathen aur Mutalia-e-Quran', *Ismat*, Vol. 73, No. 4, October 1944, pp. 209–212.

Ahmed, Iftikhar, *Nazir Ahmed: Ahwal wa Asar*, (Lahore, 1971).

Ahmed, Nazir, *Mauzuat-e-Hasna*, (Delhi, 1876).

——, *Banat-un-Nash*, (Lucknow, 1877).

——, *Marat-ul-Arous*, (Lucknow, 1896).

Ahsan, Muhammad, *Zad-ul-Mukhaddarat*, (Bareilly, 1871).

Asghar Humayun, Sughra, 'Auraton ke Fariaz', *Ismat*, Vol. 56, No. 1, January 1936, pp. 46–48.

Asif, Sultan, 'Aurat ka Nasbulayn', *Tehzib-e-Niswan*, Vol. 48, No. 15, April 1945, pp. 325–27.

Azam-un-nisa, Begum, 'Aurat aur uski Ghulami', *Tehzib-e-Niswan*, Vol. 49, No. 16, April 1945, p. 188.

Aziz-ul-Hasan, Begum, 'Kushgawar Zindgi', *Ismat*, Vol. 60, No. 3, March 1938, p. 189.

Bano, Siddiqa, 'Razamandi ki Shadi', *Ismat*, Vol. 74, No. 2, February 1945, pp. 88–89.

Begum, Jamila, 'Hamari Talim ka Maqsad', *Ismat*, Vol. 57, No. 3, September 1936, pp. 303–304.

——, 'Mazhibi Talim', *Ismat*, Vol. 60. No. 2, January 1937, pp. 111–12.

——, 'Hamari Shakhsiyyat', *Ismat*, Vol. 64, No. 1, January 1940, pp. 413–15.

——, 'Tansikh-e-Nikah Act', *Tehzib-e-Niswan*, Vol. 48, No. 37, September 1940, pp. 930–32.

——, 'Salgirah *Tehzib-e-Niswan*', *Tehzib-e-Niswan*, Vol. 143, No. 27, July 1940, pp. 632–33.

Begum, Salma, 'Aurat Ghulam Nahin', *Tehzib-e-Niswan*, Vol. 48, No. 2, February 1945, pp. 84–86.

Begum, Shahjahan, *Tehzib-e-Niswan*, (Delhi, 1889).

Chirgahuddin, Sakina, 'Aurat aur Mard ki Jungh', *Ismat*, Vol. 59, No. 5, November 1939, pp. 409–10.

Faizi, Zuhra Begum, 'Aap Biti', *Khatun*, Vol. 6, No. 6, June 1910, pp. 278–80.

———, 'Tehzib-e-Niswan ke Bani', Tehzib-e-Niswan, Vol. 43, No. 27, July 1947, pp. 633–35.

Fatima, Gadhir, 'Larkiyon ki Talim', Ismat, Vol. 26, No. 1, January 1939, pp. 55–56.

Fatima, Mushir, 'Shadi aur usky Lawazmat', Ismat, Vol. 74, No. 4, April 1945, pp. 239–42.

Garcin de Tassy, J.H., Histoire de la Litterature Hindoustanies, 2nd edn, translated into Urdu under the title of Khutbat-e-Garcin de Tassy, (Hyderabad Deccan, 1935).

Ghulam Rasul, Begum, 'Hum Bechari Auraten', Ismat, Vol. 59, No. 4, October 1937, p. 313.

Gohar, Mumtaz, Muntakhabat-e-Tehzib-e-Niswan, (Lahore, 1988).

Hali, Altaf Husain, Majalis-un-Nisa, (Lahore, 1874).

———, Ek Bevah ki Munajat, (Delhi, 1892).

Hasan, Begum A.Z., Roshnuk Begum, (Lahore, 1944).

Hasan, Begum Z.D., 'Badalte hue Mashriq par ek Nazar', Ismat, Vol. 40, No. 4, April 1932, pp. 292–97.

Hashmi, Naseeruddin, 'Hyderabad ka Zenana College', Ismat, Vol. 66, No. 1, January 1941, pp. 46–48.

———, 'Osmania University ky Niswani Maqalat', Ismat, Vol. 74, No. 1, January 1945, pp. 43–44.

———, 'Hyderabad ki European Talim yaftah Khawateen', Ismat, Vol. 74, No. 4, September 1945, pp. 243–44.

Hashmi, Naseeruddin, 'Madras ki Ala Talim Yaftha Khawateen', Ismat, Vol. 76, No. 3, March 1946, pp. 194–95.

Husain, Inayat, Mufid-ul-Khaliaq (Allahabad, 1869).

Husain, Riffat, 'Aurat Ghulam Nahin', Tehzib-e-Niswan, Vol. 48, No. 9, March 1939, pp. 129–31.

Ikramullah, Shaista, 'Kaproh se Mutaliq Chand Bathen', Ismat, Vol. 56, No. 2.

Imtiaz, Begum, 'Barhthe hue Wazan par Qaboo Pana', Ismat, Vol. 73, No. 5, November 1944, p. 283.

Iqbal, Gohar, 'Nagma-e-Bedari', Ismat, Vol. 61, No. 4, October, 1938, p. 298.

Iqbal, Rabia, Urdu Adab aur Tabqa-e-Niswan (Hyderabad, 1990).

Jafar, Fatima, 'Sayasit Main Aurton ka Hisa', Ismat, Vol. 57, No. 3 and 4, September, October 1936, pp. 313–14.

Jafri, Raza, 'Jinsi Rishtay aur aunka Intikhab', Ismat, Vol. 77, No. 1, July 1946, pp. 33–37.

Jamiluddin, Muhammad, Arsi Mushaf (Agra, 1874).

Karmania, S.R., 'Maon ko Hidayat', Ismat, Vol. 50, No. 4, April 1933, pp. 265–66.

Kazia, Sultana, 'Saz-e-Dilbari', Tehzib-e-Niswan, Vol. 48, No. 2, January, 1945, pp. 20–22.

————, 'Zehniyyat', *Tehzib-e-Niswan*, Vol. 48, No. 25, January 1945, p. 385.

Khan, Abdul Rahim, *Chasmah-e-Khirad* (Agra, 1876).

Khanum, Safia, 'Insaf ya Zulam', *Ismat*, Vol. 47, No. 4, October 1937, pp. 300–302.

Khatun, Rafia, 'Hindustan main Niswani Taraqqi ka Mafhoom', *Tehzib-e-Niswan*, Vol. 43, No. 35, August 1940, pp. 825–54.

Kiswar Ara, Sayyeda, 'Aurat aur Tarbiyat-e-Kirdar', *Ismat*, Vol. 76, No. 4, April 1946, p. 245.

Mansoori, Badar, 'Dawaten aur Hum', *Ismat*, Vol. 76, No. 5, May 1946, p. 342.

Munir, Sayyed, *Larkiyon ki Talim* (Allahabad, 1869).

Munshi, Fatima Begum, 'Muslim Ladies Conference and Zenana Sanati Numaish', *Ismat*, Vol. 48, No. 2, February 1932, pp. 144–45.

————, 'Mission Askool ki Talim Zaroor Rang Layegi', *Ismat*, Vol. 51, No. 6, December 1933, pp. 452–55.

Muslihuddin, Muhammad, *Kuhl-ul-Jawahir* (Agra, 1873).

Naqvi, Safia, 'Kaghaz ki Nao', *Ismat*, Vol. 75, No. 4, October 1941, pp. 325–38.

Naseeruddin, Begum, 'Musalman Auraton main Qaumi Bedari', *Tehzib-e-Niswan*, Vol. 49, No. 25, January 1946, pp. 385–86.

Nazli, Amina, 'Roshan Khayal Dulhan', *Ismat*, Vol. 67, No. 4, October 1941, pp. 325–38.

Qadir, Mahmoona, 'Talim ke Mukhalifon se', *Ismat*, Vol. 68, No. 5, May 1942, pp. 273–75.

Rahim, Abdul, *Rando ki Shadi* (Allahabad, 1873).

Rizvia, Mahmooda, 'Aurat ki Zindagi par ek Nazar', *Ismat*, Vol. 76, No. 2, February 1939, pp. 115–16.

Salana Reports: All India Muslim Ladies Conference, 1917–40, (Karachi), n.d.

Shaheed, A., 'Tarbiyat ke Chand Usool', *Ismat*, Vol. 72, No. 1, January 1944, pp. 21–22.

Siddiq, Shafiq, 'Mujhe Bhool Jana Meri Piyari Amman', *Ismat*, Vol. 78, No. 1, January, 1947, p. 32.

Thanawi, Ashraf Ali, *Bihisthi Zewar* (Karachi, 1962).

Wahi, Amut-ul, 'Rasmi Purdah', *Ismat*, Vol. 61, No. 6, December 1938, pp. 451–52.

Zahiruddin, Muhammad, *Fawaid-al-nisa* (Lucknow, 1873).

Zamiruddin, Saeedahe, 'Ma ki Sehat', *Ismat*, Vol. 58, No. 1, January 1937, pp. 25–26.

(English)

Balfour, Margaret, and Ruth Young, *The Work of the Medical Women in India*, (Bombay, 1929).

Caton, A.R, 'Home and Marriage' in A.R. Caton (ed.), *The Key Progress of Women: A Survey of the Status and Condition of Women in India* (London, 1930).

Desai, N. and Bhansali, K., 'A Struggle for Identity: A Case Study of S.N.D.T. Women's University', in P.R. Panchamukhi, (ed.), *Reforms Towards Equality and Relevances: Studies in Educational Reforms in India, Vol. 111*, (Puna, 1989).

Devji, Faisal Fatehali, 'Gender and Politics of the Space: The Movement for Women's Reforms 1857–1900', in Zoya Hasan (ed.), *Forging Identities: Gender, Communities and the State* (New Delhi, 1994).

Dickinson, Richard and Nancy Dickinson (eds.), *The Directory of Information for Christian Colleges in India* Madras, 1967).

Dora, White, 'A Sketch of Zenana Medical Work in Hyderabad', *The Indian Magazine, February* 1887, pp. 66–71.

Fuller, Marcus B., *The Wrongs of Indian Womanhood* (New York, 1900).

Hafeez, Sabiha, *The Girl Child in Pakistan: Priority Concerns* (Islamabad, 1990).

Hardy, P., *The Muslims of British India* (Cambridge, 1973).

Hensman, Mona, 'Report of the First International Conference of Women in India', *Stri Dhrma*, Vol. 19, No. 4, May 1936, pp. 126–27.

Husain, Aftab, *Status of Women in Islam* (Lahore, 1987).

Husain, Niaz, 'The Purdah (veil) System Amongst the Muslim Women in India', *Islamic Review*, Vol. 17, No. 9, September 1923, pp. 1–18.

Husain, Salma Tasaddeque, 'Saviour of Muslim Women', *Quaid-i-Azam and Muslim Women*, (Karachi, 1976).

Ikramullah, Shaista, 'Women in Politics', *Quaid-i-Azam and Muslim Women*, (Karachi, 1976).

———, *From Purdah to Parliament* (London, 1963).

Jahan, Roushan, Begum, *Sultan's Dream and Selection from the Secluded Ones*, (New York, 1988).

Jalal, Ayesha, 'The Convenience of Subservience: Women and the State of Pakistan', in Deniz Kandiyoti (ed.), *Women, Islam and State* (London, 1991).

Jayawardane, Kumari, *Feminism and Nationalism in the Third World* (London, 1986).

Kaura, Uma, *Muslim and Indian Nationalism: The Emergence of the Demand for India's Partition, 1928–40*, (New Delhi, 1977).

Khan, Abdul Rashid, *The Contribution of the All-India Muslim Educational Conference to the Education and Cultural Development of Indian Muslims, 1886–1947*, (Unpublished Ph.D. Thesis, University of London, 1991).

Kraemer, H., 'Islam in India Today' *The Muslim World* (August 1931), pp. 151–176.

Kumar, Radha, *The History of Doing: An Illustrated Account of Movements for Women's Rights in India, 1800–1990* (New Delhi, 1993).

Lapidus, I.M., *A History of Islamic Societies*, (Cambridge, 1988).

Lateef, Shahida, *Muslim Women in India: Political and Private Realities 1890–1980*, (London, 1990).

Mahmood, Tahir, *Muslim Personal Law: The Role of State in the Subcontinent* (New Delhi, 1977).

Maithreyi, Krishnraj, and Karuna Chanana, *Gender and the Household Domain: Social and Cultural Dimensions*, (New Delhi, 1989).

Mayo, Katherine, *Mother India* (London, 1929).

Memorandum on the Franchise of Women by the Women of Bengal (Calcutta, 1932).

Menon, V.P., *The Transfer of Power in India* (Princeton, 1957).

Metcalf, Barbara, D. (trans. and ed.), *Perfecting Muslim Women: Maulana Ashraf Ali Thanawi's Bihishti Zewar* (Berkeley, 1982).

———, 'Reading and Writing about Muslim Women in British India', in Zoya Hasan, (ed.), *Forging Identities: Gender, Communities and the State* (New Delhi, 1994).

———, 'The Making of a Muslim Lady: Maulana Thanawi's Bihishti Zewar', in Milton Israel and N.K. Wagle, (eds.), *Islamic Society and Culture* (New Delhi, 1983).

Minault, Gail and David Lelyveld, 'The Campaign for a Muslim University 1892–1920', (Modern Asian Studies 1974), pp. 1489.

Minault, Gail, 'Hali's Majalis-un-Nisa: Purdah and Women Power in Nineteenth Century', in Milton Israel and N.K. Wagle, (eds.), *Islamic Society and Culture* (New Delhi, 1983).

———, 'Making Invisible Women Visible: Studying the History of Muslim Women in South Asia', *Journal of South Asia*, Vol. 9, No. 1, June 1986, pp. 1–14.

———, 'Sayyed Karamat Husain and Education for Women' in Villette Graff, (ed.), *Memories of a City: Lucknow, 1772–1991*, (Oxford Press, New Delhi, Forthcoming).

———, 'Shaikh Abdullah, Begum Abdullah and Sharif Education for Girls at Aligarh', in Imtiaz Ahmed, (ed.), *Modernization and Social Change among Muslims in India* (New Delhi, 1983).

———, 'Sisterhood or Separatism? The All-India Muslim Ladies Conference and the National Movement', in Gail Minault, (ed.), *The Extended Family: Women and Political Participation in India and Pakistan* (Columbia, 1981).

———, 'The Extended Family as Metaphor and the Expansion of Women's Realm', in Gail Minault, (ed.), *The Extended Family: Women and Political Participation in India and Pakistan* (Columbia, 1981).

Mirza, Sarfraz Husain, *Muslim Women's Role in the Pakistan Movement* (Lahore, 1969).

Mumtaz Khawar and Farida Shaheed, *Women of Pakistan: Two Steps Forward, One Step Back* (London, 1987).

Nag, K.C., 'Women and Our Final Emancipation', *Modern Review*, Vol. 27, No. 164, August 1920, p. 188.

Napier, L.E., 'Anaemia in Pregnancy in India: The Present Position', *The Indian Journal of Medical Research* (April 1940), pp. 1009–40.

Nelson, Cynthia, 'Biography and Women's History: On Interpreting Doria Shafik', in Nikki R. Keddie and Beth Baron (eds.), *Women in Middle Eastern Society: Shifting Boundaries in Sex and Gender* (Yale, 1991).

Nurullah, S. and Naik, J.P., *A History of Education in India During the British Period*, 2nd edn. (London, 1951).

Pirzada, Sharifuddin, *Foundation of Pakistan* (Karachi, 1970).

Ramusack, Barbara N., 'Catalysts or Helpers? British Feminists, Indian Women's Rights and Indian Independence', in Gail Minault (ed.), *The Extended Family: Women and Political Participation in India and Pakistan*, (Columbia, 1981).

Robinson, F.C.R., *Separatism Among Indian Muslims: The Politics of the United Provinces' Muslims, 1860–1923* (Delhi, 1993).

Sayyed, R.A., 'Muslim Women in India: An Overview', in Anjum Mohani (ed.), *Muslim Women in India* (Delhi, 1992).

Seal, A., *The Emergence of Indian Nationalism: Competition and Collaboration in the Later Nineteenth Century* (Cambridge, 1968).

Sinha, Mrinalini, 'Reading Mother India: Empire, Nation and the Female Voices', *Journal of Women's History*, Vol. 6, No. 2, 1994, pp. 6–40.

Smith, Wilfred Cantwell, *Modern Islam in India: A Social Analysis* (London, 1946).

Sorabji, B., *Changing Status of the Women of the Orient* (Bombay, 1914).

Stocks, Mary, D., *Eleanor Rathbone: A Biography* (London, 1949).

Zaidi, S.M.H., *Muslim Womanhood in Revolution* (Calcutta 1937).

INDEX

Thanawi, Maulana Ashraf Ali, 11, 23–4, 115–16
Tehzib-e-Niswan, 25, 214–16, 217, 218

U

Ud-Din, Khawaja Kamal, 30
University (first women's), 47
Urdu
  emergence as the common language, 12
  journals and newspapers in, 24–8, 214–18
  literature in, 13–14

V

Vote, women's right to, 170–71
Voters
  number of female, 172
  qualifications for female, 187
  registration of female, 192–4

W

Wardah Education Committee, 57
Widows, remarriage of, 19
Womanhood, reassessment of Muslim, 229–36
Women
  beauty care and products for, 117, 118
  British feminists and political rights of Indian, 179–81
  community politics and Muslim, 195–200

  consciousness of social rights, 245–6
  election constituencies for, 190–91
  emancipation of Muslim, 4–5
  European women's efforts for emancipation of local, 34–5
  expansion of social activities, 76–8
  extra-curricular activities, 74–6
  government's efforts for medical relief, 94–5, 97–100
  individuals' efforts for medical relief, 96–7
  in medical education, 110–13
  new trends in health behaviour, 113–18
  political enfranchisement of, 168–205, 260
  prefessional opportunities for, 78–80
  professional training of, 80–83
  provision of *mehr* for Muslim, 325–6
  inferiority complexes, 241–2
  reservation of seats for, 185–6
  role of health care arrangements in emancipation of, 90–119, 258–9
  selection of life partners by, 243–5
  social exploitation of, 237–40
  traditional health status of Muslim, 92–100
Writings, nature of women's, 218–19

Z

Zenana schools, 12